THE SANYASI WHO BECAME A KING

The true story behind the mystery of the BHAWAL RAJA

SONIA CHATTERJEE

An imprint of
Srishti Publishers & Distributors

Srishti Publishers & Distributors
A unit of AJR Publishing LLP
212A, Peacock Lane
Shahpur Jat, New Delhi – 110 049

editorial@srishtipublishers.com

First Published by Bold
an imprint of Srishti Publishers & Distributors in 2025

10 9 8 7 6 5 4 3 2 1

This is a work of non-fiction based on the author's research about the subject. Some events have been fictionalised for dramatic effect. While due care has been taken by the author and publisher to verify contents at press time, any inadvertent miss that is brought to their notice shall be duly verified and updated subsequently. Actual names of people and places have been used with a view to provide firsthand information.

Printed and bound in India.

Dedicated to the three men
I call my pillars of support, strength and sanity –

my son Tuneer Banerjee,
my husband Dr Tanmoy Banerjee,
and my father, Prof Radhanath Chatterjee.

Thank you for always having my back.
I hope I do justice to your unwavering faith in me.

Contents

Author's Note

I started working on 'The Sanyasi who became a King' 2023 onwards. Until then, I was happily weaving detective stories around my female sleuth, Raya Ray. The idea of a true crime novel came from a brainstorming session with my literary agent, Mr Suhail Mathur, of The Book Bakers. I figured out the availability of numerous books and write-ups on this subject in both English and Bengali, in India and Bangladesh. Case judgment at various levels is freely available in the public domain. Some books were based on thorough research and brought out undistorted facts, making history come alive through their writing. Dr Partha Chatterjee's book deserves a special mention for being a treasure trove of information on this topic. Some books took a different approach and fictionalised the story. Others were a mix of the author's creativity and true incidents.

My biggest challenge was to figure out a new approach to retelling the story. The thought of sticking to the truth but making the story vivid enough for a reader to visualise the events gave me sleepless nights. I went through the available resources, especially the court judgments. It was only when I peeled off the layers of the primary characters that I could understand their emotions and actions better. That's when I knew I wanted to look at the facts through the emotions of the characters.

While most readers acquainted with the Bhawal case know what had happened, how many of us could fathom the emotional turmoil the people involved might be going through? 'The Sanyasi who became a King' is an effort at delving into the human psyche and analyzing the emotions of the primary characters in this story. I have made a sincere attempt to stick by facts, events, and their sequence while bringing uniqueness to its narration. I apologise in advance for any inadvertent mistakes. I hope you enjoy reading this book as much as I loved writing it.

Heartfelt gratitude to the team at Sristhi Publishers, especially Mr Arup Bose, for being so supportive and encouraging of my work.

P.S. – The books and the articles I referred to, while writing this book, find a mention in the Table of References at the end of the book.

THE FAMILY TREE OF BHAWAL RAJ PARIVAR

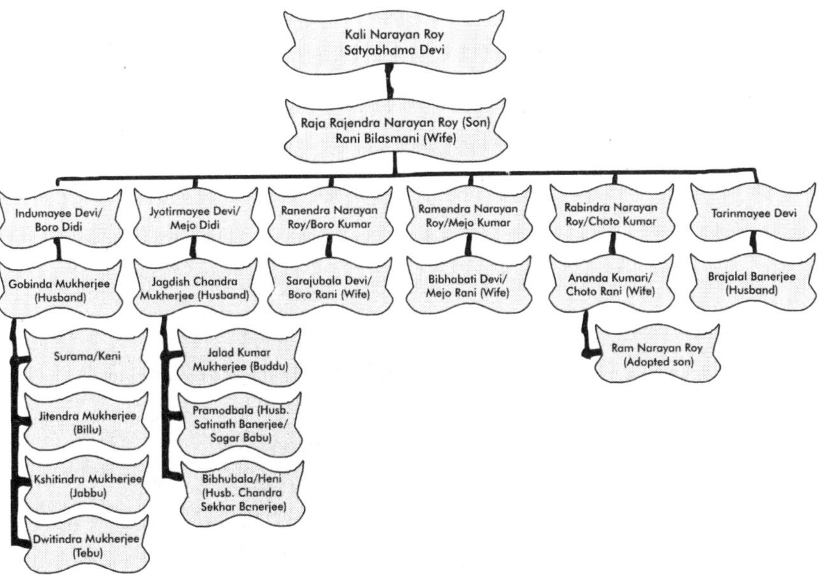

Additional members

Satyendra Nath Banerjee/Satyen Banerjee/ Satya Babu/Sala Babu	*Bibhabati's brother*
Malina	*Bibhabati's sister*
Phulkumari	*Bibhabati's mother*
Dhara Devi	*Ramendra's second wife*
Phani Bhushan Banerjee/Phani Babu	*Cousin of Bhawal Kumars*

Prologue

5th May, 1921

He felt claustrophobic in a room full of people. He could hear two familiar voices. But where was she, the one who should have been beside him at this moment? He wailed like a baby. "Help! Give me medicine. I can't tolerate it anymore." Suddenly, a face appeared with a glass of liquid.

"Gulp it down." The face helped the man swallow the liquid, and another figure appeared next to him.

"You will be fine in no time. Trust us! It's the last medicine you need..." The man couldn't hear the complete sentence because he vomited out as his body writhed with pain. Before he passed out, the man heard a female shriek in the background.

When he opened his eyes, he could barely breathe. The man realised he was covered from head to toe. He tried moving, but his legs and hands were tied. He screamed, but the wet cloth stifled his voice.

"Save me! Save me, please. I'm alive." The man with brown hair, *kata* eyes, and fair skin muttered in his sleep. He woke up drenched in sweat. It took him a couple of moments to realise it was a nightmare, and he was sleeping on a bed in a house that belonged to the one who trusted him more than herself.

6th May, 1921

The woman stared at the dead body in front of her. It was too sudden, too unexpected. What would she do now? She trembled before passing out.

When she woke up, she found a familiar face near her bed. "Get a grip on your emotions. Don't force me to lock you up here." He spoke in a stern voice before exiting the room. She shuddered.

The next moment, she closed her eyes, only to see the dead man's face laughing. "I have come back to you," he said.

"No! No! It's impossible!" she screamed out.

The face, accompanied by two hands, stretched towards her. "I knew you would wait for me."

Suddenly, the familiar face pushed the dead man's face and yelled, "Imposter!"

The woman woke up shivering. "It can't be true. He can never return. He is dead," she muttered to herself as she poured out water from an earthen jug.

7th May, 1921

The tall and dark-complexioned man had given the letter for publishing. No one could distract him from his mission. The previous night, the face haunted him, yet he hadn't budged. Instead, he yelled at it, "You are dead, and dead men don't return! You are a fraud. And I'll prove that." But the dead man's face had laughed like a maniac, and he woke up screaming again.

Chapter 1
A Sadhu at Buckland Bund

Dhaka

On a chilly morning in December 1920, a hefty stranger walked down the streets toward Buckland Bund. He had spent the night at the station before moving towards the Sadar ghat in the wee hours. His thoughts switched between the desire to stay back and the rationality to leave. Until some months back, he was just another sanyasi. But he had gradually figured out his truth, bit by bit. Every wave of memory led to an emotional roller-coaster ride, a trial he had to undergo to validate his existence.

He knew nothing would be the same once they figured out who he was. It wouldn't be easy to look at known faces and stay indifferent. But he wasn't ready to expose himself to the world yet. As he smeared the ash on his body and face, a part of his brain hoped that people wouldn't observe the resemblance.

Just as the first ray of sunlight woke up the neighborhood, he spotted the first visitor. A gentleman walked past, holding a lathi in one hand. He didn't even look at the sanyasi. A few people going about their work casually glanced at the sanyasi, but most didn't pay him attention. Though he felt a wee bit disappointed, he couldn't deny experiencing a sense of relief.

Soon, the residents grew accustomed to seeing the sanyasi with long, matted hair and a long beard covered in ash and dirt, wearing only a loincloth seated in the same spot every day. A week passed, and the sanyasi felt convinced that he looked much different from his younger self, making it difficult for the passers-by to identify him.

A couple of days later, a group of men approached him with a request for medicines. They asked the sanyasi to give special herbs to their insomniac friend to cure him. Until then, he had been polite to everyone, but this time, the sanyasi shooed them away, stating he had no treatment to offer.

Little did he know this was the first of the many instances when people would approach him for quick-fix treatments. He grew tired of refusing and explaining, and slowly started handing over some ash to them.

When some people asked him about his identity, he stated he was a nomad. Sometimes, he pretended not to remember. At other times, he spoke about his home in Punjab. He mentioned a wife and child to some people. But it was interesting how he never shifted his seat, irrespective of the weather.

A couple of months passed, and people grew curious about the good-looking sanyasi, conversant in Hindi. On a fine morning, a middle-aged man approached the sanyasi. The man sat at his feet and exclaimed with his jaws dropping, "Mejo Kumar, you have finally come back!"

Tears streamed down the man's eyes as he moved forward to touch the sanyasi's feet.

The sanyasi retreated before scolding the man in Hindi. Yet, the man kept addressing him as Mejo Kumar.

"God has sent Madhyam Kumar to set things right," he cried. Soon, more people started arriving to meet the sanyasi.

The crowd spoke of a strong resemblance between the sanyasi and Raja Ramendra Narayan Roy, the second prince of the Bhawal estate. The prince had died more than a decade ago in Darjeeling under questionable circumstances. Soon, the news of this mysterious sadhu reached far and wide. But the sanyasi seemed indifferent to the theories. He stayed mute while people grew inquisitive about the possibility of the return of the Mejo Kumar.

Most people who came to see him returned disappointed, listening to the Hindi-speaking sadhu with no association with the Bhawal estate. A group didn't even shy away from labeling him as a fraud. Many tested if the sanyasi could speak Bengali, but the latter only answered in Hindi. Yet, the rumours refused to die.

Some months later, the news of the sanyasi reached the Bhawal Raj family. Bhawal was an estate in the Madhupur forest. It spread over 579 sq. miles and comprised 2274 villages with a population of over five lac. Even though the family initially brushed it off as baseless, they couldn't ignore it for long.

Chapter 2

Jyotirmayee Meets the Sadhu

Jaidebpur

Bhawal Parganas spread over Dhaka and Mymensingh. The Bhawal Raj family owned the bulk of the Parganas as zamindars. Jaidebpur, located in the centre of the Parganas, was their headquarters. A railway line ran to the east side of the Raj Bari in Jaidebpur.

The sanyasi sat near the Kamini tree adjacent to Madhab Bari on the Raj Bari premises. Madhab was the family deity, and Madhab Bari was the temple. Raj Bari's original inmates didn't live there anymore. The brothers were long gone, while the elder and middle sisters shifted to their houses within a mile of the palace. The youngest sister, Tarinmayee, lived in Dhaka with her husband.

The Raj Bari comprised various building complexes. Raj Bilas, the palace where the Kumars resided on the ground floor, had their wives living on the first floor in the women's quarters. This white, spacious building faced the river.

The news of the sadhu's arrival soon reached the friends and relatives of the Bhawal family. By evening, small groups of people arrived to satiate their curiosity.

"Look at his hands and feet. They're the same as Madhyam Kumar's."

"He has some common physical traits with Mejo Kumar, but he's a different man."

"Is he a ghost, or has Mejo Kumar come back?"

The sanyasi heard them, but he had grown accustomed to such judgments, and they stopped bothering him.

The sadhu spent the night meditating under the tree as the *dhuni* kept burning. The following morning, he walked around the place with an uncanny familiarity. A few hours later, he sat on the verandah of the Raj Bilas building with a lost look in his eyes. The secretary to the estate, Jogen Banerjee, arrived with his brother, Sagar Babu. Sagar had married Jyotirmayee Devi's daughter, Mani. Both observed the sanyasi closely.

On the way back, Sagar Babu couldn't hide his excitement. "He looks the same as Mejo Kumar with those brownish eyes, his build, small hands and feet, his mannerisms, his gait, and his way of looking at us."

The sensible Jogen Babu hushed him. Such statements could have a long-lasting impact.

Jyotirmayee had been pacing back and forth down the hall ever since the news of the sanyasi reached her. She was unusually fair and had brownish hair and hazel eyes. Even though Buddhu couldn't conclusively state his feelings, Jyotirmayee was confident a sister's eyes would never mistake identifying her brother.

"Ma, I heard you were looking for me." Buddhu's voice echoed in the hall.

"The sanyasi is at our ancestral home. Radhika went to meet him."

Radhika Goswami was a nephew of Satyabhama Devi, Jyotirmayee's grandmother. Satyabhama, addressed as Choto Thakurma by her grandchildren, lived with one of her three granddaughters, though she was a little more affectionate towards the gentle Jyotirmayee. Her second granddaughter was as god-fearing and spiritual as Satyabhama. Her eldest granddaughter, Indumayee, was a strong and decisive lady whose opinion was sought even by her eldest grandson, Boro Kumar Ranendra Narayan. The youngest Tarinmayee was a bright woman but still a child at heart. Only Jyotirmayee had gone around the country looking for her dead brother every time a rumour of his reappearance surfaced.

Buddhu faced his mother. "So, what is his opinion?"

"Same as yours. Radhika isn't sure."

"Hmmm … guess we'll have to leave it at that."

"Of course not! You go to the man and request him to be our guest for the day. Tell him I sent you. If he's my brother, he will come."

"But Ma … ?"

"I need to know who he is, Buddhu. We heard various stories about Mejo's untimely death in Darjeeling. So many aspects don't match up. Yet, we had made peace with the circumstances. But God has given us a second chance." Jyotirmayee's eyes welled up.

Buddhu knew no logic could convince his mother to change her mind. So, he headed towards the Raj Bari.

The sanyasi was meditating on a mat near the Kamini tree. Buddhu waited till the man opened his eyes.

Extending his greetings, Buddhu narrated the reason for his visit. "I'm here as a messenger of my mother, Jyotirmayee Devi, the sister of Bhawal Kumars. She sent me personally to fetch you. Please come to our house."

The sanyasi smiled but refused to go along. After some persuasion, he assured Buddhu of a visit in the afternoon. "It's not possible for me to start now. Please don't take the trouble of coming again. Instead, you may send anyone who could lead me to your house."

He had recognised Buddhu when he laid his eyes on the young man.

It was evening by the time the sanyasi reached Jyotirmayee's place. He sat on the verandah. When Jyotirmayee saw him, she was taken aback. The man sat with his head slightly down and looked at people from the corner of his eyes. It was the same way her brother would glance at the surroundings and subjects. Jyotirmayee's heart raced, and her emotions clouded her thinking ability. But she shook them away, aware the stakes were high.

Over the next couple of hours, she observed every detail – his features, his style of speaking, his walk, his smile, and his gestures. When he got up to leave, she noticed the first dissimilarity. The man was slightly stouter and had a beard, unlike Mejo Kumar. Also, his utterance of words sounded indistinct.

After his departure, Jyotirmayee heard the divided opinion of her relatives. When Buddhu asked her what she felt, she replied, "I'm thinking of extending another invite to him for a meal tomorrow." She wanted to verify his features and gestures in the broad sunlight.

Chapter 3
Declaring his Identity

The following morning, the sanyasi roamed along the verandah of Raj Bilas, peeping inside the rooms. Some people saw him staring at Mejo Kumar's room for a long time. In the afternoon, he went to Jyotirmayee's house again.

The widow had invited her late sister Indumayee's family members like the previous day, since she wanted more family members to meet the sanyasi and give their opinion. Though their grandmother, Satyabhama, was aging, Jyotirmayee asked her to be present at the gathering as Choto Thakurma had seen Ramendra since childhood. Indumayee's husband, Gobinda Banerjee, their three sons, their only daughter Keni who had become a young widow, Jyotirmayee's two daughters, and Buddhu, were seated with Satyabhama Devi.

The sadhu looked far more comfortable that morning. He spoke in Hindi while enquiring about the identities of the gathered people; he showed a tender attitude towards the delicate Satyabhama. The sadhu familiarised himself with Jyotirmayee's children, Indumayee's children, especially the widow Keni. He broke down after seeing a picture of the Second Kumar.

The environment in the room was sombre as the memory of Mejo Kumar suddenly hit everyone. Jyotirmayee wiped her tears and spoke, "The picture you saw is of my second brother, Kumar Ramendra Narayan Roy. He died in Darjeeling. We don't know if they cremated him as per the proper rituals or his body was…."

Before she could finish, the agitated sanyasi spoke, "No, no! How's that possible?"

Jyotirmayee blurted, "You resemble my brother in many aspects. Is it you, Mejo?"

Disappointing the gathering, the sanyasi vehemently denied any association with the Second Kumar. Though everyone else took the sadhu's words to the face, Jyotirmayee didn't. She observed every gesture, movement, and physical trait. Despite the ash smeared on his body and the long beard, Jyotirmayee didn't miss the brownish eyes, perfectly even teeth, the small size of his hands, fingers, feet, and toes, his way of eating with his index finger jutting out, and his voice. She didn't want him to leave Jaidebpur since she needed to watch him closely. Jyotirmayee was a practical woman; it didn't escape her rationality how easy it was to fall into the trap of an imposter.

Unfortunately, the sanyasi wanted to return to Dhaka. Jyotirmayee didn't have a valid reason to hold him back.

A week later, Buddhu went to meet him again at Buckland Bund, at the behest of his mother. He found out the sadhu was traveling to other religious places.

On the 30th of April, Buddhu took him back to their Jaidebpur house. The sanyasi didn't object. Jyotirmayee minutely observed his movements and behaviour. She wished to verify the birthmarks on the sanyasi's body. So, she coaxed him not to smear ash; he refused. Jyotirmayee didn't want to annoy him, but she couldn't come to a conclusion without inspecting the finer details. It took a lot of effort to convince him not to put ash on his body after taking a dip in the river.

On the 3rd of May, he relented. Buddhu checked for marks that Mejo Kumar's body had. The complexion, the injury mark left by the carriage wheel, the rough skin on selected body parts, and the sadhu's facial features convinced Jyotirmayee that Ramendra had indeed returned. She assembled the relatives.

Almost everyone in the room concluded that Mejo Kumar had come back when they saw him without the ash on his body. Jyotirmayee knew she had to tread cautiously.

On the following morning of 4th May, Jyotirmayee checked all the marks and specific features again. She couldn't leave any loopholes since she was sure the non-believers would be ready to pounce on her.

Jyotirmayee looked straight into the sanyasi's eyes. "Who are you?"

"I'm just an ordinary sanyasi who has renounced the world."

"You're my brother Ramendra Narayan Roy."

The sanyasi was taken aback. "No! You're mistaken."

"Every mark, every trait, every part of your body resembles that of Mejo Kumar. Even your gait, gestures, and mannerisms are like his." Jyotirmayee stood with her arms folded over her chest.

The sadhu denied vehemently.

Outside, a crowd of over ten thousand people had assembled to find out the truth about this mysterious sadhu.

"Please tell everyone the truth about who you are. I know you remember your identity. They are here to welcome their beloved ruler."

The sadhu didn't budge. When Jyotirmayee realised it was impossible to convince the man to confess, she retorted to emotional blackmail.

"I'll not touch a morsel of food or water until you declare who you truly are. I've spent twelve years hoping Mejo is alive. I *know* you are my brother." She slopped on the chair, sniffing.

The crowd kept increasing and hours went by. Unable to bear it any longer, the sadhu gave in.

"Yes! I'm Ramendra Narayan Roy, your brother. You are right." His voice trembled.

It was an emotional moment for the brother and sister to reunite after years. Jyotirmayee wanted to speak to him in private, but she couldn't ignore the masses waiting outside.

Soon, the sadhu stepped outside with Jyotirmayee. The crowd

erupted in joy. Thousands of people were waiting for one glimpse of the man. At the behest of a male voice, the crowd finally became silent.

"Who are you?" a voice screamed from the crowd.

The sanyasi spoke in a voice befitting the Second Kumar. "Kumar Ramendra Narayan Roy."

"Who is your father?" another voice asked.

"Raja Rajendra Narayan Roy."

"And your mother?"

"Rani Bilasmani Devi."

A collective gasp emanated.

"Everyone knows the names of the Raja and Rani. Tell us your wet nurse's name."

It didn't take him even five seconds to utter the name, "Aloka."

The crowd broke into a frenzy as they welcomed the Second Kumar. The cries of 'Jai Mejo Kumar er jai!' filled the air. They sang his praises and showered him with love. The sanyasi felt claustrophobic in the unfamiliar situation; he fell unconscious. Jyotirmayee and the other ladies swiftly sprinkled water on his face and fanned him.

While he recovered, Jyotirmayee consulted with Buddhu and other relatives about the security of the sadhu. They decided to send him to Tarinmayee's home. Buddhu and other male members convinced the crowd to return home.

While the drama unfolded in Jyotirmayee's house, a couple of estate employees who had attended the gathering updated the estate manager, Needham, about the new developments.

On 5th May, Needham wrote a letter to the collector and district magistrate in Dhaka, Mr Lindsay. He narrated the sequence of events right from the first day the sadhu arrived at Buckland Bund five months ago to the sanyasi declaring himself as Mejo Kumar in front of the tenants the previous evening. Needham expressed his concern at the massive acceptance that the sadhu had gained in Jaidebpur. He ended the letter requesting Lindsay to arrange for an immediate inquiry into the matter.

Needham dispatched copies of the letter to the Ranis of the Bhawal family, including Ramendra's wife, Bibhabati Devi, in Calcutta.

On the evening of 5th May, the estate secretary Jogen Banerjee and the manager's assistant Mohini Mohan Chakraborty met the sadhu to interview him.

A few days later, the sanyasi returned to Jyotirmayee's house for good. She immediately allotted one of the vacant rooms to him, for she was sure her brother had returned.

The sadhu started wearing ordinary clothes. Eventually, he shaved off his beard, though he retained the *jata*.

Chapter 4

Satyen and Bibhabati

Calcutta
Lansdowne

Satyendra Nath Banerjee lived at 19 Lansdowne Road with his family, including his sister Bibhabati, the widow of Ramendra Narayan. The lawyer at Calcutta High Court was now an honorary magistrate. Lansdowne was home to the new urban upper-middle-class Bengalis. They were bhadralok comfortable in their skin, language, and culture. Satyen was a prominent bhadralok residing in a two-storied building with a portico, beautified by a gigantic Krishnachura tree.

After Ramen's death, the lawyer displayed concern about her sister's future. What if her marital family plotted to deprive Bibhabati of the money she rightfully inherited? Hushed rumours of a new deed had reached his ears. He coaxed his sister to take her share and move with him to Calcutta. But Bibhabati was equally stubborn.

Satyen had persisted. He vividly remembered the meeting with Ranendra Narayan, the eldest Kumar, a few months after Bibhabati became a widow. Ranendra had looked into his eyes. "Why is Mejo Rani distancing herself from the family?"

Satyen hadn't expected a direct line of questioning. "She's depressed and upset. Besides, she thinks Mejo Kumar's death jeopardised her position in the family."

"And who's putting such dangerous thoughts in her head?"

Satyen reacted immediately. "No one's putting ideas in her head. Everyone knows who's planning to deprive her of her share of the property."

Ranendra stood up. "Rubbish! Satya, I don't appreciate an outsider's involvement in our family matters. It's time for you to focus on your family. You are a newly married man. You must return to your family. We are here to take care of Mejo Rani from now on."

That finality in his tone had sealed the exit option for Satyen. Not the one to give up, he soon returned to Dhaka, accompanied by his mother and wife. Though he didn't live in the Raj Bari anymore, he made several trips on the pretext of checking in on his widow sister.

Finally, Bibhabati relented to Satyen's wishes after a year. In November 1909, she applied for the life insurance claim and received Rs 30,000 after both surviving Kumars of Bhawal forewent their shares. She also received a monthly allowance from the estate, which went up from Rs 1100 to Rs 7000 with the increase in revenue generation. Satyen utilised a portion of her money to buy the present house. Before that, he had shifted his family, including his sister, to a rented house on Harrison Road in Calcutta in 1910.

He moved within the elite circles and often mentioned how Bibhabati was lucky that she had the option of living a comfortable life away from her marital home. The family fell into a set routine as they made Calcutta their new home. Bibhabati didn't have a child of her own; she grew to love her brother's son as her own.

On a morning in May, Satyen received Needham's letter. Though addressed to his sister, he considered it normal to tear it open and read the contents. Bibhabati knew how to read and write, yet societal conditioning ensured her dependence on the male head of the family. When he finished reading it, he stared at the front walls. With a loud sigh, he went indoors.

Bibhabati saw Satyen pacing back and forth when she entered his room. "Dada, you wanted to speak to me?"

"A letter arrived from Needham, the Bhawal estate manager. It has upset the situation like never before."

Bibhabati raised her eyebrows. Satyen read out the letter to his sister before voicing his opinion. "I don't understand how this matter blew up. The man is an imposter and must be here for money and power. The commoners might lack sense, but I expect better from your sisters-in-law. Madhyam Kumar died in Darjeeling. Doesn't it occur to them that a dead man can't return?"

Bibhabati took the letter and read it. Their mother had ensured primary education for the girls, despite their upbringing in extreme circumstances at Satyen and Bibhabati's maternal home after their father passed away. Bibhabati spoke softly, "My husband died in front of my eyes. I saw his dead body taken to the burning ghat. You were present when they lit the pyre. His family was aware of every incident ever since we arrived in Darjeeling. It's been twelve years since that fateful day. Whoever this fraud is, what was he doing for over a decade if he is indeed the Second Kumar? I don't understand how Mejo Didi can accept any random person as her brother. Even if there are some odd similarities between her brother and this cheater, the family members should've handed him over to the law. Instead, they are fuelling the rumours and encouraging a false narrative."

Satyen spoke through gritted teeth, "Of course! They know if they can establish this man as Ramendra Narayan Roy, he can claim his rights over the estate, and they will benefit from it. I sense a conspiracy hatching. Once the authorities start probing, they are sure to find some insider hands-in-gloves with this imposter. But I'm Satya Banerjee, and I'll do anything to foil their plans. Don't worry, Bibha."

Despite his chaotic thoughts, Satyen dressed impeccably before meeting Mr Lethbridge, a member of the Board of Revenue at the

Writers' Building. Satyen needed to understand the actual situation for himself.

In her room, Bibhabati sat on the bed, contemplating the life she left behind in Jaidebpur a decade back. She had let the memories fade away, adjusting to the ambiance in her brother's house. But the communication had triggered her brain and brought back incidents she preferred to leave behind.

Chapter 5
Bibhabati Reminisces

Jaidebpur

Bibhabati's mother, Phulkumari, belonged to the Zamindar family of Uttarpara. Circumstances forced Bibhabati and her siblings to return to their maternal home after her mother became a widow. Phulkumari single-handedly brought up her two daughters and a son. Her elder daughter Malina was married into the family of a Bengali Prime Minister of Jaipur. Phulkumari was keen on a similar match for her younger daughter.

Bibhabati was thirteen years when she was married to the eighteen-year-old tall, muscular, and athletic Ramendra Narayan in May 1902.

Ramendra was very fair, well-built with brownish hair, and had cat's eyes called kata in colloquial language. His moustache was a lighter shade of brown. The beautiful Bibhabati, with a fair complexion, silky hair, rosy lips, and glowing skin, had attractive eyes. Because of the disparity in their social status, the bride's family went to the groom's palace in Bhawal for the marriage ceremony.

After marriage, Bibhabati lived in the women's quarters on the first floor of the primary residential building. Ramendra lived on the ground floor. The family maintained a strict purdah system. The young Bibhabati rarely saw her husband unless he sent for her through an aide. She played with her dolls as the senior women displayed a tender attitude toward the teenage bride. But with time, she found the ambiance claustrophobic, with multiple restrictions imposed on the married women.

Soon, she heard rumours related to her husband's debauched lifestyle. Surrounded by a flock of useless men, her husband and his group believed in merry-making. Most of his lowly companions stuck around and buttered him for free privileges. Ramendra, however, did not drink, unlike his alcohol-addicted elder brother. He was a sportsman of the highest calibre and enjoyed hunting.

Ramendra wasn't interested in running the estate and relied entirely on his elder brother to cater to the business needs. He was fond of music, dance, and cultural gatherings. Pomp and splendour attracted him like fire pulled a moth.

Bibhabati had expected her husband's love. Instead, she received negligence from her spouse. Phulkumari maintained regular correspondence with her daughter through letters. She didn't appreciate that none of Ramendra's female family members guided Bibhabati on how to charm her husband. So, she tried giving explicit instructions through letters to Bibhabati on how to spend time with her husband. It bothered Phulkumari that Bibhabati often felt exhausted. She perceived her daughter was suffering from a critical ailment. She recommended ways for Bibhabati to stay happy since it was the only solution for every illness and the secret to marital bliss.

Bibhabati gradually learned about her husband's vices. Ramendra nurtured a strong liking for female companions. He was so attracted to a dancer called Elokeshi that he brought her to Raj Bari's premises. Eventually, he moved her to an individual house in Dhaka after facing flak for his action. He had a string of mistresses though Elokeshi stayed his favourite.

People knew about his wild parties on boats, and frequent visits to prostitutes. But Ramendra's emotions for Bibhabati were restricted to societal expectations. She visited his room on random nights only at his behest. Otherwise, she didn't see him for weeks or even months.

The young wife was more comfortable with the women in the family compared to her husband, who rarely displayed any emotion.

By the time she turned sixteen, her husband had developed syphilis. His unrestrained lifestyle led to his illness. Though he started treatment and lived in moderation, he returned to the same life after recovering.

In 1906, Bibhabati fell sick and went to Calcutta for treatment. It was a case of anaemia, and gradually she returned to normal. A year later, her mother-in-law, Rani Bilasmani, passed away.

Five years after Bibhabati's marriage, Satyen obtained his B.A. degree, enrolled in the law course in Calcutta, and married a girl from Uttarpara. He visited Jaidebpur on the pretext of getting a job but showed no desire to return. Phulkumari sent multiple letters to Bibhabati, asking her to send Satyen back. Her mother worried about Satyen getting comfortable with the luxury in his sister's marital home.

Eventually, all three Kumars and their spouses travelled to Calcutta for Ramendra's treatment in December 1908. A few months back, Ramendra had won the Viceroy cup for a race. But his condition grew so bad that gummatous ulcers broke out on his arms and legs. Even the alcoholic Ranendra suffered from multiple ailments.

When Ramendra refused to control his urges, Dr S.P. Sarbadhikari, the doctor he consulted in Calcutta, warned him of dire consequences. Satyen returned to Uttarpara, but Phulkumari was concerned about Bibhabati as her anaemia had worsened. In 1909, the Kumars returned to Jaidebpur. They chalked the plan for the Darjeeling trip in response to the doctor's suggestion.

"You must spend time at a hill station for a quick recovery. Between Mussoorie and Darjeeling, which one would you prefer?" Satyen enquired.

But Ramendra hesitated, "Sala Babu, you just got married a few months ago. You should spend time with your wife now." Satyen had brushed aside Ramendra's concerns.

After Ramendra decided on Darjeeling, he called for his secretary, Mukunda Guin. "You and Sala Babu go to Darjeeling and find a suitable house for us."

Satyen and Mukunda finalised a place called Step Aside near the Darjeeling Mall. They returned after a week. On 18th April 1909, Mejo Kumar, Bibhabati, Satyen, and Dr Ashutosh Dasgupta left with an army of twenty-one people. Dr Ashutosh was the son of Dr Mahim Dasgupta, the family physician of the Bhawal Kumars. They arrived in Darjeeling two days later.

Three knocks on the door brought Bibhabati back to the present. Her sister-in-law was calling out to her. Bibhabati wiped her face and answered. Claiming that she had dozed off, Bibhabati wondered what Satyen intended to do about the letter.

Chapter 6
The Imposter Notice

On 9th May, Satyen Banerjee published a letter in *The Englishman of Calcutta*. It mentioned how his sister Bibhabati became a widow because of the sudden death of the Second Kumar of Bhawal in Darjeeling twelve years ago. He claimed to be present along with other friends and relatives when the last rites were carried out, thus ruling out any possibility of the man in Jaidebpur being Bibhabati's husband. He also specifically highlighted the names of the notable civil surgeon of Darjeeling – Lieutenant Colonel Calvert, who attended to Kumar's sickness, and the Deputy Commissioner of Darjeeling – Mr Crawford, who issued the death certificate.

Satyen had returned home with a copy of the newspaper.

"This should end all speculations, and the fraud would understand he can fool the sisters but doesn't stand a chance with us. Even the magistrate must initiate an investigation into this strange incident. Hopefully, better sense will prevail on your sisters-in-law, and they will disassociate themselves from this imposter," he told Bibhabati.

But he didn't mention meeting Lethbridge and asking the latter to get the evidence about Kumar's death in place after handing over the copies of the death certificate and insurance claims.

Bibhabati shrugged. She didn't want to disappoint her brother, but she knew her sister-in-law better. Indumayee passed away in 1920, and Tarinmayee wasn't a strong-minded woman. But Jyotirmayee was the most devoted to her brothers. If Jyotirmayee had decided to support this man, it would be difficult to change her mind.

Later that night, Bibhabati recollected a heated conversation she overheard. Her sister-in-law wanted Satyen to meet the sadhu. Satyen was furious.

"You want me to meet a fraud to confirm if he's a cheater? Mejo Kumar's body turned into ashes in front of my eyes. How can a dead man return to life unless it's a ploy to trap us!"

"It's about your sister's future, so...."

But Satyen had cut off the conversation even before his wife finished the sentence. "Bibha's fortunate to be living here with us. Even when her husband was alive, her life was miserable in the women's quarters. After Kumar's death, she neither had the power nor the position to continue residing there. The life of a widow in her marital home, in the absence of empathetic women relatives or friends, is nothing short of hell. After spending a decade breathing in the fresh air, why would anyone want to return to the suffocating life?"

"I agree with what you say. But can you at least decide about the imposter after meeting him once?"

"I told you it's not needed. There's no need to speak to Bibha about our conversation. I decide what's best for my sister." He dismissed her with a hand gesture.

His wife turned towards the door. She knew how Phulkumari had tried to stop Satyen from interfering in Bibhabati's life after his sister became a widow. Phulkumari had objected to him using Bibhabati's money for this house, but Satyen had ignored her.

* * *

Jaidebpur

Every day, hundreds of people gathered for a glimpse of the sadhu. Most of them went satisfied that Mejo Kumar had returned. On 15th May, people from nearby and faraway places boarded trains to reach the estate for a public meeting. Thousands of people waited in anticipation at the *chatan* of Raj Bari as Adinath Chakrabarty, a Bhawal talukdar, spoke.

"Dear all, today we have assembled here for a special cause. But before I share further details, I want to tell you all about the life of Mejo Kumar twelve years ago."

Adinath narrated the sequence of events beginning with Kumar's presumed death, the rumours related to his cremation, the time-lapse of over a decade, the appearance of a sadhu, and subsequent incidents that established him as Ramendra Narayan Roy. He detailed the meticulous and thorough process Jyotirmayee and other relatives followed to verify the man's identity. "They even verified his physical traits, body gestures, identification marks, and other parameters before ascertaining him as our Mejo Kumar."

Thundering applause followed his statement. Adinath continued, "Most of us believe our Kumar has returned. But I would like to know your thoughts. I request everyone who believes in my opinion to raise their hands." Thousands of hands of both the talukdars and tenants went up. "Now, I wish to see those who don't believe in this theory."

However, not a single hand went up. They passed a resolution with unanimous support from the talukdars and tenants about identifying and verifying the sanyasi as the Second Kumar of Bhawal.

To give this moment a dramatic end, the sanyasi, now addressed as the Mejo Kumar, made a startling appearance riding an elephant. The crowd went berserk and their collective voices cheered his presence 'Jai, Madhyam Kumar, er jai!' as the women gave *ullukar*.

They sent copies of the resolution to the Governor, the Board of Revenue, the district magistrate, and the divisional commissioner. They formed an association called Bhawal Talukdar and Praja Samiti next. It raised funds so that Kumar could seek legal ways to regain his power and position. Gobinda Banerjee, along with Jyotirmayee Devi and Tarinmayee Devi, sent a petition to Lindsay about wanting to present evidence related to the sadhu and validate his identity as Mejo Kumar.

On 29th May 1921, the presumed Mejo Kumar, with his lawyers and a local zamindar, met Lindsay, the collector. They wanted to establish the sadhu as Kumar and sought the requirements to proceed further. Lindsay guided them about filing a petition in court. He also offered an option where the man could provide evidence to the collector. Kumar agreed to avail the second option as per his lawyers' suggestions. There were unaware of the caution message the authorities had already sent to the estate employees on the previous day about not displaying any support to the sadhu.

Lindsay keenly observed the man sitting in front of him. The man's skin showed no signs of syphilis. When Lindsay asked him about what happened in Darjeeling, the man said, "I had pneumonia and was sick for three to four days. Then I lost consciousness. My guru, a Naga sanyasi, found me in an unconscious state, completely drenched, on the ground. I didn't regain my senses for nearly four days."

Lindsay observed that the man couldn't recollect most of the events. He didn't even remember the name of the house in Darjeeling. The conversation seemed amicable, but Lindsay had already formed a biased opinion.

By the end of May, the authorities had selected Mamtazuddin Talukdar, a police officer, and Surendranath Kumar Chakrabarty, an estate official, to trace Dharamdas, the guru of this sadhu, in Punjab. They were to seek his testimony validating or negating the sadhu's statement.

On 4th June, the authorities served a public notice to the tenants. When a talukdar read it out to the sadhu, his eyes shone brightly. It stated how the Board of Revenue possessed conclusive proof about the death of the Second Kumar in Darjeeling and that his body burnt into ashes twelve years ago. So, if anyone claimed otherwise, the man was an imposter. It warned the tenants about the consequences of paying rent to this fraud. Lindsay had lent his name to this notice. As a drastic measure, it also prohibited the sanyasi from entering Jaidebpur in the future.

When they scheduled the announcement of the notice to the public in Mirzapur on 10th June, the crowd created a ruckus leading to the police opening fire. A man died by gunshot.

"I knew they would never let peace prevail," the sadhu muttered under his breath when a talukdar brought him the news of violence.

The notice, followed by the hostile attitude of the Board of Revenue, had already hinted at the impending doom. It was nothing short of a war for those who believed the sadhu was indeed the Second Kumar. Little did they know that their fight for justice would soon blow out of proportion, shaking the nation's judiciary.

Chapter 7

Pamphlets and Foul Play

Calcutta

Satyen had deployed sources to update him about the happenings in Bhawal. When Satyen heard about the notice, the lawyer breathed a sigh of relief. Though he believed the Board of Revenue would never give in to this rubbish claim, he worried about the consequences of emotions triggered in the estate.

Satyen informed Bibhabati about the notice. He was hopeful the fraud would back out after realising that he held no ground for his claim. But Bibhabati countered his statement, "Even if he wishes to, people surrounding him won't let the sadhu get away so easily. Those who have already established their faith in him consider him a saviour. It won't be easy to shake their conviction."

Satyen couldn't help but admire her clarity of thoughts. "I guess we must start gathering evidence so that if this stretches to the court, we have facts to support our statements," he spoke to himself.

Bibhabati returned to her household duties in the kitchen. As she chopped the vegetables, her mind wandered back to her life as a new bride in Jaidebpur.

Jaidebpur, 1903

The fourteen-year-old Bibhabati had heard about Elokeshi Khemtawali from a maid in Raj Bari. The new bride was getting to understand the duties of a wife through the letters from Phulkumari and the words of the senior females. She tried to follow her mother's advice, but Ramendra was already engrossed in the unrestrained life he led. He would send for her only as per his whims. Sometimes, she wondered if he did it out of duty or because of societal pressure.

His relationship with Elokeshi went beyond physical attraction. It affected Bibhabati's young heart. Unfortunately, senior women in her life didn't echo her sentiments. While Phulkumari blamed her daughter for not taking care to attract her husband, Malina called Bibhabati a fool. Malina's letter to her younger sister was full of advice on keeping Ramendra happy through smiles and sweet words.

If only it could be so easy, Bibhabati sighed. Nothing could change Ramendra's habits, not even syphilis.

"Ooh Ma," blood oozed out of her right-hand index finger. She fought back her tears as her sister-in-law rushed to bandage the wounded finger.

* * *

Jaidebpur, 1921

It didn't take long for the influential people to realise the Board of Revenue wasn't willing to accept the sadhu as the Second Kumar. It would jeopardise its means of income and shake the power the authorities held over the estate. So, the talukdars sought innovative measures to establish the king's return.

Durganath Chakrabarty, a talukdar cum poet, played an active part in public meetings to help the sadhu regain his position in the estate. He wrote an elaborate speech equating the prince to God's child. According to this story, God returned the Second Kumar to the earth so that he could resume his responsibilities towards his subjects. It asked them to stand in solidarity and announce their loyalty to their king. It was the first pamphlet that spread across places. Soon, others published many pamphlets praising the king.

There were two primary intentions behind publishing pamphlets. They were supposed to answer questions about the sadhu since influential people and Kumar's close associates had met and recognised him. The second purpose was to describe what happened in Darjeeling before the sadhu returned to his ancestral place.

The first purpose was easier to serve since the pamphlets printed a long list of people who identified the sadhu as the Second Kumar. It began with Jyotirmayee and Ramendra's family members, relatives, close friends, acquaintances, prominent zamindars, talukdars, and tenants. Some pamphlets detailed the meeting of these people with the sadhu to verify his identity. The sadhu usually spoke about a unique incident or an item known only to him and the person who had come to meet him. Listening to the sadhu recall those memories convinced the other person that he was indeed Mejo Kumar of Bhawal.

But these talukdars knew how people were curious about the sanyasi's life in the gap of twelve years. Based on what the sadhu disclosed and after adding some aspects from their imagination, the plot of foul play related to his cremation process was acknowledged in public for the first time through a pamphlet.

"I felt sick after they administered the last dose of medicine. I don't know what happened afterward since I lost my senses. Four to five days later, I woke up and found a group of Naga sanyasis taking care of me. I travelled with the group across the country for years," the sadhu had admitted. He displayed the tattoo of his guru, Dharamdas Naga, on his left arm.

The declaration made people wonder about Dr Ashutosh Dasgupta's role in Ramendra's death. It raised questions about the circumstances under which Dr Henry Calvert issued the death certificate.

The supporters wanted to address the questions and gain sympathy for the wronged king. A pamphlet narrated what had happened at the cremation ground. It stated that when they took Ramendra's body for cremation, a sudden cloudburst and hailstorm forced the accompanying people to take shelter in the nearby areas. They left the body unattended. When they returned later, the body had disappeared. Since it would lead to questions, they lit the empty pyre and circulated that they cremated the body as per rituals.

A group of Naga sanyasis was passing by when they heard sounds from the pyre. They found Ramendra alive and in pain inside it. They took him away since there was no one in the vicinity and nursed him back to health. The young sanyasi lost his memory and became a disciple of Dharamdas Naga. A couple of years ago, the group came to Dhaka, where they clicked a photograph, making it evident that the sadhu had no memory of his identity.

Even newspapers like the *Herald* of Dhaka or the *Dainik Basumati* of Calcutta carried stories about the foul play faced by the sadhu. It highlighted the way Jyotirmayee Devi identified her brother despite the challenges. Now the pamphlets ran those details, citing the newspaper articles to establish credibility. It had become a strange cycle.

By then, Lindsay had already launched an official inquiry into the sadhu's case through his instructions to Needham, the estate manager. Needham, in turn, had sent the assistant manager Mohini Mohan Chakraborty to interview the sadhu.

When Mohini Mohan met him, the latter confirmed the details he had already given in the public gathering. But he refused to answer specific questions, which led to Mohini Mohan doubting the authenticity of his claim. By then, it was clear the sanyasi had managed to win people's trust. Unless the administration took strict action and negated his declaration, Mohini Mohan felt it would become difficult for the Court of Wards to retain control.

He couldn't forget the last words of the sadhu before the latter dismissed the meeting. "I know who I'm, and if needed, I'll prove it to those who can decide the consequences of my declaration. But to the rest, I don't need to provide any evidence."

Lindsay was alarmed by the update. He included his perspective and sent his version of the events to his superiors in Calcutta. Lindsay didn't forget to mention the suspicion raised about the cremation process in Darjeeling. Naga sanyasis supposedly took the Second Kumar after they found him alive and unattended. However, he negated the theory by citing the medical certificate issued by Dr Henry Calvert.

He also possessed the death certificate issued by Mr Crawford and certificates from Satyendra Nath Banerjee and C.J. Cabral confirming the completion of Ramendra's cremation in Darjeeling. Cabral was a servant of the upper menial kind. A clerk of the P.W.D. sub-division, Darjeeling, had also issued a similar statement. Lindsay inferred the certificates provided conclusive evidence about the death of Kumar.

Chapter 8
Lindsay Makes a Move

In Lindsay's mind, the sadhu was already an imposter. His report indicated the steps he and the police took to establish the same. It began with how the man could only speak Hindi and not Bengali. Jyotirmayee Devi and other relatives were grooming the sadhu to influence the tenant's minds. The situation had already worsened when the subjects displayed an immense will to pay the rent to the sadhu instead of the authorities and fought against the police. They were willing to guard the sadhu with their lives.

Lindsay realised the more restrictions he imposed, the stronger the subjects would sympathise with the sadhu. So, he decided to wait and watch. He consulted with the Superintendent of Police, the manager, and the Government pleader about giving the man enough time and opportunity to make mistakes. Alternatively, they also felt that the initial buzz would die if the sadhu stayed inactive for a long time.

Lindsay's next move was to figure out the true identity of the sadhu and prove he wasn't Ramendra. The sadhu's guru, Dharamdas Naga, was spotted in Punjab and shown his picture. Dharamdas identified the sadhu as his disciple Mal Singh of Aujla, who he called Sundardas.

Lindsay communicated with Dr Calvert. The latter confirmed treating the Second Kumar in Darjeeling. Kumar suffered from 'gallstones' and developed biliary colic during his stay. However, he refused a morphine injection, worsening his health. Calvert confirmed the presence of Dr Dasgupta and Kumar's untimely demise. Armed with the evidence, Lindsay issued a notice prohibiting the sadhu from entering the Bhawal estate.

He met Gobinda Mukherjee next for a detailed discussion and hoped to make the family see sense.

"The Board of Revenue holds enough proof of the sadhu being an imposter. There's no point in approaching the Government with his claims about being the Second Kumar of Bhawal. His only option is through the court. Does he have the guts or financial and social support to take this step?" Lindsay smirked.

Gobinda looked pensive, though Lindsay's statement wasn't unexpected. "You have little idea about the chunk of the population who identified the sadhu. Do you think they'll let go of the return of their king without a fight? Even we have evidence that contradicts things informed to us. They didn't cremate Ramendra's body in Darjeeling."

"Interesting! I hope you are aware Ramendra Narayan's wife doesn't hold the same opinion." Lindsay couldn't stop himself from making the jibe.

"Mejo Rani wasn't even in the vicinity of the cremation ground when they put fire to Ramendra's body?"

"Well, if you insist on this point, I could arrange for Needham's wife to meet her when they visit Calcutta next." Lindsay smiled, but Gobinda didn't respond.

When Lindsay left, he felt uncomfortable about the rising possibility of a rebellion against the administration because of the sadhu. Soon, he issued a notice to caution employees to not encourage rumours. He claimed the authorities had identified the man as an imposter.

Then he started collecting the list of rent collectors who supported the sadhu. Lindsay secretly employed people to gather the list of sadhu's prominent supporters. But he also advised employees to proactively make the tenants understand that if they paid rent to the imposter, the Government held every right to confiscate their property for non-payment of taxes.

The imposter notice issued by the authorities on 4th June backfired. People didn't take it kindly. They raised funds for the sadhu to fight it out in court. Lawyer and social activist Ananda Chandra Roy led a campaign to re-establish the sadhu in his place.

Another lawyer, Surendra Nath Mukherjee, was convinced about the return of Ramendra Narayan after meeting the sadhu. He went to Darjeeling to do background research and returned with the belief Satyen Banerjee had a massive role in Ramendra's death and that the Government was taking his side for its vested interest. Suren Babu spoke at various gatherings, claiming to possess evidence about the truth of Second Kumar's cremation in Darjeeling. The incident took a political turn as more influential personalities started associating with it.

The Board of Revenue called an urgent meeting to deal with the imposter and expose his intentions. "People in this country love to credit miracles for events that don't fit into their idea of possible occurrences. So, it's easy for them to stick to the theory of God giving Ramendra a new life. However, we live by logic and rationality. We already possess enough materials to believe a smooth cremation of the Second Kumar occurred in Darjeeling. Besides, there was no rainfall on the 8th and 9th of May. However, it would also be beneficial to strengthen our perspective."

Another member proceeded, "To negate all claims, we have prepared a list of questions for every prominent Bengali bhadralok present in Darjeeling at the time of Ramendra's death. Based on their statements, you must construct the sequence of events as close to the truth as possible."

The list of questions included details of the weather on the day they cremated Kumar. It queried if they knew Kumar personally, if they were part of the group that attended his cremation and whether they stayed until the body turned into ashes. The last questions were about the description of the body before cremation and if they remembered anything unusual or particular during the procession and cremation.

On 7th June, the Board sent the list of inquiries to the commissioner of Darjeeling, while the authorities issued another warning notice to the employees, asking them not to support the sadhu's cause.

Chapter 9

Kedarnath Chakrabarty's Scathing Words

Satyen Banerjee felt disappointed that the imposter was set free. "They shouldn't have just barred his entry from Jaidebpur, but put him behind bars too," he confided in Bibhabati.

He grew restless. Dr Ashutosh met him in Calcutta four to five days after Needham sent the letter to Lindsay and the three Ranis. Satyen then travelled to Darjeeling and met people who could vouch for the completion of Mejo Kumar's cremation. The team representing the Court of Wards had arrived separately.

Together, they started an anti-sadhu campaign. According to their statements, the government had figured out he was a Punjabi with an uncanny resemblance to the late Second Kumar of Bhawal. The parties who conspired against the administration for their gains had brought the man to Dhaka, misled Ramendra's sisters and family, and played with the emotions of the tenants. The primary reason was to help the imposter gain control of the estate as the only surviving heir since they weren't benefitting from the Court of Wards' control. There were articles in the newspaper about how the sadhu couldn't speak any language except Hindi and claimed no recollection of his whereabouts over the last decade. However, most of these campaigns didn't pick momentum.

The first blow to the sadhu's popularity came when Kedarnath Chakrabarty, newspaper *Rayat's* editor, published a series of articles to prove the man a cheater. Kedarnath focussed on why a sadhu possibly turned up in Dhaka after twelve years. He believed there was nothing to debate about Ramendra's cremation since everything happened in the presence of his relatives. However, it intrigued him that twelve years later, a man appeared out of nowhere claiming he was the Second Kumar. Kedarnath questioned, "Why would the sadhu take twelve years to announce his return? What made the erstwhile estate manager, Meyers, retract his statement after initially identifying the sadhu as Mejo Kumar?"

Kedarnath was the first man to compare the sadhu's appearance with the case of the imposter Pratapchand in Burdwan a century before. The editor believed the guardians of the Bhawal estate would draw inspiration from the same story and reject the sadhu's absurd claim.

Kedarnath's bold approach made him unique. He didn't shy away from naming and blaming people he thought were a part of this ghastly conspiracy. According to Kedarnath, the widows lived a miserable life under Jyotirmayee and Indumayee after the death of three Kumars. They approached the Court of Wards that instructed the sisters to move out of the Raj Bari. They left but bore grudges. Since none of the widows had given birth to a child, the sisters were hopeful of gaining their share of the property after the wives passed away. However, the youngest Rani decided to adopt an heir. Much to the sisters' resistance and dismay, she got the requisite permissions. Feeling deprived of the right to the property, Jyotirmayee hatched a plan with her sisters to bring a look-alike sadhu to Bhawal and portrayed him as Ramendra Narayan Roy.

He also mentioned the reason for the sadhu's mass acceptance. It was related to a sense of belonging to the zamindari. Despite the atrocities, familiarity worked wonders between the king and his subjects. The emotions were missing during the rule of the Court of Wards. Besides, the Court of Wards limited the tenants' access to natural produce in the Bhawal Forest.

Kedarnath exposed the sadhu's game. "The sanyasi claims he has renounced the pleasures of the world. So, he would give away his property to the tenants after gaining control of his estate. However, once the power dynamics change, will anyone remember his promise?"

Kedarnath forecasted the administration would fight it out in court and not accept the sanyasi's claims. The court cases would stretch for twelve to fifteen years until the case reached the highest authorities in London. Even if he won the case, the Court of Wards would still control two-thirds of the estate until the adopted son of the youngest widow turned eighteen.

He struck the final nail in the coffin by disclosing the evidence the administration had collected. The authorities had rubbished the story of the rains and hailstorm since the records clearly showed no rainfall occurred on the day of his cremation, three days before and four days after Kumar's death. Then, he mentioned a list of respected and influential bhadraloks who came forward to issue an official statement about the cremation process. They had accompanied the relatives of the late Kumar to the cremation ground and were present when the funeral occurred.

He included the letter from Dr Calvert to the eldest Kumar of the Bhawal estate, where he confirmed attending to a critically unwell Ramendra. Dr Calvert mentioned the treatment he suggested and Kumar's lackadaisical attitude to following remedies. Though he treated Ramendra for fourteen days, it was during three days that his biliary colic got worse. Ramendra's refusal to follow the doctor's orders led to a deterioration of his health and eventually death. This letter absolved Dr Ashutosh Dasgupta of the blame for not consulting senior and experienced surgeons.

Kedarnath mentioned the reputed Indian doctor in Darjeeling, Dr Nibaran Chandra Sen, who catered to Kumar for three days. He highlighted the list of people who contested the claim of the sadhu.

Letters from his maternal uncles proved they didn't find any similarities between the Second Kumar and the sanyasi. Many talukdars and tenants discussed how the sadhu wasn't anything like what their late Kumar was. Mukunda Gain was a prominent name in the anti-sadhu camp.

Mukunda, Ramendra's private secretary, had initially identified the sadhu as the Second Kumar, but later he wrote a letter disputing the sanyasi's claims. Mukunda was personally present when they took the body for cremation. However, Mukunda wasn't present when it turned to ashes. He spotted dissimilarities in physical traits between the sadhu and the Second Kumar. The former was taller, and his nose and lips were wider. The logic of yogic exercises leading to the widening of Kumar's nose didn't convince Mukunda. Kumar's behaviour befitted his royal lineage, while the sadhu was an ordinary man eager to please others. Mukunda claimed to have asked multiple questions that led to dissatisfactory answers.

The sanyasi's inability to speak Bengali was baffling to many people. The anti-sadhu camp reasoned it was because he was a Punjabi, faking as a Bengali. But the supporters blamed it on his loss of memory.

A few people changed camps from being the sadhu's staunch supporters to proving him an imposter. One such lawyer wrote a long article in the newspaper justifying how he figured out that the man was fooling the people of Bhawal. The sadhu's inability to converse in any language except Hindi alarmed the lawyer. Also, the sadhu needed tutoring about the events from Ramendra's past since he could barely answer questions. Even their appearances didn't match. The sadhu's stories about Ramendra's cremation were a bunch of lies since his Guru Dharamdas had met, recognised, and cursed the man for playing with the emotions of the tenants.

Chapter 10
Defamation Suit

The family of Second Kumar and the administration were on the lookout for Dharamdas Naga, the sanyasi's guru. Buddhu suggested, "Once we locate Dharamdas and convince him to meet the man, he can confirm Kumar's words. If he agrees with how one of the Naga sanyasis saved Mejo Kumar from the pyre, it'll also be easy to prove why it took the sadhu twelve years to return home."

Jyotirmayee's elder son-in-law, Chandra Sekhar Banerjee, discovered Dharamdas Naga in Haridwar. Dharamdas wasn't keen to be a part of the ongoing drama initially. However, on 26th August 1921, he agreed to come to Dhaka since the situation required his intervention. Five days later, he went missing from Jyotirmayee's house without making a declaration.

The supporters claimed the police had harassed the man and even bullied him for a statement against the sanyasi. Scared for his life, he decided not to get involved. However, the anti-sadhu camp came up with a different version. According to them, Dharamdas identified the sadhu as his disciple, not as Second Kumar, so Ramendra's family forced him to leave to keep up the pretence.

Rani Bibhabati declined any possibilities of interaction with the sadhu. Her supporters argued Rani was with Ramendra when he died. When Bibhabati knew that her husband was dead and cremated in Darjeeling, how could she even consider meeting any random stranger?

An unidentified assailant stabbed Mukunda Guin in broad daylight in September 1921. Just before his death, he issued an official statement to the police about ruffling the feathers of influential people, leading to his life being cut short.

The sadhu's supporters attempted to convince the administration to accept the sadhu as the Second Kumar. They wanted to sort it out instead of dragging it to the court. But the new district magistrate didn't even acknowledge the letter Rani Satyabhama Devi had sent in July 1922.

In the letter, the aging grandmother stated her belief that the sadhu was her grandson Ramendra. She also felt convinced about the poisoning of Ramendra in Darjeeling that led to his mysterious death. She didn't fail to mention the cremation theories, which proved Ramendra was still alive. For the first time, she blamed Satyendra Banerjee as a suspect in the foul play. She justified Bibhabati's reluctance to meet the sadhu after hearing about Ramendra's cremation from her brother; Bibhabati wasn't present in person. Satyabhama sought the evidence the administration had collected about the sadhu being an imposter since she wanted to consult her lawyers and justify the claims of the sanyasi. She made it clear that though many old employees supported the sadhu secretly, they couldn't voice it out because of the fear of losing employment.

Six months later, in December 1922, Satyabhama Devi passed away. In August 1923, Jyotirmayee wrote to K.C. De, a member of the Board of Revenue. He was visiting Dhaka; she requested an appointment which he agreed to but asked her to send her son-in-law instead. When Chandra Sekhar Banerjee met De, the latter guided him through the process.

"The sadhu must give a petition with all his claims. Only then the Board of Revenue can initiate some action. Until now, the people who have claimed the sadhu is Ramendra Narayan are just his well-wishers."

Chandra Sekhar mentioned the details of the meeting to the sadhu and other relatives. Yet, it was only in December 1926 that the sadhu filed a petition claiming to be Ramendra Narayan Roy.

In July 1921, Purna Chandra Ghosh of Harbaid created a big uproar through his pamphlet, which put the story of the sadhu/fakir directly blaming Satyen Babu and Dr Ashutosh Dasgupta for the death of Raja Ramendra Narayan. He mentioned Satyen as the brain and Dr Ashutosh as the hand that killed Ramendra by separating him from his family.

Until then, Dr Ashutosh knew that the sadhu's version of the cremation had jeopardised his reputation as a physician. But no one dared to make a direct allegation till Purna Chandra Ghosh published his name in the scandal. The doctor, unable to bear this character assassination, filed a case against the author cum publisher, the man who printed the pamphlet/booklets, and the bookseller.

The magistrate pronounced Purna Chandra Ghosh guilty and sent him to prison for three months. However, he appealed against the judgment. The judicial authorities approved his request for a retrial.

The sanyasi was sitting outside Jyotirmayee's house in Armanitola in Dhaka when a prominent talukdar brought him the news of the retrial that had happened the previous day. Lindsay's notice had made him shift to Jyotirmayee's house in Dhaka from Jaidebpur.

"What did they say?" the sadhu asked in Hindi when he noticed the man standing.

"The doctor said he executed the orders of Dr Nibaran Sen and Dr Henry Calvert. He didn't act according to his will but attended to Kumar as per their instructions. The pamphlets directly accused him of conspiring about Kumar's death."

"And Purna Chandra? What was his opinion?"

"He believed in the words he had written and acted in good faith for the good of the people. He says he bore no ill will towards the doctor."

The sadhu sat in contemplation even when the sun had set. He knew the case would open a can of worms.

The medical certificate mentioned Kumar suffered from biliary colic, but the court refused to accept it as a public document since it was for insurance claims. The court found Dr Dasgupta's statement that Kumar was suffering from biliary colic intriguing since no prescription or any doctor mentioned it elsewhere. Even Dr Dasgupta hadn't bothered to inform Dr Sarbadhikari about Kumar's biliary colic.

After discovering the prescriptions from Kumar's Darjeeling trip, the judge found that none of the drugs had anything to do with biliary colic. Certain prescribed drugs could've aggravated his diarrhoea and led to the worsening of his health. The second discovery ran a shockwave since a suggested drug contained a small dose of arsenic as an ingredient in the mixture. It couldn't be a coincidence that Kumar's symptoms on 8th May mentioned pain in the abdomen, irregular pulse, perspiration, bloody stools, severe diarrhoea, thirst, and collapse – the signs of arsenic poisoning. Since there were multiple drugs administered to Kumar based on his health, it was plausible that this drug by Dr Dasgupta led to the deterioration of his health and eventually, his death.

When the same talukdar visited the sadhu a couple of months later, he beamed excitedly. "The court had asked for the truth about the cremation. Though the doctor claimed following Hindu rituals for cremation, a few witnesses said the body was taken out during the night from Step Aside. Most of them weren't present till the last moment, though they heard the rains stopped the funeral. A witness stated the funeral proceedings began the next morning, but he found it strange how they had covered the body from head to toe. Since the dead body of a local was missing, rumours about a local's body replacing Kumar's body went around. Finally, some people confirmed they had seen Kumar alive a few days after the cremation."

Two days after the judgment, the sadhu heard the magistrate had pronounced Purna Chandra not guilty. The magistrate said there was no clarity about Kumar's death or why the doctor used arsenic in the drug. Dr Dasgupta's role in the death of Ramendra Narayan was becoming questionable. The sadhu had waited for this judgment and the consequences of the seeds of doubt that had slowly developed in the minds of the Bhawal tenants.

The Government filed a suit against the judgment. The lawyer on behalf of the Government claimed the pamphlet was an unnecessary item after twelve years of Ramendra's death, especially when it was doubtful if Purna Chandra was even aware of the evidence when he published it first. According to him, Dr Dasgupta didn't need to administer the drugs personally. It was interesting how the government got involved in a private case. Since Dr Dasgupta was the full-time medical attendant to Ramendra, he must have prescribed the drug to Kumar.

But the judges too considered it impossible for a lower court judge to assess and raise questions about a medical practitioner's actions in treating his patient. Dr Dasgupta couldn't prescribe any drug without the knowledge of the senior doctors. Also, it was questionable if the amount of arsenic in the mixture could lead to the death of an individual. It also doubted whether Purna Chandra knew about the evidence when he wrote the story. The court found Purna Chandra guilty and sentenced him to one month's imprisonment and a fine of 1000 rupees.

In the rented house on Harish Mukherjee Street in Calcutta, the melancholy didn't reflect on the sadhu's face, though he was affected.

"These are moments when I feel we shouldn't have raked up the past and made it inconvenient for our people. Look where the pursuit of truth is leading us at this moment," the sadhu lamented.

Jyotirmayee stood with a stoic face. She was equally upset at the verdict, but the step taken by the administration made their uncanny interest in the case quite obvious.

Chapter 11
Bibhabati's Refusal

Satyen stayed in touch with the secretary of the Board of Revenue in Calcutta after providing him with documents like the medical certificate from Dr Calvert. He supported the Government in proving Ramendra's natural death and cremation.

Satyen accompanied Sasanka Ghosh, the government pleader, to meet Mr Lees in Darjeeling. Bibhabati's brother also took the representatives to places and introduced them to people who certified the cremation of Ramendra's dead body as per rituals. He collected the weather reports, which proved no rainfall had occurred on the day of Kumar's death.

While Satyen tried defending his sister's interests (and his own), a lot was happening at Jaidebpur. Satyabhama wrote a letter to the Raja of Bardhhaman, seeking confirmation on Ramendra's demise in Darjeeling. Since the Raja couldn't state much with absolute surety, she wrote a letter to the district magistrate next. The aged woman wanted to see things settled while alive. She sent her second granddaughter-in-law a letter.

Bibhabati refused to accept it since she was sure about its content. Satyabhama wouldn't leave any stone unturned to convince Bibhabati about meeting the sadhu once. Almost every relative of her late husband was confident that if she met the sadhu, she would change her mind. But Bibhabati felt disgusted. She knew the dead couldn't return. Later, she informed Satyen about the letter.

"What if it contained something important or contradictory to what you believe?" Satyen wasn't in favour of her emotional reaction.

"Impossible! I know how the minds of the Bhawal Raj family function. They would need nothing but my validation to prove their claims. But we know the truth, so there's no point in dragging this further." She stayed firm in her decision.

Bibhabati recollected how Jyotirmayee would visit Calcutta and update her with probable sightings of Ramendra at various places across the country. Jyotirmayee travelled to those places hoping to spot Ramendra, rumoured to have become a sadhu in the company of other religious men. While Jyotirmayee latched on to every ray of hope, Bibhabati moved on to a new life of acceptance of fate and widowhood.

After the sadhu shifted to Calcutta with Jyotirmayee's family, including Jyotirmayee and Satyabhama, Bibhabati saw him a few times when the man drove down with Buddhu in front of her house. In the first instance, the phaeton had stopped a little away from her residence. Buddhu had pointed at the Krishnachura tree. She also spotted him at other places though they never exchanged a word.

One day, her sister-in-law took Bibhabati inside her room, and asked her the dreaded question. "Did you see the sadhu? I know you hid behind the Krishnachura tree when his vehicle passed in front of our house. Does he resemble your—"

She didn't get the time to finish the sentence. Bibhabati hissed, "No! My husband died in Darjeeling in front of my eyes. The sadhu doesn't resemble him in any way."

Bibhabati stopped herself from saying how Jyotirmayee and Ramendra's relatives' intentions could be equally evil. She resolved not to entertain any more conversation about the sadhu with her family or relatives.

"I told your brother to meet him. But when has he ever listened to anyone?"

"I'm glad he refused. We both know why the man can't be my husband."

That ended all possibilities of having a conversation about Bibhabati's future related to the sadhu.

While Bibhabati dealt with nosy relatives sternly, Satyen tried to strengthen their perspective by accumulating evidence of the death of Ramendra Narayan. His sources informed Satyen how the sadhu had collected rent from the tenants. After his declaration, the tenants voluntarily paid him the rent. However, after the Government threatened them, they started paying rent to the Board again. When the sadhu realised the Government wouldn't accept him as the Second Kumar without a legal battle, he moved to Dhaka and continued collecting rent for his share of one-third of the property.

He wasn't ready to give it up because the estate belonged to his father, and the three princes, including him, had inherited it. Why would the Board of Revenue enjoy the benefits which rightfully belonged to him? Eventually, the collection in the Government accounts dropped. The authorities sent a letter to the eldest Rani Sarajubala Devi, widow of Boro Kumar, asking her to advise people to exercise caution against the imposter and not pay him any rent.

Chapter 12

Public Support for the Sadhu

The sadhu's supporters felt charged up. They circulated another round of pamphlets highlighting fresh discoveries. The famous lawyer Suren Banerjee, the legal advisor to the sadhu, wrote about the involvement of Satyen Banerjee and Dr Ashutosh Dasgupta in Ramendra's death. Kumar wasn't in a critical state when he left for Darjeeling but died within three days of the treatment there. Thus questions about the doctor's role in his death were unavoidable. There were stories about Kumar lying unattended until the afternoon of his demise. Most didn't know what had happened and people heard a twisted version, further distorted with time and circumstances.

Banerjee wrote about the lack of transparency in Kumar's cremation. Questions about the body cremated on the night of 8th May and again on the 9th morning made people wonder whose body it was. It was eerie that other than Satyen and Ashutosh, no one had come forward to state they were present at the time of cremation and had witnessed the body of Kumar turn into ashes. Banerjee also mentioned how after Satyabhama's demise, the sanyasi performed the last rites of his grandmother, as per her dying wish.

A few weeks before Suren Banerjee published his article, Kumar carried out the annual rituals for his late Choto Thakurma on her first death anniversary. The tenants, talukdars, relatives, and friends had witnessed and accepted the sadhu performing his duties as a grandson.

Suren Babu ended the letter with a sarcastic jibe at the British administration. He struggled to understand how the super-efficient machinery of the Government failed to expose the true identity of the sadhu if he was an imposter, while the people of Bhawal accepted the man with open arms. Suren Babu claimed it was because the people had realised the man was Kumar himself, and the administration had no way to prove otherwise.

Even though the administration banned him from visiting the Bhawal estate, he lived as a member of Jyotirmayee's family in Armanitola in Dhaka city. His acceptance by the majority as the Second Kumar was evident in how people welcomed him at social gatherings, or his presence at events like Satyabhama's cremation went unquestioned.

In 1924, he shifted to Calcutta when the defamation case of Purna Chandra versus Dr Ashutosh began in the Calcutta High Court. He rented a house called Bose Park on Harish Mukherjee Road in Bhawanipore and lived there for five years, accompanied by Jyotirmayee, Buddhu, and other relatives.

Soon, he declared his interest in visiting Sarajubala Devi at her father's house in North Calcutta. Sarajubala belonged to an illustrious family of traders. Her grandfather had owned the Bowbazar market in Calcutta. Her father, Surendranath Matilal, was a lawyer at the High Court and owned some properties. Matilal also served as a manager under Rani Bilasmani in 1901. Meyers succeeded him. Even Sarajubala's family had gone to Jaidebpur to get her married to Ranendra Narayan since the Bhawal Raj family held a higher status. She had birthed a son who passed away after three months. By her marriage to Boro Kumar in 1901, she knew Ramendra well.

"Do you recognise me?" Sarajubala's mother had asked the sadhu, fully aware of the last meeting with Ramendra almost sixteen years ago. The sadhu not only recognised her but also answered her questions correctly.

When Sarajubala met him, emotions ran high. Her brother Sailendra Matilal had met the sadhu two years back in Dhaka. But his narration did not convince her. But after a look at the man in front of her, she knew he was no fraud.

Many other family members of Sarajubala interacted with the man and believed the Second Kumar had returned. Over the next few years, he found support in his eldest sister-in-law as the court case got murkier.

Jyotirmayee hoped Bibhabati would meet the sadhu. "I'm certain she will realise her mistake and thank the Almighty for bringing you back to the world."

The man shook his head. "I doubt it. Bibhabati had every possible way of getting in touch with me if she wished to. Even now, the Bhawanipore thana police told me in no kind terms that I must maintain a distance from her residence."

"You aren't bound to listen to them. Bibhabati is your wife." Jyotirmayee found it silly how the police were getting involved in the personal matters of a husband and his wife.

"They will arrest me if I violate the order," he sighed.

On certain nights, he reflected on his bond with Bibhabati. The years they spent as a married couple were nothing special since he couldn't recollect any tender moment to hold on to. But he hadn't expected her stubborn resistance. Ramendra believed women didn't rebel against men, especially their husbands. Did he regret his past behaviour? He wasn't sure.

When the newspaper *Dainik Basumati's* correspondent interviewed the sadhu in Bengali, the latter voiced his displeasure about the order. But he didn't forget to mention that Bibhabati had seen him a few times when he drove down in his car.

Soon, realisation dawned on the sadhu and his family. They understood that unless the man got involved directly, the Board wouldn't take corrective action. In December 1926, the sadhu presented a memorial to the Board of Revenue to confirm his identity and withdraw the imposter notice. But the Board rejected his plea on 30th March 1927, stating that the investigation would be a waste of time if they found him an imposter. On the other hand, if he was Ramendra Narayan, the administration still needed to follow a legal process to hand over the estate to him.

The Board could only prevent his formal recognition. The sadhu had made a name in the eminent social circles of the city and had purchased shares and properties. He occupied social positions and held power as Ramendra Narayan. He became the Bengal Landlords association's member and attended parties as the Mejo Kumar of Bhawal. During this period, he attended many events, including the upanayana ceremony of his cousin Phani Bhushan Banerjee's son at Phani's father-in-law's house. He rode to the function in Dhaka on a tom-tom, just like Mejo Kumar.

Chapter 13
Filing a Suit

Soon after, Bibhabati, fully aware of the restriction order on the sadhu, went to Jaidebpur to address the tenants about the fraud sadhu and his ill intentions. She declared the Government had collected evidence to prove him an imposter but was holding it back to produce in the court if the need arose. Mejo Rani intended to discourage them from paying rent to the cheater. Though it was debatable if Bibhabati acted as per the Government's instructions or out of her own will, she had her interests to protect since lesser rent collection meant lower monthly income for the widows.

Bibhabati had heard how the sadhu conducted the Punyaha festival in 1929 and openly asked for rent from the tenants. It was a festival celebrating the bond between a ruler and his subjects. The estate hadn't seen a Punyaha ritual after Boro Kumar passed away. The rebellious act was an open challenge to the authorities as the tenants flocked to offer tribute to their Mejo Kumar. Another notice issued in April 1929 forbade the sadhu from entering Jaidebpur. By then, the man had enough and fought back, stating that he was the lawful owner of the property.

The news of Bibhabati arriving at Jaidebpur reached the sadhu through one of his trusted talukdars. "Rani Ma is visiting the estate. She will advise the talukdars and tenants not to go against the administration."

"Carry on. I'm sure there's more. Since Mejo Rani has travelled from Calcutta to Jaidebpur after so many years, her speech must include some fiery statements."

"She says you are…" the man didn't know how to proceed.

"Imposter, cheater, fraud? Of course, she must mention that. How else will the people stop paying me the rent?"

After the talukdar left, the sadhu kept wondering about Bibhabati's presence. There was a possibility of Satyen influencing her decision to come down. It was also likely the Government was a part of this ploy. But he couldn't shake away the feeling that Bibhabati might have realised the need to do this based on her requirement for money from the estate. If the last was true, the chance of reconciliation was nearly impossible. To him, Satyen's reaction was the outcome of things he knew about the Darjeeling events. But he had expected Bibhabati to be a better judge of character. He sighed. It wasn't the time to ponder and fret. He called for Buddhu.

"We shouldn't wait any longer. I want to file a suit, requesting the court to declare me the Second Kumar."

Soon, the sadhu, his sisters, and their families consulted their lawyers for their next move. As per their suggestion, he filed a declaratory suit on 30th April, 1946, in the court of the first sub-judge of the Dhaka district, claiming his identity and his share of the Bhawal estate. In his plea, he narrated his history, what happened in Darjeeling, how the Naga sadhus saved him, his travel stories across the country, and his homecoming after twelve long years. He described the mass acceptance he received from the people of Jaidebpur after they came to know of his true identity.

In the next part, he specified that his wife, Bibhabati, and her brother, Satyendra Nath Banerjee, hatched a conspiracy influencing Lindsay to issue an imposter notice against him. Bibhabati felt prejudiced by their thoughts and refused to meet her husband to validate his identity. She was the first, and Sarajubala was the second defendant in the suit. The adopted son of the youngest Rani was the third, and the last Rani was the fourth.

Hearing Sarajubala Devi's name, the sadhu hesitated. "Why should Boro Rani's name be mentioned beside the tainted souls? She has always been warm and welcoming. Even her mother has accepted me as Ramendra Narayan."

But the lawyer persisted. "It's not about your equation with Boro Rani. You must understand you are filing the case against the manager of the Bhawal estate under the Court of Wards. All three Ranis and Ram Narayan, the adopted son of Choto Rani, receive a portion of the rent as income every month. So, you can't leave out one." He reluctantly agreed.

Before filing the case, the sadhu's lawyers had a detailed discussion of the instances where the miraculous return of a prince or king was celebrated or proved to be a well-laid-out trap. It included Pratapchand of Burdwan Raj, Rudra Narayan Roy from Midnapur, Raghubir Singh of Landhaura, and the Tichborne case of England.

They knew the sadhu's case would follow a similar pattern. They noted six steps in all these cases of miracles. The protagonist was flawed, and some people close to him hatched a conspiracy. The plan usually involved a female, a cremation that went wrong, and the reappearance of the protagonist after a time gap as a changed character. Finally, he fought against the administration to claim what rightfully belonged to him.

When the sadhu filed the suit, Alan Henderson was the district judge of Dhaka. The Government pleader met him and requested a young European officer as the special subordinate judge. Henderson was curious since Indian judges usually heard such cases.

The pleader explained, "If a Hindu judge of Dhaka is in charge of the case, his judgment will always be biased. It's a matter of emotions associated with the caste and religion of the country. The Hindu public will forgive no one who hurts their religious sentiments. These Indians are obsessed with magic and miracles. Even in this case, they would rather put their faith in the imposter since the story of divine intervention sounds fantastic. Try to show them the reality; you'll face their wrath. Even the Indian judge will become prejudiced despite the absurdity of the events."

Henderson felt concerned about the situation. But he decided not to forward the request since he worried the High Court might reject it. Eventually, the case came up for trial in the court of the subordinate judge of Dhaka district, Mr Pannalal Basu, a professor turned lawyer.

The sanyasi was seated on the bed when Jyotirmayee entered. "It begins tomorrow." Her voice broke. "If only she hadn't been this rigid, we wouldn't be going through this. I don't understand why she can't meet you once."

The sadhu didn't respond. There wasn't any emotional bond between them. But he hadn't expected Bibhabati's stubbornness. When he returned as a sadhu, he had assumed she would be one of the first to welcome him.

"You aren't saying anything." Seeing the man sit in silence, she continued, "it must be that brother of hers poisoning her mind."

The sadhu looked away.

"They must have celebrated after killing you. Do you know Satyen bought the house using your share of the money? Shameless! A lawyer at High Court and still living off his sister's income. *Chhi!* I'm sure he's giving her ideas about how the income will stop after you establish your identity. I don't understand why the police never questioned Ashu doctor and Satya after suspicions about the cremation became stronger. I only pray God does justice and be with us in our journey to the truth." Jyotirmayee folded her hands and touched them to her forehead.

The sadhu snapped at her. "If only the court functioned as per your orders! I need some quiet time to think. The lawyers will come to meet me after lunch."

Jyotirmayee gave an indulgent smile and walked out. The sadhu focussed on those incidents or instances that could strengthen his claims to prove his identity. He would need to repeat events from the Darjeeling phase umpteen times in and outside the court. It was critical to maintaining consistency in his statements.

Chapter 14

Darjeeling from the Sadhu's Perspective

Ramendra had attached little importance to the doctors who treated his syphilis. Every time it started healing, he would immediately return to his old habits. It grew so bad that he had to travel to Calcutta to see a renowned surgeon.

The doctor stayed within his limits while voicing his opinion. It irked him to see that the patient wasn't serious about his treatment.

"If you don't lead a controlled life from now on, your syphilis will only get worse. Already ulcers have broken out in your arms and legs. You keep scratching them, drawing blood out of the skin." He ran his hands through his hair.

"Doctor, I'm not fond of people dictating the terms and conditions of my lifestyle. Instead of telling me where I went wrong, can you say what I should do now to recover fast?" Ramendra looked straight into his eyes.

The doctor was well-versed in dealing with rich people. "You need to restrain your urges, stick by the prescribed medicines, and go for a change, preferably to any hilly place for a couple of months."

When Ramendra informed his family, Satyen jumped in and asked if Kumar would prefer Darjeeling or Mussoorie. Eventually, they zeroed in on Darjeeling. Satyen, accompanied by Mukunda Guin, went to the hill station to make the requisite arrangements.

When his family physician, Dr Mahim Dasgupta, heard about the impending trip, he met Kumar.

"Take Ashu with you. He has just passed his medical exams and is a doctor now."

Ramendra had laughed at the elderly's suggestion but he persisted. "If you need any medical assistance, Ashu can help out urgently as an assistant to facilitate your recovery."

When Ramendra left on the train, Bibhabati, Satyen, Dr Ashutosh Dasgupta, Mukunda Guin, and an entourage of estate officials, guards, servants, cooks, and maids accompanied him.

After reaching Step Aside, their accommodation in Darjeeling, Ramendra found the weather suitable. He looked forward to the fresh air and hoped to return to Jaidebpur soon. However, he fell critically sick. Diarrhoea with bloody stools and continuous vomiting made him weak. Ashutosh administered the medicines suggested by the foreign doctor, Henry Calvert. But they didn't help.

The doctor suggested a morphine injection to stop the diarrhoea. The sadhu couldn't remember most of the conversation because he kept moving in and out of a dazed state of mind. On that fateful day, he remembered shivering and feeling hollowness in the stomach. The pain had worsened and his chest was burning. Suddenly, he collapsed and fell unconscious.

The sadhu had no memory of what happened next. He had woken up at the sound of the hailstorm and shivered inside a cloth drenched with rainwater. A grunting sound came out of his mouth as he tried screaming for help. Unable to bear the chilly air and cold rains, he vigorously moved his loosely tied foot.

While he struggled to set himself free, he felt another hand on his foot. He used all the energy left in his body to grunt before collapsing again. When he woke up next, he saw a group of sanyasis around.

"*Amı kothay?*" tumbled out of his mouth.

"Oh, you are finally awake. How are you feeling now?" The man spoke in Hindi.

"Do you know who I am?"

"No! I have known you only for the last four days, as a living man put on the funeral pyre. Who are you?"

Unfortunately, his memory was blank. He could neither recollect his name nor his place of residence. The sanyasi narrated how he and his fellow sanyasis had saved him.

"There was no one near the pyre. I felt shocked upon seeing an unattended body on the cremation ground. I assumed whoever had accompanied the body had run away to find shelter from the rains. Then, I waited to see if anyone would turn up. Since you were getting drenched, I took the help of my group of sanyasis. We carried you to this shed and catered to your ill health."

They also spoke about a kind man who provided the group with a blanket and medicines that revived Ramendra's health. He was fit to go after a while, but the man's memory hadn't thrown up any event or clue for him to connect to his past. He decided to accompany the sadhus, who happily welcomed him. With time, he became a disciple of Dharamdas Naga.

The nightmares began a couple of years later. The sadhu often saw people or incidents in his dream. Their faces were always hazy. At times, he dreamt about grief and death, while a few times, he saw faces.

Then the faces started becoming more visible, and he almost visualised the events. Over the last couple of years, he started recollecting his past as he remembered names, places, and events. Finally, when he knew who he was and where was his ancestral home, he turned up in Dhaka, alone.

He assumed he looked different. Besides, he smeared ash on his face and body. He felt most people wouldn't identify or relate him to Ramendra Narayan.

But the people of Dhaka surprised him as they connected the sadhu to the Second Kumar. Even when Buddhu came, the sadhu felt he could get away without revealing too much. But Jyotirmayee had stood firm on her conviction. Despite people telling her that the sadhu had no connection with Ramendra, she decided to follow her heart.

It was painful for him to see the anguish his family, especially his sisters, went through in his absence. On the day he proclaimed his identity, he felt a burden lift off his chest. He didn't have to pretend to be someone else.

Of course, there were nay-sayers even in his case. Some refused to believe he was Ramendra. Then some, like Mukunda Guin, accepted him, then took a U-turn. But he didn't bear them any grudge. He understood their doubts and concerns. He also knew about the pressure on his subjects to issue statements contradicting their beliefs.

Bibhabati's stand shocked him. While he didn't expect his wife to feel overjoyed at his reappearance, he thought she would be more than happy to meet and validate his identity. Living the life of a married royal Hindu woman was far more prestigious and respectable in society than being a widow. Bibhabati refused all forms of correspondence. She hadn't even shown the basic respect of accepting Satyabhama's letter. It irked the sadhu how she brought a police order about not wanting to meet him.

These days, he often wondered how much Bibhabati knew about what happened in Darjeeling. The more he thought about it, the more convinced he felt about the foul play where his brother-in-law and Ashu doctor planned to kill him. At times, he suspected Bibhabati's involvement in the crime.

He would have forgiven her hadn't she come to Jaidebpur and triggered his opposition camp by certifying him as an imposter. Now, he knew the road to reconciliation looked dubious.

Chapter 15
Bibhabati in Jaidebpur

Calcutta

Satyen had returned early in the day. The last few weeks were full of disappointment for Bibhabati and Satyen.

He addressed Bibhabati, "The administration, the honest people of Bhawal, and the employees of the Bhawal estate need you to step up as the widow of the Second Kumar of Bhawal. This sadhu is fooling people and earning rent, affecting the income that you and the other widows rightfully deserve. He's making a place in the minds of innocent people in the name of a man who's no longer alive. Eventually, they'll rebel against the administration if they feel the Court of Wards isn't giving the sadhu what is rightfully his. You know how disrespectful that'll be to the memory of our beloved Kumar."

Bibhabati had listened to Satyen with undivided attention, but his speech was repetitive, and she was bored of hearing the same saga of the sadhu. If the administration was so capable, as her brother believed, she couldn't decipher why they did not curb the movement and speech of the sadhu, especially if they had resources and evidence to take action against him.

"What do they want from me?" she responded curtly.

"Your sisters-in-law are blinded by their love, or they are a part of the plan. Boro Rani has accepted him as her brother-in-law. The youngest Rani of the estate hasn't responded, but her interests are protected. She has adopted a son, who has the rights to the estate after he becomes a major. It's you I'm worried about."

Bibhabati's heart melted at her brother's concern. Everyone in the family, especially the female members, had wanted her to continue living at the Raj Bari as a widow. Even now, they wished for her to meet the sadhu and check if he was Ramendra. Not her brother, who supported her during her worst phase. He always had her best interests in mind. So what if he considered her money as his? Didn't a sister have the right to share her resources voluntarily?

"Please tell me what I must do to ensure our safe future and that the property doesn't fall into the wrong hands," she assured him without a second thought.

"Visit Jaidebpur at the earliest and meet those talukdars not convinced by the sadhu's statements. Take them into confidence and address the tenants as Rani Bibhabati, widow of Ramendra Narayan Roy. Try to convince them why he's an imposter. Let your speech be a mix of emotional plea and hard-hitting facts. The first part will come from your experience as Kumar's widow. The second part can arise from the cremation details, as per records and the administration's perspective towards the sadhu. Your presence will make them understand why they shouldn't believe the sadhu. After you leave, the number of people in the anti-sadhu camp would have grown manifold." Satyen's nostrils flared up.

A mild shiver ran down Bibhabati's spine. She hadn't been to Jaidebpur or the Raj Bari for a decade. To return to a place that was now a battleground between her family by blood and marital family wasn't an easy decision. But education and experience had made her a wise woman. She went to Jaidebpur a fortnight later after communicating the details to the Bhawal estate manager. Though she felt butterflies in her stomach, it was reassuring to know that the Board had barred the sadhu from entering Jaidebpur. It also meant that Ramendra's sisters were away from the town, thus ruling out all possibilities of a showdown between Jyotirmayee and Bibhabati.

The familiarity of the place made her feel nauseous. She recollected the years she spent as a married woman and the months as Ramendra's widow. Strangely, she had felt similar emotions in both phases.

After resting for a while, she spoke to Jogen Babu from behind the screen in Raj Bari. She wanted to meet the talukdars who didn't believe the fraud sadhu. Bibhabati stayed on for a couple of days. She met many talukdars and even addressed the tenants from behind the purdah.

"You know your dearest prince had an untimely death in Darjeeling twelve years ago. We got the best doctors to attend to him. Unfortunately, his condition grew critical. After his demise, his cremation process adhered to the Hindu rituals. Our friends and relatives were a part of this funeral from the procession to when his body turned to ashes. A huge number of people are willing to come forward and vouch for the truth. Even the authorities possess multiple pieces of evidence related to Kumar's death and cremation in Darjeeling. They will produce it as and when needed." Bibhabati stopped. She heard rounds of murmur from the assembled crowd.

When the buzz died, she continued, "Now I hear a strange man has turned up in Dhaka, a sanyasi who claims to be the Second Kumar. He is conning and collecting rent from innocent people like you. It's part of a bigger conspiracy, and the authorities know who's behind it. But they'll disclose the truth only when the right time comes. Many people supported him initially. But those who dug deeper left his side as they soon realised the man was a fraud and only spoke statements tutored by someone who knows the royal family closely. You have seen the imposter notice by the Government. It didn't happen overnight. I understand and sympathise with your sentiments but I'm worried about all of you. Some of you continue to hand over the rent to this sadhu, swayed by false stories. What if the Court of Wards takes action against those who fail to pay rent to the authorities?" she sighed.

By then, the people sounded agitated. The crowd felt divided over their opinion towards the sadhu and loyalty towards Bibhabati. A section had expected Bibhabati to confirm the sadhu as Mejo Kumar. But for some tenants, her presence and speech took away the guilt or indecisiveness in not acknowledging the sadhu as Ramendra Narayan. They supported her choice and thought process.

One talukdar spoke, "Rani Ma, how can we disown him? Our Raja Babu has returned."

Another one spoke next, "Please meet him once, Rani Ma. You'd understand that he's no imposter."

Bibhabati felt annoyed at every random person asking her to meet the sadhu. "You are all delusional. How can you be so irrational? Don't you understand this is just a conspiracy hatched by our enemies?"

Soon, the talukdars siding with the sadhu realised it was useless to convince the Rani about meeting the sadhu. But a section also wondered if it was because Rani knew better than all of them about the truth of Kumar's death.

When Bibhabati sat in her room that evening, she knew her words had instigated doubts in the mind of the non-believers and fear in the heart of the tenants. She had completed her mission in Jaidebpur and was to leave for Calcutta the next day.

During the night, she tossed and turned. The surroundings and familiar faces brought back memories of her past.

Chapter 16

Darjeeling from Bibhabati's Perspective

They had rushed to Calcutta to meet a renowned doctor. Ramendra's syphilis had worsened, and rashes broke out on his arms and legs. When he returned, Ramendra asked Satyen to find a suitable hill station. After zeroing in on Darjeeling, Satyen visited the town with Mukunda Guin and finalised Step Aside for their stay. She smiled, recollecting the excited face of her brother.

She learned about Dr Ashutosh Dasgupta joining them on the trip. The senior Dasgupta was her husband's family doctor; it was assuring to have his son as her husband's medical supervisor.

On the day they reached the house in Darjeeling, Bibhabati supervised the staff as the family settled down. Step Aside was a large mansion on a mountain slope. With multiple entrances, gardens, and terraces, the house felt welcoming. It was double-storeyed with five rooms on each floor. The front rooms faced south and opened to a verandah which led to a small garden in a tiny compound downstairs. The back had the servant's quarters and kitchens. Her husband's face radiated happiness as he showed signs of recovery in the initial days.

Satyen dedicated every moment attending to Kumar's needs. Dr Ashutosh turned out to be a valuable resource. She started seeing a ray of hope before Ramendra's health deteriorated for the first time in Darjeeling. They immediately consulted Dr Calvert and sought advice from the senior doctor, Dr Nibaran Chandra Sen.

Far away from the Bhawal Raj Bari, Bibhabati had found peace in the company of familiar people. But she had no idea that her happiness was short-lived. Ramendra showed a faint chance of recovery before his health worsened. Satyen later told her Ramendra was obstinate in refusing an injection to get quick relief. It made his already serious health condition critical.

After Kumar collapsed, Bibhabati's world came crashing with her husband's untimely and shocking death. She had followed the rituals drafted for a Hindu widow about giving up jewellery, sindoor, and all colours. She shortened her hair and wore a white saree.

She wasn't allowed to accompany the funeral procession or be at the cremation ground. She howled and cried as they took away Ramendra's body to the cremation ground downhill from Step Aside.

When Satyen returned, he was too exhausted to speak to her. She had stayed up, weeping and shivering at the impending doom. The following morning, Satyen updated her about the cremation. Satyen and Dr Ashutosh had arranged to inform the family about Kumar's death and their return journey.

On reaching Jaidebpur, Satyen stayed back taking care of her before her marital family deemed it intrusive. Her brother returned to Calcutta. Soon, he was back in Dhaka with his wife and their mother, living in a rented house. He advised her at frequent intervals personally and sometimes through letters, "Claim the life insurance and come with me to Calcutta. You never know when these people will turn against you and leave you penniless. We can restart our life in Calcutta."

She had hesitated because the move would set tongues wagging.

But by the end of the year, Satyen had convinced her to send a notice to Ranendra Narayan for the claim of Ramendra's life insurance policy. Boro Kumar had already received another intimation of Bibhabati appointing Satyen as her manager and agent in dealing with matters related to the estate. She had consulted her brother at every stage before discarding her old life in Jaidebpur. Mejo Rani gave up her title and share of the estate for a fixed sum and a monthly allowance of 1100 rupees. Soon after receiving the amount, she moved to Calcutta.

In 1910, Ranendra, already suffering from multiple ailments because of alcohol addiction, passed away. Soon after, the Court of Wards took over the share of Bibhabati, followed by that of Rabindra Narayan and Sarajubala, under the pretext of efficient management. Rabindra, unable to bear the move, passed away in 1913, shattering the family. Jyotirmayee and Indumayee started dominating the household and behaved rudely with their brothers' widows. Eventually, the torture became unbearable, and Boro and Choto Rani decided to move out of the Raj Bari to settle in Calcutta. Choto Rani moved back to her home in Dhaka after a few years. Bibhabati had already received a substantial amount from the life insurance claim since the other Kumars let go of their share.

Over the past decade, Bibhabati grew accustomed to living with her brother and his family. Though she maintained cordial relations with her marital family, especially Jyotirmayee, it had more to do with societal expectations. But she never returned to Jaidebpur.

Bibhabati knew Ramendra's family, especially his sisters, believed in a mystery element related to his death. It also had to do with the fact that the other brothers passed away at their ancestral home while Ramendra's demise occurred in Darjeeling, far away from his residence. The circumstances made it easy for people to speculate and spread rumours about the reasons behind his sudden death.

But was she as unaffected as she portrayed? Only she knew how she woke up in the middle of the night feeling like someone was choking her. She never mentioned it to anyone, especially Satyen.

Bibhabati dozed off as she dreamt of her life back in Calcutta. The following morning, she took leave of the estate manager after re-emphasising the need for the people of Jaidebpur to stand by the Court of Wards.

Bibhabati's presence in Jaidebpur had reached the sadhu's ears. A few of his supporters were concerned since the Rani had shown no inclination to meet the sanyasi, but was publicly supporting the administration. Public sympathy shifted based on what moved people. Though a majority of people had shown their faith in the sadhu as the Second Kumar of Bhawal, it was a fact that many didn't believe his story. On the other hand, they had always known Bibhabati as the widow of the late Mejo Kumar. If she had openly refused to acknowledge the sadhu, it was bound to raise doubts in people's minds.

The sadhu spoke to his lawyer, Bejoy Chandra Chatterjee, late in the morning. "The administration is taking advantage of our domestic discord. Satyen is hands-in-glove with Lindsay in playing up Mejo Rani's emotions. Let's not give them another chance to sabotage the efforts of those who believe in me," he spoke in a calm but firm tone. They had set the battlefield; it was time for war.

At Satyen's house, Bibhabati received a warm welcome from her brother. An anxious Satyen got updates from Jaidebpur through his sources. While the locals feared the administration, they were far more affected by the emotional appeal of the widow Rani. People were already questioning the authenticity of the sadhu. The general buzz stated if he was the Second Kumar, wouldn't his wife be the first to know?

Satyen knew only a legal resource could settle this conflict. He didn't want an Indian judge to hear the case.

"They will never give an unbiased judgment. Who'll go against the prince, for he's one amongst them?" He'd often been vocal about his thoughts. "They have made Ashu doctor's life miserable. Why can't they let us live in peace? We, especially you, have suffered enough." Satyen lamented.

"God is seeing it all. He will serve justice," Bibhabati assured him. But Satyen knew better. It would take more than the Almighty to deal with the situation. He was glad about collecting evidence beforehand and grateful for the backing of the influential in fighting the cheater.

Back in her room, Bibhabati stood in front of the window. She had seen him pass through the streets. The phaeton never stopped barring the first time, but it would make multiple rounds to make her aware of his presence. If she judged him from a neutral perspective, she would've noticed the striking resemblance. But to her, the Second Kumar was dead.

Her sister-in-law had refrained from passing any further comment, but Bibhabati was aware of people gossiping. Happiness had eluded her since childhood. She hadn't known marital bliss even when Ramendra was alive. Her mother and sister had refused to understand her. Not Satyen! He felt his sister's pain in the Raj Bari and didn't stay indifferent to her suffering.

She heard many rumours about Satyen, the primary being that he was the main conspirator in Ramendra's death. She'd only known bits and parts of the allegations until she reached Jaidebpur. She heard stories about the doctor prescribing harmful drugs and Satyen poisoning her husband in Darjeeling.

Satyen had told her about the pamphlet which assassinated their characters. It eventually led to the defamation case, where the Government got involved in the last stage. Despite the outcome, people's perspectives toward Ashu doctor had changed. She shuddered to think of the statements the tenants were passing about her and Satyen in private. She felt they were paying the price for their dignified silence.

Chapter 17

Shariff Khan and Birendra Banerjee

Lawyer Bejoy Chandra Chatterjee or B.C. Chatterjee, a Hindu nationalist, was appointed as the counsel on behalf of the plaintiff, the sadhu. Suren Banerjee assisted him. He was the lawyer involved in the case from its nascent stage when the sadhu first declared his identity. Lawyer Arabinda Guha and a dozen other lawyers were part of the plaintiff's team.

Amiya Nath Chaudhuri or A.N. Chaudhuri acted as the counsel on behalf of the defendants. He led a westernised life and was a part of the elite social clubs in Calcutta. Since the defendants were widows with limited opportunities to present their cases, the Court of Wards stepped in and requested Chaudhuri to take up the case.

Sasanka Coomar Ghose was the pleader on behalf of the Government. In July 1930, E.J. Bignold, the estate manager, handed over the statement of facts to the Board of Revenue. It mentioned how Kumar died at midnight on 8th May 1909 in Darjeeling, and Dr Calvert and Crawford confirmed and validated his death. The details also included how the Board of Revenue conducted an exhaustive investigation about the sadhu claiming to be Ramendra Narayan before concluding that he was an imposter.

In August 1931, Ghose was to travel to England to instruct the counsel about examining Calvert, Lindsay, and Crawford. They had retired from services and settled down in England. J.M. Pringle, a retired

ICS officer, was chosen as the counsel. While the Board of Revenue made watertight arrangements to ensure the defendants were well represented and had sufficient evidence to back their claims, the expenses related to fighting the case came into question.

At Sarajubala's residence, all hell broke loose when she heard the suggestion of bearing the cost of the case from her share of the estate. "No! I won't allow my share for expenses related to the suit. It's between Ramendra and Bibhabati. Let them do the needful. Don't drag my money into this," she had firmly objected.

The Board of Revenue turned to Bibhabati next. And she was left with no choice but to agree to it.

"I don't think it'll take more than a year or two for the court to dismiss his plea and declare him a fraud. It's our good luck that the Board has taken a keen interest in the case and is providing us with the best lawyers. Yes, this means bearing the expenses for a while. But it's better than losing out our income to a fraud," Satyen assured her.

Bibhabati agreed, but she knew they didn't have any option to decline the offer.

Soon, it was evident that the sadhu's lawyers were hell-bent on proving Satyen as the reason behind the biased attitude of the Government officials. They sought documents, but the Government declined to produce them. In May 1932, Pannalal Basu asked for specific documents in court. Sasanka Ghose stepped in to suggest the communication between the officials and the estate related to the imposter notice was confidential and privileged information. The district commissioner, Nelson, stated it wasn't possible to produce the documents in court because of confidentiality.

At Satyen's residence, Bibhabati bore an austere look when Satyen came to her room. "Nelson is the right man on the job. The sadhu's team is crying foul and blaming it on me, like always. They think I'm influencing the authorities. They have such a high opinion of me." He laughed as Bibhabati gave a faint smile.

"Bibha, are you not feeling well?" Satyen looked concerned.

"It begins in two days, and only God knows when our trial will end."

It often irked Satyen how the female folk shifted responsibilities as per convenience to the Almighty and let their faith overrule the hard-hitting facts. "I told you we have every evidence to prove his death and cremation. It won't even take beyond a couple of years for the judge to dismiss the plea. I doubt if they'll seek a retrial after losing the case." He sounded confident.

But Bibhabati was an ordinary woman who had matured much before age because of circumstances. She didn't want to spoil his jubilant mood. She meekly said, "I hope your words come true, like always."

At the sadhu's place of stay, the mood was urgent. The lawyers had left after a detailed discussion with the sadhu. Jyotirmayee reappeared. She prayed continuously for her brother's well-being since filing the suit. She saw him standing near the window.

"Are you anxious?"

"No! I lost everything, including my life. But Madhab was kind to return everything to me. I have you, Tarin, my family, and my people standing in solidarity with me. Why should I be worried?"

"So many things will be spoken and dissected, some pleasant and some not-so-pleasant. Your life as Ramendra will be analysed and judged. Every minor act of importance to the case will get magnified. It'll get uncomfortable, Buddhu told me."

"I'm not bothered about what happens to me, my image, or my reputation. But I'm not the only one who'll face judgment for every small thing." He stopped.

"Are you thinking of..." Jyotirmayee stopped. She didn't need to know further details from him, but she was sure her brother worried about the effects of the case on a personal level. Bibhabati was going to get dragged into the mudslinging game just like the other women of Ramendra's family.

Ramendra's marriage had been a sincere attempt to curb his wayward ways and domesticate the wild Kumar. His mother presumed her son would get attached to his young and beautiful wife. Unfortunately, Ramendra showed no signs of giving up his old company or habits.

Jyotirmayee felt annoyed and impatient with Bibhabati's inability to attract Ramendra toward a stable life. Most of the time, Bibhabati complained of weakness and fainted. Though Jyotirmayee sympathised with the teenage wife and even took the initiative to nurse her to health, she couldn't help but notice how Bibhabati never proactively initiated steps to make her husband happy. It wasn't unusual for men of Ramendra's stature and lineage to keep mistresses, but the wife got the status, power, and often his wealth.

Jyotirmayee never understood if Bibhabati's failing health, lack of interest, or frustration made her withdraw into a shell. That Bibhabati's presence made a negligible difference in Ramendra's emotions, duties, or lifestyle, was clear. It bothered her how the same woman held such strong opinions in the current scenario. Even if Satyen was brainwashing her, it went beyond Jyotirmayee's understanding of how a married woman could stand against her husband in the court. She felt confident that Ramendra nurtured similar thoughts about Bibhabati. But the husband was also concerned that his wife might face judgment and hate from people.

Years ago, Bibhabati had returned to the palace as a widow. When Satyen persisted in speaking to her, her patience snapped. On a particular day, she yelled at her brother about how her family made her a queen, only to be brought down to the status of a beggar eventually.

Jyotirmayee remembered the people who had returned with Bibhabati and Satyen after Kumar's presumed death in Darjeeling.

She thought of the Durban Shariff Khan, who first hinted at Mejo's unnatural death.

Boro Kumar Ranendra Narayan was a fat but tall man of 5 ft 10 inches with darkish skin, a squint in his black eyes, no hair on his face, and his mouth twisted on one side when he spoke or smiled. Khan had sobbed uncontrollably in front of Ranendra and Indumayee as Jyotirmayee stood behind the curtains. Between Boro Kumar and her Boro Didi, her tall and dark-complexioned elder sister was a dominating personality. Indumayee had easily slipped into the role her mother played as a Rani.

"It was poison, Huzur. My shirt had a hole where Kumar's vomit fell." It became difficult to follow Khan's thought pattern, as he seemed to miss the sequence of events. Ranendra calmed him down, "Tell me from the beginning."

"When he fell sick for the first time, Mejo Rani panicked and insisted on sending a telegram here. But doctor babu gave him excellent medicines, and he started recovering. So, Mejo Rani's brother sent another telegram assuring you of his well-being. But the next day, Kumar was in severe pain. Doctor babu gave him a liquid to drink, after which he vomited out when we were trying to carry his bed from near the window to the centre of the room. The vomit fell on my shirt. Immediately, there was a hole. It could happen only if there was poison in what he drank. Sala Babu asked me to leave and change my clothes. After that, I came to know Mejo Kumar was dead."

But it wasn't the only worrying thing. Shariff also spoke about the evening cremation gone wrong. "The rain and storm forced the *shamshan yatris* to take shelter elsewhere, and they left the body unattended on the cremation ground. After returning, they spotted the empty charpoy. The corpse was missing."

Shariff wasn't the only one. Many other servants shared strange stories about Kumar's death and botched-up cremation. Though some claimed to witness the cremation when they returned to the ground, most of the servants' statements didn't match. According to another servant, they lit the empty pyre. However, these stories reached Indumayee and Ranendra through other sources since the servants kept their mouths shut.

Birendra Banerjee met Ranendra next. He accepted carrying out the rituals for Kumar. Satya Babu had asked him to do it. Birendra hadn't taken a bath before the cremation process and confessed an uneasy gut feeling related to Kumar's death and his cremation. Jyotirmayee wasn't sure if Birendra had spoken of the evening cremation since she had gone indoors before Birendra's arrival. The two people who could testify were dead now. Indumayee had told her about Birendra's statement but her words held no value since Banerjee had retracted his words and refused to accept his statement about the evening cremation.

Chapter 18
Trial Court Proceedings

The sadhu was almost sure about Satyen's role in his presumed death and cremation. Whether Satyen planned it alone or had company was debatable. His lawyer was confident about the role of Dr Ashutosh in executing Satyen's plot. But Chatterjee's question about Bibhabati's equation with the doctor caught the sadhu's attention.

'Did they know each other from before?'

'Were they comfortable in each other's company?'

'Did you notice anything unusual? Of course, you couldn't do much, but did anything strike as odd in their behaviour towards each other?'

'Did you see your wife, the doctor, and Satyen together frequently?'

He couldn't recollect much about Bibhabati and the doctor. He had no idea if he saw them together. Also, he doubted if it was possible for Bibhabati to have met the doctor before their Darjeeling trip. Yet, he couldn't be sure. It took him a while to understand that the lawyer was suggesting a liaison, not just between the doctor and Satyen, but a scandalous possibility of the doctor's association with Ramendra's wife.

The implications of these questions annoyed him. Ever since he could recollect who he was, he hadn't experienced any powerful emotion towards his wife. Society had set fixed benchmarks about how a wife must behave with her husband, but not vice versa. Bibhabati's denial of his identity and refusal to meet him didn't make him sad. He directed his anger at her stupidity and stubbornness.

But he couldn't shake off the uncomfortable feeling of Bibhabati nurturing a soft corner for someone else. The emotion rose out of a sense of betrayal, for marriage bound her to keep him as her priority. His relatives reaped the seed of unfaithfulness in his mind even when they casually mentioned Bibhabati's loyalty towards her brother or the doctor. He had heard she quashed all claims of inappropriate medical treatment by Dr Ashutosh toward Ramendra.

After meeting his lawyer, he had paced back and forth inside the room. There was an urgency to contact her without drawing attention. After thinking for a while, he planned to visit the Ganga ghat the following evening. He called Buddhu, who usually played the role of a mediator, and asked him to pass on the information to Bibhabati through his trusted sources. In the past, his path had crossed with Bibhabati's in front of Victoria, on the strand, and near the college square, but they never interacted.

The news reached Bibhabati the following morning while arranging the handmade *boris* to dry. A maid was telling her sister-in-law about the sadhu, now addressed as Mejo Kumar. Bibhabati overheard their discussion. The Kumar hoped to regain his power and position soon. He wanted a relaxed mind before the court case commenced the next day. That's why he wanted to have a quiet time at the ghat.

Bibhabati pretended not to be interested in the ongoing conversation. But she left the house early evening and rode to the ghat. Ramendra sat in the phaeton, speaking to Buddhu when she spotted them. She didn't want to come face to face, so she stopped a little away behind the trees. After waiting for almost an hour, Ramendra and Buddhu drove away, assuming that Bibhabati hadn't cared to show up.

Bibhabati turned towards her home after seeing the car leave. She chided herself for falling weak, albeit momentarily. The idea of the court case was still repelling for her, but every time she looked at the sadhu, her inner voice screamed, 'Your husband is dead!' With a stoic face, she returned home.

Her brother looked at her with raised eyebrows as she stepped in. Bibhabati smiled. "I went to the temple to seek blessings for us." She touched his forehead with a flower from the pooja thali. He smiled.

Inside her room, Bibhabati's mind was full of chaotic thoughts. Despite knowing that Ramendra couldn't be alive, a tiny part of her brain couldn't stop thinking about all possibilities of 'what ifs?'

On 30th November, 1933, the proceedings began in Pannalal Basu's court in Dhaka. The 51-year-old Basu was the subordinated judge of the Dhaka district. Chatterjee presented the plaintiff's story and furnished the statements of Dr Calvert, Sarajubala Devi, and Dr Pran Krishna Acharya.

Dr Acharya was a renowned surgeon from Calcutta who was present at the time of Ramendra's death in Darjeeling. He mentioned he had been to Step Aside on a May morning around six. He received a call from a nurse at his villa on the Darjeeling mall to check on the Second Kumar. The doctor had found a body on a cot, covered from top to toe with a white cloth. He attempted to remove the sheet; the onlookers protested. Since the doctor was a Brahmo, they didn't want him to touch the body. He felt disgusted by their attitude and left without a clear conclusion.

Sarajubala Devi described meeting the plaintiff at her Calcutta home and accepting the sadhu as Ramendra Kumar. Sarajubala met him for the first time three years after the latter's appearance in Dhaka. They shared a cordial relationship, but she declined the charges of providing him financial assistance for fighting the case. However, the opposition lawyers counter-argued that she was supporting the sadhu only because of her grudges. She was against the young Rani, Ananda Kumari's adoption choice since Sarajubala wanted the widow to adopt her brother's son. Bibhabati had supported the eldest Rani for years. However, when Bibhabati switched loyalties, Sarajubala decided to stand with the sadhu. But Sarajubala denied the allegation, stating that she had shown solidarity with the sadhu way back in 1925 and provided evidence for the same.

N.N. Sircar, the lawyer who cross-examined Sarajubala, believed the eldest Rani felt prejudiced in her belief that the sadhu was indeed the Second Kumar of Bhawal. According to him, Rani's brother had voiced his faith in the sadhu, which affected her opinion. It manifested in how she received the sadhu in her room in their first meeting. Sircar was sure Rani hadn't recognised the sadhu as Kumar in their first meeting, but she already held a biased perspective about the man's identity much before she came face to face with him.

Ramendra's aunt, Kamal Kamini Devi, also testified in the sadhu's favour. She mentioned vital information about Bibhabati when she met her after Ramendra's demise. "When I sat with Bibhabati, she burst out crying. It was an expected reaction. Soon, she spoke about his unexpected death. Eventually, Bibhabati lamented how she wasn't allowed to be with her husband in his last moments because many important and influential people were present, and she couldn't go to the front room." Chatterjee made a note of the information.

Kamal Kamini met Bibhabati again after the sadhu revealed his identity. The former felt convinced about the return of Ramendra, and told the same to Bibhabati. But Kamal Kamini couldn't convince her. She asked Kamal Kamini the reason for her faith. The latter spoke about Satyabhama Devi identifying the sadhu and the sadhu performing her last rites.

A.N. Chaudhuri wanted the sadhu in the witness box since nine years had passed after the latter's first appearance in Dhaka to the case filing. Chaudhuri had considered it a sloppy case, with the plaintiff's side having no chance. Like typical folklore, it had the plot of a king with no moral values and a suspicious death-like situation because of the conspiracy hatched by his near ones. But the reality was far from such fantasies, and miraculous returns were often plans hatched by conspirators. Chaudhuri was confident he would prove the man an imposter once he got him in court.

Unfortunately, Jyotirmayee's son, Buddhu, passed away during this period. Considering the situation's sensitivity, the court excused him for a couple of weeks.

Chapter 19

The Plaintiff in the Witness Box

The sadhu, claiming to be Ramendra Narayan Roy, was called into the witness box around mid-December 1933. Thousands of people flocked to the court to hear his version.

His counsel asked him to narrate his childhood, his relatives, and his life as the Second Kumar. The man detailed his physical traits and the similarities he shared with his parents and siblings. He spoke about his broken tooth and the marks when a carriage wheel had run over his legs. But people were keen to hear what happened in Darjeeling.

"I fell sick within a fortnight of arriving in Darjeeling. Ashu doctor attended to me for a day before calling a Sahib doctor the following day. But his prescribed medicines were of no use. In the evening, Ashu doctor gave me a glass of medicine. A couple of hours later, I vomited and fell critically sick. I was restless and even sensed burning in my chest. Despite my condition, the European doctor came only the next day. The following morning, my condition grew worse as I had loose motions. Blood came out along with my stools. I can only recollect till here since I passed out immediately after."

The counsel asked him, "What happened after you regained consciousness?"

"I saw four-five sanyasis around me. I was so weak I could barely speak. The sanyasis nursed me back to health. I didn't know who I was; the sadhus became my family. So, I accompanied them to Benares, and after four months, we headed to Amarnath. In Amarnath, my Guru Dharamdas gave me the mantra. By his blessings, I could faintly recollect moments of my past."

"Oh! Did you share this incident with your Guru Ji or other sadhus?"

"I discussed with Guru Ji. He asked me to be patient. He assured me it would come back in time, and I would return home when I had to. So, I travelled with them everywhere, from Punjab to Benares and Dhaka. I suddenly had a flash that Dhaka was my hometown."

"So you visited Dhaka immediately after this?"

" I spoke to Guru Ji again, and he asked me to reunite with my family. Guru Ji assured me I was welcome to return to the sanyasi group if I didn't like what I experienced."

"Did you make the trip to Dhaka after this conversation?"

"I took a train to Dhaka and stayed on the banks of the Buriganga river for three to four months. Eventually, people started approaching me with queries in Bengali. I replied in Hindi. Guru Ji guided me to reveal my identity only at the right time. Next, I went to Jaidebpur with Atul Prasad Roy. Though I knew who he was, I neither disclosed my identity nor let him know that I recognised him. Even when I met my sister Jyotirmayee and other relatives, including my grandmother, I continued conversing in Hindi, though I knew Bengali. By then, my memory had refreshed."

A.N. Chaudhuri and Sasanka Ghosh had made a list of parameters to judge if he fitted the criteria of being the Second Kumar. So, Chaudhuri asked him questions about his education, his knowledge of Bengali and English, and his ability to write or read letters. When they showed the sadhu some signatures and read out a few letters Ramendra wrote to Bibhabati, he identified a handful of signatures as his and the rest as forgeries. For the letters, he was confident he hadn't written them. He had no qualms about accepting his illiterate status. He was forthright about Mr Wharton, the tutor of the three princes, revealing how Wharton spent his time in the stables and not with his pupils. He was questioned about the marks on his body because of syphilis and a tiger's paw.

The sadhu could barely recollect events from the phase the sanyasis saved him. He insisted that the mantra by his guru brought back flashes of his memory. It grew clearer with time. When he had travelled with the group, he didn't know whether he was a Bengali or Hindustani. But in Dhaka, he understood his ethnicity.

"You remembered everything the moment you reached Dhaka station," Chaudhuri smirked.

"Of course not! But the place felt familiar. I heard voices saying I was Mejo Kumar. But I didn't know that I was a prince. When I sat surrounded by people in Buckland Bund, I knew who I was, where I belonged, and remembered my family members."

For the defence counsel, the sadhu's inability to speak in Bengali was a vital point. He cross-checked on why the man couldn't pronounce certain words or continued speaking in Hindi, even while at Dhaka. A tumour under his tongue had made him incapable of pronouncing certain words, but he insisted on deliberately speaking in Hindi despite knowing Bengali. He feigned ignorance of English.

The subject of sports came up next, and the sadhu had no idea about cricket, the items used to play the game, or the rules. Even for billiards, he remembered his elder brother's fondness for the game, but he hadn't played it. When the topic of racing came, he spoke about riding the horse that won the Viceroy's Cup in Calcutta. However, he couldn't answer questions related to the details of the game.

The sadhu had claimed to be a *sikhari,* a hunter. When Chaudhuri queried on the technicalities of hunting or the firearms, the sadhu could hardly understand or reply. Chatterjee requested intervention since the sadhu had confessed his lack of knowledge about English.

Chaudhuri then kept throwing questions related to the Viceroys, magistrates, Bengali writers, and prominent personalities. The sadhu answered a few but expressed his inability to respond to most. Some names like Rankin and Garth were familiar, but most sounded new.

Chaudhuri queried about Bibhabati Devi. "You claim Bibhabati Devi is your wife. As her husband, what is it you are aware of but unknown to everyone else?" Chaudhuri asked.

The sadhu took a deep breath. "A cyst left a mark on one side of her private body part. Only her husband can have this knowledge."

Chaudhuri and Ghosh continued questioning him about Ramendra and Bibhabati's family. He answered most of the questions with ease.

Suddenly, Chaudhuri seemed worked up. "When it comes to the family and relationships, it's strange how the plaintiff seems to know it all. I wonder if he's tutored about these aspects by someone close to him."

B.C. Chatterjee took offence and objected. The two lawyers threw allegations at each other, and the judge, Pannalal Basu, had to intervene to bring back order.

Chaudhuri ended the cross-questioning round by asking what the sadhu intended to do if he inherited the property. Though he initially claimed he was going to use it for the welfare of others, the sadhu lashed back at the defence council, "I'll use it like a rich man uses his wealth – for enjoyment, on women, liquor, elephants and horses!" Basu adjourned the court for the day.

Chapter 20

Satyen's Mystery from the Past

Back in his house, the sadhu felt physically and mentally exhausted. Chatterjee seemed satisfied with the way the proceedings had gone.

Jyotirmayee, coping with the loss of her dear son, came to meet her brother. The sadhu held her hand as he noticed her tear-stained face. "You need rest, Mejo Didi. You've become so weak."

Tears rushed down her cheeks as she held on to her brother's hand. They were both united in the loss. She had lost her son; he had lost his identity, his wife's trust, and their ancestral property.

Satyen eagerly waited for the following morning to get a detailed update about the case. The court summoned the sadhu to the witness box for the first time. Satyen wished the sadhu's façade would blow away once Chaudhuri grilled him. But he knew the conspirators had prepared the fraud well. He had avoided meeting Bibhabati during the evening as the last thing he wanted was for her to witness an anxious brother. It would only add to her worries.

He soon came to know of the happenings of the case. When he was about to enter his room, Bibhabati called him softly. "Dada, did you hear anything?"

"It went off as expected. Our lawyer was good with the pointed questions, so the sadhu often fumbled. He failed to answer many questions related to Mejo Kumar. It was a neutral day since none of the sides gained any advantage over the other. But you must understand that this is just the tip of the iceberg."

Bibhabati mumbled a few words and left.

Satyen sat in the dark for a long time. He recollected his bond with Ramendra Narayan. Though Kumar wasn't fair in his treatment of Satyen's sister, he didn't object to Satyen staying at the Raj Bari at a stretch. When they chose Darjeeling, Ramendra sent Satyen to the hill station to finalise the house. Over the last decade, Satyen had woken up from nightmares at odd hours.

"Call the doctor. I can't bear the pain."

"What are you giving me in the name of medicines? Why am I not getting better?"

"Take me back to Jaidebpur. My health is getting worse here."

"Tell Ashu I can't breathe."

Ramendra's voice would echo in Satyen's ears. As he recollected those moments, a shiver ran down his spine. A sight flashed in front of his eyes.

The year was 1912. A much younger Satyen opened a locked wooden drawer. His hands ran down to the bottom of the drawer, and he took out a diary. Satyen sat on the floor and pulled the lantern closer to read the contents.

He had recorded every crucial information of their stay at the hill station. It was full of entries about Kumar's deteriorating health, the consulting doctors, their timings, and the prescribed medicines.

His eyes ran through the entries. '*Dr Henry Calvert has agreed to come on the house call and take Kumar as his patient. Ashu is already following the senior doctor's orders as he attends to the patient round the clock.*'

The entries over the next few days were about Kumar's sickness and fluctuation in health as they altered medicine doses based on the senior doctor's prescription. His fingers stopped at the next entry. '*Dr Calvert insists on a morphine injection. He says it'll act fast and stop the bloody stools. But Kumar is adamant about his refusal. His mother died after the physician administered an injection into her body. Dr Calvert looked unhappy and irritated.'*

But the detailed entries of 8th May, 1909, occupied multiple pages as he had listed everything that had happened before, during, and after Kumar died. *'Bibha is having fits.'*

He closed the diary, covered it with a red cloth, and kept it back.

When he returned the following day to take it out, he found the diary missing.

Satyen was jolted out of reverie by the sounds of a mild knock on the door.

"Were you sleeping? I have been knocking for so long." His wife shut the door behind her.

He didn't respond. His wife sat beside him, "Why don't you or your sister share anything with me? I keep telling her to speak about her concerns with me. Irrespective of whether I can help, venting it out will lift the load off her chest."

Satyen looked at his wife. She meant well but lacked the maturity to handle situations. Also, her ability to keep a secret was non-existent, a trait that Satyen and his sister had learned to perfection.

"I'm sure she'll tell you when she wishes to. Bibhabati's a recluse and prefers to keep things to herself. She must be worried about the ongoing things. We all are in the same boat." Satyen patted her shoulder.

"And why are you worried?"

"A random stranger pulls a trick on Mejo Kumar's family and friends with insider assistance. Instead of putting him behind bars, the Bhawal Raj family supports the imposter. Can't they understand how it might jeopardise Bibhabati's honour and social position as the late Ramendra Narayan's widow? Besides, there are financial implications to consider in the long run."

"You and your sister should have met the man once. He might be a fraud. But you could've judged it better while interacting with him face to face." She spoke with a tinge of frustration.

Satyen sighed. His wife continued, "You saw Mejo Kumar dead and cremated him at Darjeeling. But miracles happen. There's a greater force that might have done wonders for Kumar."

Satyen regretted letting the conversation flow to this phase. He wished he had pretended to be tired or not encouraged her to go on.

But his wife was still not done. "A woman's marital home is where her happiness and honour lie. As much as you care for her, it won't be wrong to say if the sadhu turns out to be Mejo Kumar, she . . . ."

Satyen's cheeks flushed. He clenched his fist and spoke through gritted teeth. "I'm tired. In case you don't remember, I have a meeting with Ukil Babu tomorrow."

He stormed out of the room to regain his composure.

Chapter 21

The Plaintiff's Supporters

Chatterjee's team prepared a list of people who identified the sadhu as Ramendra Narayan Roy. It comprised his close family, relatives, friends, acquaintances, tenants, talukdars, current employees, and former employees of the Bhawal estate. They intended to call these witnesses into the stand individually and ask them why and how they believed the sadhu was the Second Kumar. Some had identified him by his looks, mannerisms, and behaviour, while few recognised him through his signature. The plaintiff's lawyers intended to bring out Kumar's childhood or youth traits that tallied with the sadhu's nature.

A set of erstwhile employees of the estate had alleged prejudice in the behaviour of the Court of Wards. As one mentioned, "The order from the Court of Wards explicitly stated no estate employee should be a part of any public meeting held by the sadhu or encourage these rumours in any manner. After seeing the sadhu, how could we let injustice happen to him? We faced the consequences in the form of a termination letter."

Another employee stated, "There is constant pressure on the tenants and employees from the administration to stay away from the sadhu's camp. We've faced unfair treatment and been penalised for standing by the truth."

Some mentioned how they faced pressure to sign a piece of paper without knowing the content. When they asked what they were signing, they received threats. The Court of Wards, through the estate employees, forced the witnesses not to testify.

The list of employees, who felt an instant connection with him after he spoke to them as Mejo Kumar, was endless. Along with identifying them, the sadhu also recollected a specific instance or story known only to that particular employee and the Second Kumar. Many eminent lawyers, musicians, sports persons, and theatre personalities also validated his identity.

Jamini Kishor Chakraborty, a former estate manager, certified, "The Kumar signed his name as R.N. Roy. I've never seen him write in Bengali or speak English. When I met him, I questioned him about childhood memories. He could recollect everything and give satisfactory answers in Bengali."

Kumar's tutor, Rebati Mohan Ghosh, confirmed his inability to teach Kumar English despite trying for three years. The young Kumar was an ill-tempered boy. When Rebati Babu went to meet the sadhu, he spoke to the tutor in Hindi-accented Bengali. When Rebati asked the man about his unclear speech, the sadhu showed him the tumour under his tongue.

The milkman, cook, mahout, personal servant, tailor, personal guard, and many others who had catered to Ramendra were convinced that Kumar had returned. Some noticed the patch of dry skin near his ankle like that of Kumar, while others remembered how the uneducated Kumar never studied or spoke English. Some confirmed Kumar spent a lot of time with elephants and mahouts, wasn't a polo enthusiast, and barely slept in the women's quarters even after marriage.

Even Bibhabati took a strong stand against employees who favoured the sadhu. After Nand Kishore, Ramendra's guard, met the sadhu, the estate secretary called the guard. Anyone who showed sympathy to the sadhu had to quit their job. Like many others, the authorities fired Nand Kishore.

Though Kumar was an avid hunter, he had failed to answer questions related to the terminologies associated with hunting. He was unfamiliar with English terms like 'target', 'cat's eye', 'bull's eye', and others. Chaudhuri had pointed it out. But Chatterjee assembled a few of Ramendra's hunting companions, and none of them had heard those English words. Most of them were illiterates but possessed sharp skills related to hunting.

A few people who met the sadhu, felt convinced of his identity, spread the message through songs and pamphlets that he was the Second Kumar, and gave him rent and *nazar* as a sign of their loyalty. But according to Chaudhuri, the plaintiff's supporters had paid the witnesses, or the witness held a personal interest in the outcome. That's why they had come forward to testify.

When these witnesses came into the box and shared their side of the story and vouched for their faith in the sadhu, some spoke about the unfair treatment and termination from work. The defence counsel justified the authorities' stand by stating that these people acted out of resentment towards the Court of Wards. Sometimes, he also mentioned the witness was indebted to one of the plaintiff's family members, mostly Jyotirmayee. The defendant's lawyers suggested the sadhu's close associates paid the witnesses to testify in his favour.

In the evening, a talukdar updated the sadhu about Sibchandra Malakar, the man who did painting and decorative work at the Raj Bari.

"Malakar confirmed identifying you as Mejo Kumar after meeting you. But Ukil Babu from the opposite side showed the court a piece of paper in which Malakar claimed you weren't Kumar. It bore his signature."

Jyotirmayee, who was standing behind the purdah, cleared her voice. "Why would he do that? He came forward and met Chatterjee Babu to testify as a witness."

"Ma Thakrun, that piece of paper created havoc in the courtroom as the lawyer counsels fought about the authenticity of the signature."

"Those brutes must have tortured poor Sibu," the sadhu lamented.

"Precisely! When Sibu refused to sign since they denied to disclose the paper's content, they threatened him with extreme consequences."

"What consequences?" It was Jyotirmayee again.

"The estate officials said he wouldn't get any work from the Raj Bari in the future. Even then, Sibu stood his ground. When they failed to break his resolve, they put him in a dark room and locked him from the outside. They said they would keep him without food and water if he refused to sign. They didn't let him go until he signed the paper."

"That's outrageous!"

"But that's just one of the many painful stories of torture we heard today. Do you remember Ashu Babu, the retired station master?"

"Of course! He used to have a beard. I remember he was posted in Jaidebpur when Lord Kitchener visited."

"He appeared as a witness and described his ordeal. While he was about to reach the court, someone stopped him and asked him to meet the officer at the police station immediately. But he declined politely. Just outside the court, another man stopped him and said Ashu babu couldn't testify since he was a government pensioner and was duty-bound to obey the order. When Ashu Babu asked him to show the order, the man sternly told him to go home. He spoke in no kind terms that Ashu would be responsible for everything that happens to his family."

"Yet he turned up to testify?" Jyotirmayee gaped at him.

The talukdar nodded. "All of us want Mejo Kumar reinstated as our ruler."

But the sadhu was skeptical about the duration he needed to cover before getting back his identity and power. The administration was hell-bent on cancelling his claims and existence.

Chapter 22

Bibhabati Agrees to Revisit Jaidebpur

By 1934, Bibhabati had met several talukdars and addressed a crowd of tenants from behind the screens at Raj Bari. While it led to a small group of people shifting loyalties, the majority still supported the sadhu. A long queue of people showed up at the court daily to testify in his favour.

"We can't do anything about the rich and influential. However, I'm in touch with those who consider the sadhu a fraud. The majority of his supporters are the tenants and talukdars," Satyen spoke.

"A section of the Bhawal estate employees is also in his favour." A lawyer from Chaudhuri's team chimed in. Bibhabati sighed from behind the curtain. Satyen had insisted on her joining the discussion.

"Right! The administration issued multiple notices, starting with the imposter notice. Many employees lost their jobs because they refused to stay away from the man. Yet tenants continue paying their rent to him, though it had marginally reduced after Mejo Rani's visit. But the crux is that people are uneducated emotional fools. We can't sit quietly and let this pass." Satyen cleared his throat.

Bibhabati knew the last part of the statement was for her. After returning from Jaidebpur a couple of months ago, she told Satyen about the suffocating feeling she experienced in the Raj Bari. He had assured her that she wouldn't need to visit again. As the case grew complicated, his demeanor changed. Chaudhuri's team suggested Rani's presence at the estate at frequent intervals. It was the only way to maintain contact and influence the subjects' thoughts.

Satyen worried about Bibhabati rejecting the idea. So, he got a lawyer to convince his sister.

The lawyer spoke in a shrill tone. "If Mejo Rani can speak to the people, make them understand, rebuke them if needed, warn them about the consequences of supporting the sadhu, the employees would understand. If the talukdars see her around, they would think twice before going against the authorities."

Satyen looked at the door. He doubted if Bibhabati was still listening or had gone indoors. He spoke to the lawyer about the witnesses who claimed the authorities were forcing them to stay away from testifying. Ten minutes later, the lawyer left.

Satyen left for work soon after, giving her time to think. Bibhabati stayed inside her room the entire day, pretending she had a headache. Her mind was a flurry of emotions with anger directed at those who supported the fraud to despair at her situation. The morning discussion gave her a hint that she had to get involved directly to handle the people.

Late evening, Bibhabati came with a bowl of fruits for her brother. "Bibha, you heard us in the morning. Many eminent personalities have come forward as witnesses and declared that they recognised the Second Kumar. Hemendra Kishor Acharya Chaudhuri, Manindra Mohan Bose, Subodh Kumar Basu, N.K. Nag and Jatindra Nath Lahiri are notable people. Most of them justified his inability to speak English or write Bengali as his poor mental skills. Kumar's friend from his youth, Edwin Fraser, came to Jaidebpur to meet the plaintiff. The man spotted Fraser and fed him snacks with a spoonful of ghee on the side, just as Fraser preferred his food. Fraser feels convinced the plaintiff is his friend Kumar Ramendra, and supports him. The plaintiff's neighbour from his Calcutta house, Ram Ratan Chibba, is a Punjabi from Ludhiana in Punjab. He said Kumar speaks in Bengali-accented Hindi, while Chibba speaks in Punjabi-accented Hindi. He validated the sadhu couldn't be a Punjabi since Chibba would've figured it out in a couple of interactions."

Satyen stopped to think of what to say next. N.K. Nag met the man; the sadhu identified him at one glance. But Nag had asked him to narrate any incident known only to the two of them. The sadhu recollected how they had gone late in the night to borrow money from Nag's father because the sadhu had to pay off someone urgently. Only Ramendra, Nag, and Nag's father knew about the incident. Satyen had a fair idea about why the Second Kumar would've needed the money but he didn't want to discuss Ramendra's visits to dance girls.

Though Satyen could never confront his brother-in-law about his escapades, most people knew about his first mistress Elokeshi, and Ramendra's obsession with a singer, Malika Jaan. There was also his much-publicised affair with an Anglo-Indian female companion who ran away, eventually.

A witness disclosed how he and Kumar would share their mistresses. When the witness showed Elokeshi's picture to the sadhu, he stated her name and mentioned the circumstances under which they shared the photo. But Satyen preferred to keep the information away from Bibhabati. Kumar's friends and companions knew these secrets of his life. To prove his fake identity, the sadhu and his team didn't even consider the impact of such scandals on Ramendra's wife or his close family.

Satyen wrinkled his nose. "Though the sadhu claimed to recognise most people, he missed identifying a few."

Bibhabati was lost in thoughts when Satyen paused. Though it wasn't for her ears, she had overheard the lawyer in the morning tell Satyen about Elokeshi. The sadhu had recognised her. He also remembered the names and relationships of his prominent female associates. She felt humiliated.

"Bibha, what do you feel?" Satyen stared at her. She chose a safe option and muttered, "I don't even know what to say."

"I understand. But I don't see any other option since the subjects will listen to you as their Rani."

"Will you come with me?" Bibhabati nudged him gently.

"Not right now. The sadhu's supporters are already portraying me as an evil man. But I have thought of someone to help you while you are in Jaidebpur."

Bibhabati raised her eyebrows. Satyen commenced. "Dr Ashutosh can arrange for meetings and pass on your message to the employees. He might know who is against the sadhu and help you have a word with them. Let him act as the mediator."

Bibhabati thought for a while and replied. "I hope his involvement will not have any negative connotations."

"He has already fought and won the defamation case about his role in Kumar's illness and death. People know he won't be affected by baseless allegations. Besides, he comes from a reputed family of doctors. However, I would still advise him to stay in the background."

"Will people consider my presence in Jaidebpur a way to influence the subjects?"

"It's possible. The court might think you are using your power to control the employees and tenants. But Chaudhuri Sahib has found a justification for your presence. Rumours about your ill health or death made you travel to Jaidebpur with the intent of assuring the anxious subjects of your health status."

Bibhabati shuddered at the mention of the word death as they discussed the tentative dates for Bibhabati to commence travel.

Chapter 23
Bibhabati's Second Jaidebpur Visit

Satyen's request reached Dr Ashutosh before Bibhabati arrived in the town. The voices spreading gossip about him poisoning the Kumar, having an illicit affair with Rani Bibhabati, and playing an associate in Satyen's plans to remove the Kumar went behind his back. He refused to pay any attention. Ashutosh openly opposed the rumours in the form of a defamation suit only when they slandered his character.

The doctor met Bibhabati inside the Raj Bari. Mejo Rani wanted to speak to the employees, talukdars, and tenants. But she planned to take a stricter approach in her interactions, unlike last time. Ashutosh assured her of help in all possible ways.

Early evening, Bibhabati interacted with a select few estate employees in the presence of either Ashu doctor or Jogen Babu. "What are you all doing? I told you last time the man is a fraud. You are still going to testify in his support?" she rebuked the group from behind the screens.

"Rani Ma, our loyalty lies with you and Mejo Kumar. We met and interacted with the sadhu. We intended to see if he was indeed a cheater. But we were mistaken. He's our Kumar, sent by God to protect us. He remembers incidents known only to Kumar and a handful of people," an employee spoke up.

Before Bibhabati could respond, another one chimed in. "Please consider meeting him once, Rani Ma. It'll clear all your doubts."

Many voices joined in to show solidarity. Bibhabati's nostrils flared. Though she hadn't expected them to give in easily, she didn't think they would have the audacity to disobey her orders openly. She drew a sharp breath, "If you feel you must render your support to a man, noted as an imposter by the authorities, I don't think any of you deserve to be under my employment. The authorities have already warned about the consequences of supporting the fraud. I must note your behaviour and act accordingly." She dismissed the meeting with the finality of her statement. Almost all the employees who testified in favour of the sadhu were fired from their jobs after they testified in court.

When the plaintiff's counsel brought up the matter, Chaudhuri defended Rani's presence in Jaidebpur. "A Dhaka newspaper carried the news of Rani's death. Some miscreants have been spreading false rumours along similar lines. Since Rani is in good health, she decided to come and assure them of her presence." He justified the termination of employees because of a conflict of interest. Most of them had their loyalty towards the family related by blood to the Second Kumar.

Bibhabati interacted with numerous talukdars with the help of the doctor. Most pleaded with her to meet the sadhu. But she was unyielding. The same people testified in court and spilled the beans of the meeting. Bibhabati stayed back for a few more days as Ashutosh set up meetings with more sadhu's supporters to interact with the Rani.

On a stormy evening, Ashutosh met her. She was planning to return to Calcutta soon. After the pleasantries, Bibhabati noticed the fidgety doctor. "Is there something you want to say?"

"Umm… yes… actually…" He wiped his forehead.

Bibhabati waited. Ashutosh cleared his throat and attempted again. "Elokeshi came to the court today."

Bibhabati stood transfixed. "I thought she wasn't…."

"Chaudhuri Babu was perplexed. Until now, the existence of Elokeshi was labelled as fiction despite the man identifying her picture a few weeks back. The defence has connections who tried convincing her about the repercussions of appearing in the court."

"Yet, she turned up! What did she say?"

"She went to see the sadhu the day after his declaration. She was certain it was Mejo Kumar at a glance. Next day, she went to Nanak Sha's *akhara,* where a religious ceremony of the Sikhs was in progress. The sadhu spotted her and came to talk to her, asking about her well-being. Elokeshi met the sadhu multiple times during this period. She validated his identity."

"Did she tell the court how she met my late husband and what kind of relationship they shared in the past?"

"Yes!" Ashutosh hoped Bibhabati wouldn't ask him to narrate further details.

"Okay! Thank you for updating me."

Ashutosh picked the cue and left for the day.

Chapter 24

Bibhabati Remembers Elokeshi

Late at night, Bibhabati sat on her bed. How often had she thought of Elokeshi – the first woman to snatch away her husband. There were many women in Ramendra's life after Elokeshi. Yet, Bibhabati hadn't felt the repulse and grudge she harboured towards the dancer girl.

Two days after the wedding, Bibhabati, the new bride, overheard a conversation between Rani Bilasmani and Jyotirmayee. "Why did he have to go to that wretched woman?"

"Calm down, mother. After Mejo Rani learns the tricks to keep her husband tied to her saree's pallu, you will find your son hovering around her."

"Mejo should've waited a week at least. It's just a few days since he brought a new bride."

"Mejo's wife looks like a sensible girl." Jyotirmayee had spotted the thirteen-year-old Bibhabati and changed the conversation.

The teenager didn't need to wait long to hear the name Elokeshi. A couple of weeks later, a female companion in the women's quarters gossiped. "Elokeshi Khemtawali enamoured Kumar when she came to sing and dance at Boro Rani's son's birth. The son didn't live for long, but Kumar coaxed Elokeshi to stay back for a month and put her up within the Raj Bari premises. He gave her cash, sarees, and other gifts when she returned to Dhaka. He brought her back within a month again and set her accommodation at Hawa Khana. Rani Ma was scandalised. It's more than a year of her living there."

Another maid giggled. "Did you hear people saw her riding the horse cart with Mejo Kumar? She wore a red silk saree; jewellery adorned her body. They laughed and chatted as onlookers stared on."

Bibhabati confronted Jyotirmayee on the same evening. "Who is Elokeshi? What rights does she have over my husband?"

Jyotirmayee sighed. There was no escape from her brother's follies. She repeated the same story the woman companion had told Bibhabati. A sense of betrayal occupied Bibhabati's mind, but there was no one to whom she could bare her heart. Jyotirmayee sympathised with Bibhabati's state, though the former avoided further conversation about Elokeshi or her brother's wild lifestyle. Bibhabati often heard about her husband's escapades through others, though no one told her upfront.

A few weeks later, Bibhabati sought Jyotirmayee out. She had set her mind on meeting Elokeshi, but she neither knew the woman nor the location of Hawa Khana, so she requested her sister-in-law to accompany her. "What are you planning to do?" Jyotirmayee asked her with wide-open eyes.

"Ask the nautch girl to leave and warn her of the consequences if she continues living in Jaidebpur," Bibhabati spoke with resolve in her tone as they got inside a palki.

Elokeshi had a round face with red lips. Her face glowed with bright makeup. Bibhabati's eyes assessed the gold and diamonds adorning her face and body. Elokeshi took a tone of indifference while speaking. But Bibhabati was red with fury, and Jyotirmayee supported her to uproot the woman causing problems in the family. "You will not stay here any longer but go away as far as possible from the town." Bibhabati didn't mince her words as she continued rebuking the dancer girl. Elokeshi, realizing she didn't hold any power against the woman of the royal family, gave in.

Later that week, when Ramendra came to meet her, Elokeshi insisted on leaving Jaidebpur. Ramendra arranged for her stay in the Begum Bazar area in Dhaka.

Elokeshi's move failed to improve Bibhabati's marital life. She continued staying upstairs while Ramendra spent most nights at Elokeshi's new place in Dhaka. Two and a half years later, Elokeshi and her mother moved into a house in Chandni Ghat. Kumar was so obsessed with her by then that rarely a night passed when he didn't visit his mistress.

"The Kumar was with Elokeshi Khemtawali in a houseboat last night."

"Kumar spends all his time at Elokeshi's house. He doesn't like to be away from her."

"Do you know he took that dancer girl to Nalgola Raj Bari? They stayed there for a week."

"Poor Mejo Rani! She stays alone in Raj Bari while Elokeshi gets all the attention."

The women's quarters were full of whispers about how Elokeshi bewitched Kumar. Forcing Elokeshi to leave Jaidebpur became a curse for Bibhabati When Elokeshi was in the town, Ramendra was at least around. Now he came only for work.

Things were great for Elokeshi until Kumar contracted syphilis. He blamed her for his condition. But she had rarely allowed anyone else to touch her. Despite his craze for Elokeshi, Ramendra couldn't refrain from liaisons with multiple women. His wild lifestyle led him to contract syphilis. But he refused to look into the mirror. They fought bitterly during his last visit. When she realised, he wasn't returning to her, she moved on to another wealthy man.

In the court, the fifty-year-old woman claimed that she heard of Kumar's death and rumours about the botched-up cremation in 1909. She was only twenty when she met him first. Despite the acridity at the end of their relationship, Elokeshi never forgot Kumar or the good times she spent in his company. From his Darjeeling visit to his cremation, she knew it all. His death was no less than shocking for her.

When the sadhu turned up in Jaidebpur, she couldn't resist seeing him once. Was he indeed her Kumar, she had wondered all the time? A glance at him and she knew he was back. His features, mannerisms, and behaviour were the same as Ramendra's. He seemed cordial when she spoke to him the next day at the akhara.

Before leaving the witness box, Elokeshi named the officer of the Kotwali police station who had warned her not to testify in favour of the sadhu since it was a case against the Government. The officer had offered her fifty rupees if she refused to testify. It became evident the officer was acting as per the authorities. Though Chaudhuri Sahib had dismissed Elokeshi as a fictional character, her presence in the court changed the direction of the events in December 1934.

Chapter 25
Jyotirmayee's Testimony

On a sunny morning, Gauranga Kabyatirthya came to the witness box. As the sub-register of Jaidebpur and an eminent scholar of Sanskrit, he attended a question-answer session with the sadhu at Jyotirmayee's house on 5th May 1921. The estate manager, Needham, led the meeting along with some prominent estate employees and Dr Ashutosh. Chatterjee asked Gauranga to describe the sequence of events.

"The sadhu had declared himself as Ramendra Narayan Roy the previous morning. Needham Babu asked a few of us to visit Jyotirmayee Devi's house based on the administration's orders. We bombarded the sadhu with questions, most of which he didn't answer. I don't know if it was because he didn't want to reply or he couldn't recollect the incidents at that moment. Then Ashu doctor queried about a bird shot in Darjeeling. He asked the sadhu to name the person who shot the bird. Immediately, someone from the group said the doctor should share the name with me secretly because I was sitting next to him. We needed to see if his answer tallied with that of the sadhu," Gauranga paused.

"Did the sadhu reply?"

"The doctor told Birendra Banerjee's name in my ears. But the sadhu said Hari Singh. Ashu doctor rejoiced while stating the answer was wrong since Hari Singh hadn't even visited Darjeeling. We called Birendra Banerjee, and he stunned everyone by stating how he had never held a gun until then. Hari Singh had indeed aimed at the bird. Ashu doctor left immediately. He didn't wait for the session to finish."

The court summoned Jyotirmayee to appear as a witness in July 1934. With Pannalal Basu as the judge, it functioned in Jyotirmayee's house every day for three weeks as she answered questions from behind a purdah. Chatterjee asked her to take the court through her childhood linked to Ramendra.

"I was the second child and was married at sixteen. We were three brothers and three sisters. Ramendra was the second brother – our Mejo Bhai. He and our youngest brother were hardly interested in getting a formal education despite the sincere attempts of tutors. Our Choto Thakurma, Satyabhama Devi, was highly indulgent towards her two younger grandsons. Because of her constant interference, my younger brothers, except Boro Kumar, escaped from any form of learning. They barely knew English and couldn't write. They spoke low-class Bengali. But Boro Kumar could converse in the languages and easily attend to foreign guests. In comparison, Boro Didi and I were grateful to be educated at the insistence of our father before his death. Since we had a majority of Hindustani servants, we picked up Hindi easily. Ramendra wasn't interested in polo, unlike my other brothers. He didn't even like cricket, football, or billiards."

Chatterjee produced the letters that Ramendra supposedly wrote to Bibhabati. Jyotirmayee glanced at them and said in an exasperated tone, "Impossible! Ramendra didn't know how to write in Bengali."

"What about the official documents?"

"The secretary would write the letter and read it to my brother. He only put his signature."

"Can you tell us what happened before the Kumar took off to Darjeeling? Were you aware of his sickness?"

"A few months before Ramendra travelled to Darjeeling, he met me. He had bandages all over his hands. I was worried after seeing him in that state. But he assured me it was only eczema and he was going away to Darjeeling so that the sores could heal fast. He asked Choto Thakurma and me to accompany him to the hills. Though I was initially reluctant since I also had my family to cater to, I gave in to his request because of his persistence. When Satya Babu came to know of the change in plans, he informed me they had booked a house in Darjeeling. It didn't have enough space for all of us. I got the hint he expected us to drop out."

"Did you think it was usual for an eczema patient to visit the hills?"

"Initially, I didn't think about it. However, when Satya Babu met me, he insisted on the urgency for Mejo to go to Darjeeling. That's when I asked him why. He disclosed Mejo had contracted a terrible disease."

"What happened after they returned without Mejo Kumar?"

"We were devastated. I heard Mejo Rani and Satya Babu's version of Ramendra's death and cremation, but the servants' and the accompanying employees' statements varied. Shariff Khan and Birendra Banerjee's stories made me doubt if the cremation had taken place and whether it followed the rituals of a Hindu funeral. While our suspicion was gaining ground, Boro Kumar received an anonymous letter stating Mejo Kumar was alive, and people had spotted him in various towns. He decided to inquire. Bibhabati lived in the Raj Bari as a widow, and Satya Babu stayed back to help her deal with her grief. When Boro Kumar's decision to investigate Mejo's death reached Satya's ears, he convinced my brother about getting the certificates from Dr Calvert confirming Mejo's death. Of course, we believed him since he was an extended part of the family. When he got the certificates, Boro Kumar decided not to pursue it further."

"How was your relationship with your brother's widow after she left Jaidebpur to stay in Calcutta?"

"Of all the family members, Bibhabati was the closest to me. I always loved her as a sister. Even after Mejo's death, we tended to her during her mourning phase. After she left for Calcutta, she stayed in touch through letters, and we met whenever I went to Calcutta. Mejo Rani wrote to my daughters frequently. But she was most fond of my son, Buddhu. Whenever Buddhu was in Calcutta, she insisted him to visit her home, have his meals at her place, and stay back for a few days. She even handed over many of my brother's European clothes and boots that fit Buddhu."

"It's worth noting the same clothes and boots now fit the plaintiff perfectly," Chatterjee mentioned as Jyotirmayee identified the clothes in the court. "What made you think the plaintiff is your brother, Ramendra Narayan?"

Jyotirmayee paused before replying. "I heard about the sadhu from people who had visited Dhaka and seen him. Then Buddhu met him." She described the journey from Buddhu meeting the sadhu at Buckland Bund for the first time to the day he declared his identity in front of the people. "I couldn't take risks. I questioned him and tested him on various parameters before feeling convinced my brother had returned. He narrated several instances of his life before the Darjeeling trip and events in Darjeeling. He recognised people from his past. When we were sure about his identity, we welcomed him to the family and my house with *bhai phonta,* wishing him a long and healthy life."

"Are you also handling the money the plaintiff accumulated from the tenants?"

"They pay him *nazar,* which he keeps in my custody. He led the life of a monk for years. He isn't used to handling money for a long time. But this case has wrecked us financially. My income has dried up, and now I have to take a loan to run the case. And here you're asking me if I handle his money!" She sounded exasperated.

Chatterjee changed the topic and described the similarities between Jyotirmayee and the sadhu, the traits she had shared with her middle brother.

"Jyotirmayee Devi has brown eyes, small hands and feet, and rough skin near her wrists and instep – a feature found in most members of the Bhawal Raj family. Her brown hair and very fair skin are features observed in Ramendra Narayan and their youngest brother, Rabindra. Her son Buddhu had also inherited these features. We can spot the same traits in the plaintiff."

Chapter 26

Billu Babu Testifies

Chaudhuri embarked on a mission ever since Jyotirmayee was at the witness box. The evening before he was to cross-examine the lady, he held a meeting with his team. "We must prove Jyotirmayee is biased so that her testimony doesn't get too much weightage. She's the lead conspirator in this fake sanyasi theory. She's trying to go against the Government, deprive her brothers' widows of their monthly income, and establish an imposter as her brother so that she and her family reap the benefits. Her changed equation with Bibhabati Devi proves how she never cared for anything except property and wealth. We need to break her strength."

On the following July morning, Chaudhuri started questioning Jyotirmayee. His razor-sharp questions, aggressive body language, and sarcastic jibes made the lady uncomfortable. Owing to the extreme weather and continuous attack by the defence counsel, Jyotirmayee fainted in the afternoon. After she recovered, Chaudhuri continued with his pointed questions.

"Why would you believe rumours related to your dead brother when your sister-in-law Bibhabati Devi confirmed the cremation took place as per Hindu rituals? Shouldn't the brother's wife be a more credible source of information than the gossiping servants?"

"When my brother left Jaidebpur for Darjeeling, he bore no signs of any disease that could lead to his death. Losing a sibling so young was never easy for my family. We heard a different version of the cremation from Shariff Khan and Birendra Banerjee. Yet, we believed what his widow told us. Years ago, a sanyasi who had visited Jaidebpur met me and Choto Thakurma. He scribbled on a piece of paper my brother was alive. How could we not believe the holy man? I was sure my brother hadn't died in Darjeeling. We actively started looking out for him. I also told Mejo Rani about it, and though she didn't share our enthusiasm, she never objected to our statements. I clutched onto every piece of information, even if it was just a rumour. We went as far as Benares to look for him but had no luck."

When Chaudhuri grilled her on the sadhu's inability to speak Bengali, she dismissed all claims of him speaking only in Hindi. "Immediately after he made a public declaration of his identity, he spoke in Bhawal Bengali. He uses Hindi words on and off, but can converse fluently in Bengali."

The questions got personal and offensive. "What makes you sure Satyen Babu is a murderer?"

"I said nothing like that."

"You suggested the same."

"Your information is incorrect. Satya Babu was the one who took my brother to Darjeeling, arranged for his stay at the hill station, and carried back the news of his death to Jaidebpur. But at no point did I ever say or suggest that he was a murderer." She stood her ground.

The next crucial witness to appear at the box was Jitendra Chandra Mukherjee, the son of the late Indumayee Devi. He was popularly known by his nickname, Billu.

"Please mention your relation with the Bhawal Raj family."

Billu Babu stated Ramendra was his uncle from his maternal side. He spoke about Mejo Kumar's lack of interest in academics and inability to sing in tune. His uncle attempted playing polo but gave up. Though he was a skilled hunter, Ramendra didn't know the English technical terms related to hunting or firearms. Even Billu couldn't state their meanings.

Chatterjee showed him the same letters Ramendra supposedly wrote to Bibhabati. Billu dismissed the idea. "My uncle didn't know to write. These are fake."

"Tell us everything you can recollect about the Darjeeling trip."

"I was a young boy keen to accompany my uncle to the hill station. Even he agreed. But Satya Babu told me the house had a single kitchen, where people cooked vegetarian and chicken items together. Since I couldn't tolerate the smell of chicken, my food came from a separate kitchen. He also insisted on how I mustn't miss school for so long since it would be a while before they returned. Because of these issues, I backed out. Mejo Mama Babu told me I could still come and visit him during my summer holidays. Unfortunately, the opportunity never arrived."

"Do you remember the details just before and immediately after Kumar's death?"

"Yes! On 6th May, we got a telegram that Kumar was unwell. On the 7th, we got an assurance he was recovering since the pain and fever had subsided. Immediately after, we got a shocking telegram that Kumar was critical and someone from the family should come to Darjeeling at the earliest. However, when Choto Mama Babu was on his way to the railway station on 9th May, we received another telegram that Mejo Kumar had died at dusk the previous day. My youngest uncle returned to the palace, devastated. The telegram also mentioned Satya Babu intended to take Mejo Rani to Calcutta directly. But my eldest uncle would not let it happen, so he asked the secretary to hurry to Poradah station and intercept the mail carrying the Second Rani and Satya Babu."

"What about the cremation?"

"Birendra Babu told me they took the body for cremation. But a storm made them take shelter away from the cremation ground. When they returned, the body was missing. I spoke to Shariff Khan, and his version was the same."

"So, they made you believe there was foul play in Kumar's death?"

"The cremation details made me think something was amiss. But after I spoke to my Mejo aunt, I knew something fishy had happened. She was close to Buddhu and me. So, she opened up to us easily. She cried and lamented how her brother hadn't let her be with my uncle during his last hours. When she pleaded for a meeting with her husband, Satya Babu scolded her. I was certain the truth associated with my uncle's death went deeper than the statements used to cover it up." He paused to think. "But two months later, two letters arrived at the Raj Bari. They had the same context that Mejo Kumar was alive. My eldest uncle couldn't ignore the letters any longer."

After days of examining and cross-examining, Billu Babu's testimony was over. Before leaving, he announced, "I came here as a witness because I believe the sadhu is my uncle."

Chapter 27
More Witnesses

The day after Billu Babu finished giving his testimony, Chandra Sekhar Banerjee, Jyotirmayee's elder son-in-law, appeared in the court. After introducing himself, he validated the statements about Kumar and his apathy toward academics.

"Mejo Kumar was so uncomfortable conversing in any language other than Bengali that he avoided the company of Europeans." He negated all claims that the sadhu spoke only Hindi. "He speaks Bengali with a Hindi accent. However, it's interesting to note he can also speak the Banua language just like before."

Chandra Babu explained how Mejo Kumar spent time with the tribals Banua and conversed with them in their language. When the sadhu spoke the same way as the Banua people, Chandra Babu was sure the man was Ramendra.

Satinath Banerjee or Sagar Babu, the younger son-in-law of Jyotirmayee Devi, offered a deeper insight into the moment the news of Ramendra's death reached Jaidebpur. "I was with the youngest Kumar en route station when the telegram arrived. The exact words were – 'Mejo Kumar expired in the evening'. We returned to inform the secretary, Jogen Babu, who was already aware of it since the previous night."

"Did you often speak to Mejo Rani?"

"She rarely spoke to me. She was comfortable interacting with Billu and Buddhu, though she spent most of the time in her room after Kumar's death. I remember seeing her cry, mostly. She didn't even speak to Satya Babu for weeks."

Chatterjee thought to himself how Bibhabati was still as rigid in her denial to meet the sadhu.

"What is your relation with Jogen Banerjee, the estate secretary?"

"He's my elder brother."

"Did he recognise the sadhu as Mejo Kumar when you saw him for the first time?"

"We both identified him as Madhyam Kumar."

"Why did he change his statement?"

"I won't be able to answer because my knowledge is limited in this case." Sagar Babu refused to reply whether the Government or Mejo Rani was influencing Jogen's actions.

Many people knew Jogen shifted his loyalty from the sadhu to the Government because of Gobinda Banerjee. The latter threw baseless allegations at the employee, irking the former. Jogen vowed to be never on Gobinda's side, irrespective of what he believed about the sadhu.

Chaudhuri grilled Sagar Babu about Kumar's education or the lack of it. But there were no two ways about Kumar's inability to write or speak English. Questions related to the Bhawal princes following European table manners came up. Sagar Babu dismissed the idea like the other witnesses before him. "There is no dining room, dining table, or cupboard in either Kumar's quarters or inside the Raj Bari."

Bibhabati's aunt, Sarojini Devi, appeared next. Sarojini was fond of the family's son-in-law Ramendra after Bibhabati was married into the royal family. Her husband, Protap Narayan Roy, also Bibhabati's maternal uncle, had arranged the alliance, and Sarojini took a personal interest in their wedding. Mejo Kumar met Sarojini whenever he was in Calcutta, Jaidebpur, or Uttarpara. When word spread about Ramendra's cremation gone wrong, Sarojini displayed great restraint by not asking Bibhabati or Satyen about the incident.

When the news about the sadhu reached her, she was keen to meet him. But her sons discouraged her from meeting the sadhu since the Government issued the imposter notice.

On a winter morning in Uttarpara, a man arrived at her doorstep. Sarojini saw him from behind a purdah. It didn't take long for her to realise that the smiling sadhu was Ramendra. "You look and speak like our son-in-law, Ramendra. Of course, you are the Second Kumar of Bhawal." She was elated.

Before leaving, the sadhu spoke to her in private. "You know I'm fighting a battle against the authorities to reclaim my identity and property. Since you know who I am, can you testify in court about how you arrived at my true identity?"

Sarojini Devi agreed. In her mind, she was not just helping an honest man but facilitating her husband's niece to lead a happy married life again.

When she stood at the witness box almost a year later, Sarojini was aware of Bibhabati and Satyen's attitude towards the sadhu. Though she didn't want to hurt Bibha, she felt it was her duty to stand with the truth.

Just like the sadhu visited Sarojini Devi, he also travelled to various other towns to make his presence known to the subjects. During most of these visits, the plaintiff was eventually treated as the prince by the zamindars and influential people, thus leading to his mass acceptance as the Second Kumar.

Jyotirmayee mentioned it to the sadhu when he was taking updates from Billu Babu one evening. "How will they stop the truth from coming out now? People aren't fools like these gora sahibs make them out to be. They can identify the true Kumar. Look at the response Mejo gets wherever he visits. Judge Sahib should consider this aspect."

Though Billu Babu nodded, he knew better. It took much more than public popularity for the judgment to go in their favour. But he didn't want to demotivate her.

"The court can't ignore the sentiments of the mass while arriving at a decision," he responded.

Chapter 28
The Witnesses from Darjeeling

A couple of weeks after the case began, B.C. Chatterjee sat on the gigantic sandalwood chair. His team, comprising other lawyers like Suren Banerjee and Arabinda Guha, occupied the opposite chairs.

"The modus operandi of the defence counsel is to prove the cremation never happened in the night. Their theory focuses on how Kumar died at midnight, and they kept the dead body in the house until the morning, after which they took the body to the cremation ground. The funeral followed the Hindu rituals. Satyen Babu and some other witnesses claim they saw the body turn into ashes. Based on this theory, the question of a botched-up cremation doesn't appear. If there was no attempt to cremate the body in the night, rain and storms driving the accompanying people away from the ground to seek shelter sound improbable. It rules out the vital aspect of a missing body from the case." Arabinda Guha paused to look at Chatterjee, who listened with his eyes closed.

"Right! When there's no missing dead body, there's no scope for Ramendra Narayan's return. It makes the cremation time a vital point for us. Based on what the plaintiff says and what we heard from his family, his old servants, and employees, a cremation was attempted late at night. It hints at how the primary defendant's associates were in a hurry. What did they fear, or were they trying to hide a secret?"

Suren chimed in, "If you observe the pattern, strangely none of his family members other than his wife could make it to the hill station from the day they commenced the journey, during his duration of stay, or even at his funeral."

Chatterjee continued, "As per the customs, we don't keep a dead body overnight, else the soul doesn't attain moksha. Since Kumar's family couldn't be there, they would need other male members for the funeral procession. So, what could Ramendra Narayan's associates do? They would try to explain the situation to the bhadraloks in Darjeeling and request them to become *smashan bandhus* for the funeral procession."

"The team appointed by the Court of Wards has already interviewed most of them through standard questions. Satyen Babu was in Darjeeling when the team reached there. He assisted them in meeting specific individuals and getting the details. I believe he helped to retrieve the weather reports on 8th and 9th May before handing them over to the team," Suren spoke.

"The entries mention no rain or storm on the 8th and 9th of May. So, witnesses who claim they ran to take shelter, leaving the body unattended, sound dubious to the court. It's another attempt to prove the body couldn't go missing." Chatterjee raised his eyebrows.

Suren nodded. "It's summer April onwards. So, gentlemen preferred to spend their days in the hills. Several clerical staff worked from Darjeeling as their reporting authorities spent the summer months away from Calcutta to escape the heat. A group of professors was residing at the sanitorium during the period. Prof Satyendra Nath Maitra is a prominent name in the group. He lived at the sanitorium with his wife from April to June 1909. Though most of these professors recollected a servant arriving to announce the death of the Bhawal prince, none of them made it to the cremation grounds. However, some random people went to the cremation, and a few returned drenched. Most of them aren't alive to state what happened that night. But we have a few people, then teenagers, in 1909, who remember a funeral procession chanting *'Hari Bol'* went through the streets that night. They recollected the announcement of

Bhawal Raja's death. The servants requested help to carry the dead body, and some people accompanied the funeral procession."

When Suren visited Darjeeling, he met Ashraf Alam, a clerk who was Shariff Khan's friend. "Shariff Khan came to me in the evening because Kumar had died. A Bengali gentleman accompanied him. He sought help in organizing the items needed for the funeral. I asked him why they couldn't wait until the morning. He said they needed to burn the body before morning as per rituals. I took him to Ram Khilan's shop. Later, I saw the procession with lanterns in their hands at night." When Suren asked him if he remembered how many people were a part of the procession, Ashraf mentioned thirty.

"Can you take me to Ram Khilan?" Suren had asked.

Ram Khilan wasn't available, but they met a man who worked at the shop in 1909. He smiled at Ashraf, the Munshi Babu. "I remember the group. A Bengali bhadralok and some porters came with Munshi Babu. They wanted things for the cremation. I gave them kerosene, ghee, incense sticks, earthen pots, and other items. A porter who carried the bulk of the materials told me the cremation would occur at night. I saw the procession later that night."

Suren had narrated the details to Chatterjee immediately on returning from Darjeeling. Chatterjee addressed Suren, "You also told me about the tea estate employee and his school teacher friend. Didn't they attend the funeral too?"

"Yes! They joined the procession. On reaching the cremation ground, a storm broke out. It forced them to seek shelter at a slaughterhouse uphill. When they returned, they saw the charpoy on which they had placed the body but couldn't spot the dead body. Someone mentioned the missing dead body in the chaotic situation. Everyone went around the place with lanterns. Eventually, they left since they weren't sure when the rituals would begin."

"Did they go to the cremation ground in the morning again?"

"No! The tea estate employee heard about the cremation the next morning, so he assumed they had found the body."

"Many people came forward with the same story. They had joined the procession, though they didn't know Mejo Kumar or his family. The body, covered with a shawl, was taken on a charpoy to the cremation ground. A storm wreaked havoc, and they ran for their lives. Some returned to their homes since they were drenched or were getting late. Most who returned to the ground left after the cremation got delayed because of the missing body. Some saw the vacant charpoy, but almost everyone was clueless about how the body went missing. No one saw the cremation taking place that night," Chatterjee pondered.

"Chandra Singh, the clerk at Kalimpong's revenue office, saw the body tied to the charpoy with ropes when he accompanied the funeral procession. He recollected the shawl's corners covering the dead body tied to the charpoy's legs. Chandra Singh gave the same version of bad weather and seeking shelter at the slaughterhouse. When he returned to the ground, he saw the charpoy was not at the original spot, the wet shawl was on the ground, and the ropes, though still attached to the charpoy, were hanging loose. He didn't wait to search for the body," Suren mentioned.

"They took the body to the old cremation ground. We established the shed of this cremation ground was in shambles through the assistant secretary of the cremation ground committee. The municipality built a new cremation ground a little away from the existing one. It became functional by the end of 1907. However, people still preferred to use the old grounds despite the non-availability of a shed. I guess the old ground was more accessible because of its location. However, the defence counsel will argue on the rationality of taking the body to the old ground because the new ground had upgraded facilities," Chatterjee sighed.

"We must remember Ram Singh Subba, the man who saw the marks on the dead body," Suren spoke again. Subba was the munshi of the owner of Step Aside.

As the lawyers continued debating the points, it was a common observation that people who went to Step Aside or joined the funeral procession on the morning of 9th May didn't get a chance to see the face of the dead Kumar. From keeping the body on the charpoy to carrying it to the cremation ground and putting fire to it, no one removed the white cloth used to cover it. Dr Pran Krishna Acharya had already certified he found it unusual how Kumar's family didn't let the doctor touch the dead body. Some witnesses came forward stating they saw two processions, unnatural black marks on one foot of the dead body, indenting a new charpoy and other materials required for the funeral for the second time, and skipping many rituals associated with Hindu rules for cremation.

"If they exercised caution to cover his face throughout, it could also signify that they didn't want it exposed to the world. What could be the probable reason?" Arabinda spoke aloud.

"If the body wasn't of Kumar because he was alive and the Naga sanyasis took him away, the only way to prove the cremation was by burning another dead body. It brings us to the question of whose idea it was to replace the body. Also, who did it? What were Satyen and Dr Ashutosh's roles in this? And the toughest question – did Bibhabati Devi know what was going on at Step Aside?" Chatterjee grabbed his temple hard.

Chapter 29

Darshandas in the Witness Box

The lawyers dispersed soon after. Chatterjee went indoors to rest for a while. He thought of Ram Singh Subba's testimony, detailed by Suren.

Ram Singh returned home around 4:30 p.m. on 8th May 1909. A few hours later, women's shrieks at the Step Aside alerted him. Someone was sobbing uncontrollably. Ram Singh rushed to check what led to such an unexpected reaction.

"It was around 7:30 in the evening. I entered the house and saw a couple of Kumar's servants huddled near the compound. They told me about Kumar's sudden demise. Shocked, I went inside. His body lay upstairs, covered with a white cloth. Three men sat in silence. I identified them as Dr Sarkar, Dr Ashutosh, and Satya Babu. I couldn't bear to stay in the grief-laden environment beyond ten minutes. I left quietly."

But it was the latter half of his testimony that made the plaintiff's counsel take notice.

"While passing the adjacent rooms, I saw Rani locked up in one of the rooms. She was crying her heart out on an iron bed."

"Didn't it occur unusual to you?"

"I thought little about it then. It was a house where death had occurred."

Dr Sarkar's presence hinted at the possibility of Dr Calvert and Dr Sen's absence at that moment. It was tough to visualise the junior Dr Sarkar treating a patient in the presence of senior doctors.

Darshandas Naga, the man who saved the sadhu from the cremation ground, was a disciple of Harnamdas, just like Dharamdas. He sat in front of the Guru as the latter's eyes pierced through his soul.

"Speak the truth. I don't want any version which you think might be interesting," the Guru spoke in a firm voice.

"I have already told you so many times over the years. Lokdas was also with me. You heard him narrate the same story."

The Guru softened his tone. "I want you to be clear about what happened that night because the situation is messy now. Both sides will try to prove they are right."

Darshandas recollected when they reached Darjeeling and took shelter in the caves near the cremation ground, he had heard '*Hari Bol*' being chanted on that unfortunate night. "I was curious, so I took Lokdas to check what was happening. People stood with lanterns on the cremation ground. We didn't know anyone, plus it started to pour. We rushed back to the cave.

"Soon, the chanting stopped, and I thought of checking the reason. I heard a peculiar sound and got a lantern to investigate. Lokdas and I visited the cremation ground and saw a body on the charpoy. The sound was coming from underneath the white cloth covering the body. Lokdas removed the cloth and heard sounds of breathing from the body. I called Dharamdas and another sanyasi. Together, we carried the body inside the cave."

The rest was known to the world when Darshandas narrated the incident as a witness in the court. "He was shivering and seemed to be in severe pain. We took him inside, changed his wet clothes, and covered him with a blanket. We found a tin shed warmer than the cave."

"Was the shed open?" Chatterjee had asked.

"No! We didn't have the time to look around for keys. We broke the chain attached to the lock and barged inside."

"What happened after that?"

"We started his treatment. Soon, a Bengali babu came to the shed and wanted to feed us since we were holy men. We requested a blanket instead. He also helped us move to a better and bigger shed nearby. The man regained his senses eventually but was too weak to communicate. Gradually, the medicines brought him to a semi-normal state, and he asked us where we were. However, we didn't understand most of his words. We travelled from there to Siliguri, Benares, Punjab, and other places. At certain junctions, we met people who identified his language as Bengali. They asked us where we met the man, but we preferred not to discuss the circumstances of his discovery. Dharamdas made him his disciple and named him Sundardas."

"Do you remember his first words after he started speaking?"

"*'Ami kothay'* meaning 'where am I'?"

"When did he start speaking Hindi?"

"Since he travelled the country with us, he picked up our language of communication. Eventually, he spoke only in Hindi."

When Chatterjee asked him to describe how Sundardas recollected his identity, Darshandas had an intriguing tale. "In Nepal, flashes of memory came to him. He remembered Dhaka and guessed he possibly lived there. Dharamdas permitted him to go to Dhaka and check for himself. It would be his choice to stay with his family or return to the life of a monk. Sundardas went to his family in Dhaka. By then, he could recollect most details of his family. We went to our Guru Ji at Nankana Sahib."

"When did you hear Sundardas was the Second Kumar of Bhawal?"

"I came to know he had returned to his family. I came to see him a year after but didn't meet him as per our Guru's instructions. Then, I interacted with one of his relatives as Gopaldas – the name I used before Guru Ji called me Darshandas. People in Jaidebpur told me their king had returned a sadhu. It was around eleven years ago."

"Why did you change your mind about getting involved in the case now?"

"Guru Ji instructed me to speak the truth. I met the man a year ago in his house when the case was already in full swing."

The man, who supplied the blanket and helped them shift to a new place, appeared as a witness. He corroborated what Darshandas stated.

Chaudhuri, during his cross-examination, highlighted the sadhus should have returned the sick man to his friends and family. But Darshandas retorted, "If his family was so concerned, they should have taken better care instead of abandoning him in such a state. I don't know if they would be as happy as we were to see a dead man come alive. As sanyasis, we felt blessed. But we were scared of their reaction since we had touched a dead body and weren't aware of what's allowed and not as per Hindu rituals."

Though Chaudhuri tried influencing his thoughts by continuously asking if Darshandas thought the family was trying to cremate a living man, he steered clear of any controversy.

Darshandas' presence substantiated the sadhu's claims of memory loss, picking up Hindi, and returning to Dhaka.

Chapter 30

Manamohan Bhattacharya Flips

Manamohan Bhattacharya was a personal clerk to the Bhawal estate manager. When he met the sadhu, he felt convinced the man was the Second Kumar of Bhawal. He spilled the beans in front of the plaintiff during a conversation.

"When the news about your death arrived, Boro Kumar wanted to probe further. There were rumours of you surviving the tragedy. But Sala Babu got the death certificate from Dr Calvert and ended all speculations. Boro Kumar didn't proceed with the queries. A few years later, Mejo Rani employed me as her clerk since Boro Kumar didn't need my services here. Mejo Rani sent a letter to Boro Babu through Satya Babu about her desire to claim the insurance on your life. Satya Babu disclosed her sister's wish to donate the amount to a sanitorium in Darjeeling. The nobility of the cause made Boro Kumar withdraw his claim. He possibly convinced Choto Kumar to forego his portion too. They submitted the requisite certificates, and the cheque with the claimed amount arrived in Jaidebpur. After encashing the cheque in Calcutta, I accompanied Satya Babu as we travelled back to Jaidebpur." Manamohan stopped as he realised that the next part of his story was inappropriate to state in Jyotirmayee Devi's presence.

The sadhu noticed the hesitation in Manamohan's voice. He turned toward the purdah. "I feel a little hungry. Will you please ask the servant to prepare a bowl of fresh fruits for me?" Jyotirmayee reluctantly walked away.

Seeing the sadhu signal him to continue, Manamohan spoke, "I observed something scandalous while we were returning on the train. Satya Babu had arranged for two prostitutes for Boro and Choto Kumar. It was his way of keeping them happy. He needed to ensure Mejo Rani got the requisite financial benefits."

"Did he tell you he brought the women for my brothers?"

Manamohan nodded. "They took the women to Nalgola Raj Bari from the steamer ghat."

The sadhu didn't look surprised. Ramendra often took Elokeshi to Nalgola Raj Bari for pleasure. Nawab Salimullah of the Nalgola Raj Bari shared a warm relationship with the Kumars, especially Ramendra.

"Anything else you want to share?" the sadhu raised his eyebrows.

"Soon after, Mejo Rani left for Calcutta permanently. The Court of Wards took over the property. But Satya Babu filed a petition stating Mejo Rani could look after her share with his help since she was an educated woman. The authorities rejected her plea. I worked with her for over two years. Then I quit and returned to Dhaka."

"Did you leave voluntarily, or did she ask you to leave?"

"We didn't see eye to eye on many matters. Also, Satya Babu's constant interference in her matters made it difficult for me to operate. When I met you for the first time, I knew you were Mejo Kumar from the way you talked, walked, and looked."

"Are you willing to testify in court?"

Manamohan was ready to support what he believed was the truth.

Manamohan met Bibhabati in 1933; Jogen Babu beckoned him. Mejo Rani spoke to the clerk in a stern voice, "You are betraying the late Kumar and me by supporting a fraud. How can you become a witness without asking me?"

When he entered the room, Manamohan had assumed the Rani wanted his help. But the conversation turned ugly when Manamohan requested Bibhabati to meet the sadhu once.

"Many people met him and felt convinced about his identity. Please give him a chance, Rani Ma."

Bibhabati made it clear that she had no intention of meeting the imposter. Besides, the trial was about to begin, and it was time to look forward.

Realising how crucial Manamohan's evidence could be since the man was privy to insider secrets of the Raj Bari and Rani Bibhabati's family, Bibhabati sought the secretary Jogen Banerjee's help to set up another meeting with Manamohan at the Nalgola Raj Bari the following year.

When Manamohan went to meet Bibhabati again, the voice that spoke to him from behind the purdah belonged to the youngest Rani, Ananda Kumari. "You must help Mejo Rani." The conversation steered in the same direction as last time. Both widows insisted on Manamohan not testifying in the sadhu's favour. But Manamohan persisted with Bibhabati to meet the sadhu once.

"Multiple letters have been produced in the court, supposed to be sent by Mejo Kumar to Mejo Rani. The letters are fake, and someone has forged his signature. You'll get into further trouble because of the forged letters. The court doesn't take it kindly when one side attempts to misguide the course of law."

But Bibhabati turned a deaf ear to Manamohan's pleas and warnings. The widows were outraged at Manamohan's audacity to argue with them.

When Manamohan took to the witness box, he narrated the same things he had told the sadhu and spoke of Bibhabati's reluctance to see the plaintiff.

"I would've done everything in my capacity to help her if she harboured the same opinion after meeting him once. I would've even helped her if she had changed her opinion. But she is adamant about her stand. I can vouch that Kumar hasn't written these letters." He gave a detailed statement about why the letters weren't genuine.

Manamohan's testimony highlighted the emotion nurtured by many. Why wasn't Bibhabati allowing the sadhu to present his side of the story? Did she not want her husband to return? Was there someone else in her life? The questions seemed unending; the possibilities turned scandalous.

Chapter 31

Elokeshi Khemtawali

In the room where Elokeshi lived, memories and tokens of her former lovers occupied a portion. Her fragile bones didn't allow her to dance any longer, but she hadn't given up on her daily ritual of practicing singing. However, she couldn't bring herself to concentrate on the music today. Every time she picked up the *sur*, her mind wandered to the conversation with a servant's wife early morning.

Elokeshi usually went to pick flowers even before the first ray of light appeared in the sky. She had encountered a woman on her way back. The slender woman swayed her hips as she carried the earthen pot. Elokeshi moved aside to let the young woman pass.

"What beautiful fragrance!" The woman stopped in front of Elokeshi and put the pot down. Elokeshi looked at the face. It felt familiar. She realised the woman was the daughter-in-law of a woman companion who had attended to the wives of Bhawal princes in the women's quarters. Elokeshi referred to her as a *'bou'*.

"Going to the ghat, bou?" she asked out of courtesy.

The woman nodded. "I heard your stories from my mother-in-law."

Elokeshi didn't know how to respond.

"Do you collect flowers every morning?" the woman continued.

"Not always. I come for an early morning stroll. If I find flowers on my way, I pick them." They spoke for a while before going in opposite directions.

Back in her house, Elokeshi thought of how the dusky beauty made her feel comfortable conversing with a stranger. However, Elokeshi decided not to take the same route for a few days to avoid meeting her again.

More than a fortnight later, Elokeshi bumped into the young woman as she carried the earthen pots full of water back home. The previous week, Elokeshi had met the sadhu. She knew it was Mejo Kumar the moment she set her eyes on him near Jyotirmayee's house. She hadn't shown any fear of voicing her opinion in front of people familiar to her and the Bhawal prince.

The woman looked exhausted as she put the pots down and wiped the sweat from her face and neck.

"Didn't you sleep last night?" Elokeshi asked.

"It's been a hectic week. Mejo Rani was in town; she left yesterday."

"Oh!" Elokeshi was well aware of the purpose of Rani's visit. Bibhabati was meeting estate employees, talukdars, and tenants with gusto.

"I had to run errands since my mother-in-law isn't well and can barely walk without support," the woman volunteered information.

"I heard about Mejo Rani's stay at the Raj Bari," Elokeshi responded.

"Yes, it's no secret that she has the time and intent to come here and interact with people but refuses to meet her husband." The venom in her voice was unmissable.

"She won't see him. That's why she's fighting a case against her husband." Elokeshi recollected the day Bibhabati came to meet her with Jyotirmayee. Mejo Kumar's obsession with Elokeshi spread far and wide after he arranged for her to stay within the Raj Bari premises. Rani Bilasmani was vocal about her displeasure about the set-up. The wife in her teens was no match for the sultry siren mistress. Bibhabati's hatred was palpable the day she warned Elokeshi to leave the town.

Elokeshi shifted to a new address after convincing Kumar the move would lead to a peaceful arrangement for all. But deep within, she took it as a challenge. She stayed away from Jaidebpur, but Kumar couldn't bear to be away from her. Their association and moments, earlier confined to her house, were now out in the open as Kumar spent time with Elokeshi on the boat and at the Nalgola Raj Bari.

Elokeshi last saw Ramendra when he returned from Jaidebpur to meet her after five months. She was worried about an unusually long gap but had no option but to wait. Ramendra had lost weight, and his skin looked dark and rough. He maintained his distance.

"What took you so long?" she spoke in a seductively sad voice. Instead of pulling her closer, he removed the shawl and stared at her. Elokeshi saw his hands were full of marks from dried sores.

"The sores are from syphilis. If you sleep with multiple partners, you contract it through…" he didn't need to elaborate further. "I spent my nights with you."

The implications of his statement were clear to Elokeshi. She wanted to retaliate by asking how many women he bedded. But she held her tongue and replied sternly, "I've never had such a disease. I think you can make it out from the texture of my skin."

Ramendra hissed, "What's the guarantee that you didn't have it before you met me?"

The argument became nasty as they alleged each other of being responsible for Kumar's illness. Ramendra stormed out of the house and never returned. Elokeshi, shocked at the sudden events, spent a few nights crying and regretting her words. With time, she became a mistress to another wealthy man.

"Kaki, why are you shivering? Are you feeling sick?" The woman's voice brought Elokeshi back to the present.

"I need to rest." She didn't bother about the woman's offer to help and left without further delay.

At home, Elokeshi thought of the day she first sighted the sadhu. She had shivered the same way as in the morning. He was back, and she would do anything to protect him this time.

Chapter 32

Scandals from the Past

Elokeshi got an intimation from the Kotwali police station asking her to meet the officer. Elokeshi's turn to appear as a witness was due soon. The interaction with the officer didn't go as expected. He coaxed her not to testify in court. Initially, his tone was of reconciliation, but the hostility grew as he realised she would not back off.

When she appeared in the court, she narrated her association with the Kumar, her identification of the sadhu as Ramendra Narayan, and her experience at the police station. The defence counsel had negated her existence as fiction until then. But Elokeshi shocked the opponents with her presence and statements.

A few well-wishers asked her to stay indoors for some days since her statement about the involvement of police and authorities in influencing the witnesses raised a storm. She eventually took off for her long pending early morning walk after ten days.

Elokeshi saw the dusky woman walk at a distance with the earthen pots. It was quite a while since she spoke to somebody not associated with the case. She called out. "Bou, why are you rushing today?"

The woman turned around and beamed at Elokeshi. She waited for the aging woman to catch up with her. "How are you, Kaki? I worried about you since I didn't see you for so many days. I thought of checking on you. But..." she stopped.

Her reason for not visiting didn't need any explanation. Society approved of men using women for pleasure but didn't think twice before branding the same woman as a social outcast.

"No, no! It's thoughtful of you, but I was busy with other things."

"Of course! I heard about the courage you displayed in the court."

"It's not only me. Many people proved their loyalty to the sadhu, our Mejo Kumar."

They spoke for a while before splitting mid-way toward their destinations.

They met almost every day as Elokeshi grew comfortable with the effervescent woman. Sometime later, the topic of Bibhabati came up again.

"Mejo Rani is arriving today. Jogen Babu has called some selective employees for a meeting with her tomorrow. Most of these people have testified in court or will appear soon. He's leaving no opportunity to showcase his support towards the Rani."

"Oh! She must have plans to meet the talukdars and tenants, too."

"Jogen Babu and doctor babu are setting up the meetings."

"Ashu doctor?"

She nodded. "I heard Satya Babu wrote to Ashu doctor to help Rani Ma. But it could also be possible she communicated directly with the doctor. After all, their bond has always been in the limelight." The woman lowered her voice.

Elokeshi didn't say a word. The woman continued, "You must have heard about their hush-hush relationship. However much they claim the gossip as fabricated lies to tarnish their images, I believe there can't be smoke without fire." She smirked.

"Ashu doctor faces multiple allegations related to Mejo Kumar's treatment. He is the hand that committed the crime planned by Satya Babu. No wonder he is active in proving the sadhu a fraud," Elokeshi muttered to herself.

"Kaki, is it true that Mejo Rani and doctor babu…" The woman paused for a second before deciding how to form the words. "Some even say Mejo Rani's womb carried his child, and she had to abort it out of the fear of a scandal. Doctor babu gave her medicines, leading to Rani Ma bleeding out the child. Satya Babu knew about it and helped to hide the secret. It's why the Rani and doctor are indebted to Satya Babu and obey his orders."

Elokeshi felt fatigued as the woman went on blabbering stories she heard from various sources at the servants' quarters.

Ashutosh had earned his medical degree when he met the lonely and depressed Bibhabati. Elokeshi heard from some women working in the Raj Bari about how sparks flew between them. Satya Babu befriended the doctor, making it easy for Bibhabati and Ashutosh to have access to each other. Bibhabati had also travelled to Calcutta at various intervals on the pretext of her poor health. There were stories of Ashutosh's absence from Jaidebpur during some of her trips, instigating people to speculate if they were meeting at a secret hideout.

Did Kumar know? Elokeshi had often thought of asking him if he had heard those rumours, but she understood she couldn't cross the line. Bibhabati was Ramendra's socially wedded wife, while Elokeshi was a mere mistress. Besides, she couldn't recollect him mentioning Bibhabati during their interactions. Beyond his sense of duty and fulfilling family's expectations, she could gauge no tender emotion towards his wife.

When Ashutosh accompanied them to Darjeeling, Elokeshi felt Kumar was unaware of the dynamics of the doctor with Bibhabati. Shariff Khan's version of the events reached her through sources. It looked like Mejo Rani was around the ailing Kumar at Step Aside, except on the day of his demise. Satya Babu had prohibited her from being in the room where Kumar yelped for a quick remedy. The doctor and the Rani carefully maintained a distance in the public eye, an aide of Kumar had told Elokeshi. But it could also mean Bibhabati and Ashutosh continued their illegitimate affair behind everyone's back.

Elokeshi didn't share the information she was privy to because of her well-spread network. She nodded as the woman continued blurting out juicy gossip. A servant saw Ashutosh creep out of the Raj Bari late at night. As much as she wanted to believe the possibility of a passionate affair, experience had taught Elokeshi to take things with a pinch of salt. Winning the case must be Bibhabati's primary focus now. Elokeshi was sure Mejo Rani wouldn't do anything scandalous to jeopardise her position.

After Bibhabati became a widow and shifted to Calcutta, she didn't come to Jaidebpur until the case started. Many people believed the initial fizz died after Kumar's death as the doctor focussed on his profession, and Bibhabati embraced a life of dignity as Ramendra's widow.

"I tell you, Kaki. Mejo Rani doesn't want to accept the sadhu as Kumar because she wants to continue her affair with the doctor."

Though Elokeshi barely added to the conversation, she nodded and gestured. Eventually, they parted, but she turned back and said, "My mother-in-law once said a woman helper saw heaps of blood-stained sarees and sheets years ago. No maid knew what happened to the clothes later. Probably, some trusted associate burnt them secretly." She walked away.

While returning home, Elokeshi remembered Jyotirmayee confirming Bibhabati was never pregnant in the years when Ramendra was alive. Did Bibhabati have a miscarriage or had she aborted the baby? Elokeshi believed if the same incident had happened far away from Jaidebpur, it was possible to hide the truth from the Bhawal family.

Chapter 33

Defence Presents Witnesses

Even after months, Chatterjee's number of witnesses seemed far from over. He ensured every person who identified the plaintiff as Kumar testified in his favour. Chatterjee knew some officials from the administration would represent the anti-sadhu camp. Their testimonies would automatically gain more weightage and credibility. So, he intended to create hysteria around mass acceptance.

The judge, Pannalal Basu, refused to let public opinion affect his rational thinking process. At some point during the procedure, he subtly mentioned the defence counsel's witnesses waiting for their turn. During this phase, the topic of Bibhabati's pregnancy in the past came up. There were claims that Rani was pregnant after a year of marriage. Did Bibhabati undergo an abortion, or did she have a miscarriage? The lady gynaecologist, dismissed all rumours about Bibhabati's pregnancy. Since she had treated Mejo Rani a few times, she was confident that she would have known if there was any truth to the pregnancy rumours.

They put the question to Jyotirmayee Devi, who Mejo Rani was closest to as a new bride. Jyotirmayee rejected stories about Bibhabati's pregnancy and abortion. However, during the investigation, they figured out how Mejo Rani's menstrual cycle had stopped for three months in 1904. She was in Calcutta then, and a male doctor had attended to her until her periods resumed.

Chatterjee shared his concern with his team. "The defence counsel is trying to portray how Ramendra Narayan and Bibhabati Devi led the normal life of a husband and wife. Their married life was running as expected, and they were physically intimate. But that's far from the truth. It's important to negate the pregnancy claims."

But another lawyer spoke from a different perspective. "There are rumours of Bibhabati and the doctor's secret affair. So, the pregnancy theory could point in the direction of Bibhabati cheating on her husband. Possibly, she went to Calcutta to get the fetus aborted to suppress the scandal."

But Chatterjee shook his head. "You forget the timeline. We are talking about the immediate year after marriage. She was a new bride. I doubt if Dr Ashutosh and Bibhabati had the opportunity to know each other. Whatever relationship sparked off the rumours must have happened later."

Chatterjee followed the same argument in the court, ruling out Bibhabati's pregnancy. The number of witnesses from the plaintiff's side totalled 1042. In February 1935, Chatterjee declared he had presented all witnesses. The stage was now open for defence counsel. By then, Pannalal Basu was the additional district judge of Dhaka.

When Chaudhuri took up the case, his strategy was to prove the Second Kumar had indeed died and his cremation happened in Darjeeling. If the defence could provide evidence that there was no loophole for the body to go missing, it would become easy for him to argue why the dead didn't return. The sadhu's claim of memory loss would become irrelevant, and the testimonies of those who declared the plaintiff and Mejo Kumar were the same would automatically turn inconsequential.

"We need to bring those who have certified about the morning cremation. Their statements can prove many points. For instance:

"Mejo Kumar was dead.

"The dead body never went missing.

"They cremated the body in the presence of many people.

"The story of an attempted night cremation is a fabricated lie.

"No missing body means no story of Mejo Kumar getting saved by Naga sanyasi.

"The sadhu's statement about memory loss becomes a plotted lie.

"The presence of the man pretending to be Mejo Kumar is part of a conspiracy.

"And this brings us to the question of who would benefit if the sadhu gains the wealth and status of Mejo Kumar?"

When the court proceedings began, the first one to appear was a cousin of Bibhabati Devi. The man worked at the Bengal secretariat and was present in Darjeeling at the time of Kumar's death.

"I visited Mejo Kumar daily during the weeks his health deteriorated. Satya tried his best. So did the doctors who attended to the ill man. On the day he passed away, I saw him in severe pain when I visited the house around 7 p.m. Later around 1 a.m. I received the message of Kumar's demise. He had passed away around 11:30 p.m. Bibhabati didn't leave his side since evening. She was inconsolable. Dr Nibaran Sen was present throughout the night. I stayed until the morning. Then I went to inform people about the tragic news. I gathered people for the cremation. They followed all the Hindu rituals with precision at the new cremation ground. They removed the clothes from Kumar's body. After bathing the body in ghee, they put new clothes on it and lit the pyre. We left after the body turned to ash."

"What about the rumours about an attempted cremation at night?" Chaudhuri asked.

"That's rubbish! He died late in the night. Where could we get the necessary items or people for the funeral? The shops were closed, and most people had slept. Besides, everyone was grieving, especially Bibha."

When Chatterjee stood up to cross-examine him, he held a document. "Is it true that your name appeared in the missing funds scam?"

The cousin swallowed hard. "It was a misunderstanding. I borrowed the money and would have returned it, but—"

"I have the details. Why did you take premature retirement?" Chatterjee asked with a stoic face.

The cousin crumbled under pressure and confessed to his association with the misappropriation of funds. He also stated the current secretary sent him to the Board of Revenue to testify.

Jagat Mohini, the nurse who attended to Kumar in Darjeeling came next. She repeated the same sequence of events and even claimed to have travelled some distance to bring Ganga water and the sacred thread needed for the last rites. She confirmed her presence at the cremation ground until the body turned to ashes.

However, Chatterjee nurtured a hostile attitude towards this woman with a dubious identity. Some claimed she was a Muslim with a fake Hindu name. The nurse accepted wearing jewellery and eating non-vegetarian items despite being a Brahmin widow. She failed to answer questions related to funeral rituals despite claiming to be a part of these rituals. Chatterjee concluded, "Why would anyone ask her to get Ganga *jal* and the sacred thread when it's quite evident that she's neither a Hindu nor a Brahmin? Why should the court trust the testimony of a witness who isn't even ready to disclose her true identity?"

The wife of the chowkidar at the Step Aside house also turned up as a witness. She confirmed seeing the face of the dead body, which was undoubtedly that of Mejo Kumar.

Chapter 34

Some Intriguing Testimonies

A few days later, Jyotirmayee sat with the sadhu on the verandah. They discussed the latest proceedings. "Many people came forward to state I died at midnight, they kept my body in the house overnight, and the funeral procession left in the morning. Someone heard Bibhabati crying through the night, someone spotted my uncovered face while they rubbed ghee on the dead body, and a few saw the Rani take off her jewellery, too." He sounded amused.

But Jyotirmayee didn't smile. "Even a doctor who agreed to testify against you for money stated he saw your face when the procession reached the cremation ground. They had the galls to bring that clown of a professor who supposedly met you a few days before the cremation, was present during the ritual, and saw the body burn. Most have received rewards in some way. Some escaped punishment for their past acts."

"It's weird how some of these guys claim to know I was suffering from biliary colic for a while." The sadhu stood up.

"What did Birendra say?" Jyotirmayee wanted to know after she heard that Kumar's clerk, Birendra Banerjee, was summoned.

"The same story others gave. I had biliary colic yet refused an injection. I was unconscious for fifteen minutes before dying. Biren dismissed the timing of death in the evening and the attempt to cremate the body in the night. And he didn't forget to mention Bibhabati was shattered and refused to leave her husband's side. Biren specifically mentioned the last part, dismissing theories about her not being allowed to be with me during the last hours."

The sadhu spoke through gritted teeth. "He took up the responsibility of lighting the pyre after applying ghee on my dead body, putting new clothes on it, and the sacred thread around it. He stayed back, along with others, until late afternoon to see the body completely burnt."

The sadhu turned towards Jyotirmayee. "He retracted from his statement given to Billu Babu about the attempted midnight cremation. That liar dared to say he remembered Shariff Khan crying at the cremation. Since he cremated the body in Darjeeling, Biren was sure Mejo Kumar was dead."

Jyotirmayee wanted to know what their lawyer asked the hypocrite Birendra. "He asked him pointed questions and mentioned his version of events was full of discrepancies. They didn't match his statements during Ashu doctor's legal case. A lawyer from the defence counsel's team prompted the replies."

"I hope Basu Sahib takes cognizance of all the lies," Jyotirmayee said before they went indoors.

The next set of witnesses were officials associated with the Bhawal Raj family. Rankin, the collector of Dhaka during Kumar's childhood, mentioned the Kumar's ability to converse in English and recollected playing polo with him. During cross-examination, Chatterjee highlighted how Rankin refused to identify the sadhu as Mejo Kumar since he had seen the man twenty-five years ago and was trying to build the image of the Kumar based on his memory. It was interesting that Rankin died of cancer a week after his testimony. When the news reached the sadhu, he told Jyotirmayee, "I had promised to seek revenge on the man for mistreating our mother when he took over our estate forcefully. What an irony of fate that he got a chance to seek vengeance by turning the tables on me before his death!"

Lindsay was interviewed in London since he took voluntary retirement from the civil services. He spoke about meeting the sadhu for the first time. When questioned about the imposter notice, Lindsay mentioned the evidence of no rainfall in Darjeeling on the night Kumar died. He gave a detailed view of the procedures followed by the authorities to validate the sadhu's identity and rubbish his claims.

Basu sought official documents during Lindsay's tenure to present in court. Initially, the authorities refused, citing confidentiality as the reason. Eventually, they handed over a few to the court, though they held back most under the pretext of safeguarding Bibhabati's reputation. The authorities blatantly mentioned official privilege for not producing the papers in court.

Meyers, the estate manager whose contract Rani Bilasmani had terminated, felt convinced the sadhu wasn't Mejo Kumar. Kumar couldn't be spiritual because of his wild nature. However, a piece of paper disclosed Meyers' initial observation of seeing the sadhu for the first time. He had casually mentioned his doubt about the sadhu being Kumar. People wondered if his sour relationship with the Bhawal family or his friendship with Rankin made him retract his initial statement.

Other estate employees came up to testify against the sadhu. Often, Chatterjee's cross-examination of these employees led to a discovery about some financial or non-financial favour bestowed by the authorities for testifying against the sadhu. Kumar's character slandering related to his wild lifestyle and female companions became a regular affair in the court.

Senior ICS officers appeared on behalf of the defence next. Chatterjee cross-questioned them about their intention to be a witness. Most hadn't met the sadhu. As the questions grew sharper, the officers' claims of interacting with the sadhu fell flat.

K.C. De was an intriguing witness. He claimed he met the plaintiff as a sadhu in Dhaka in 1926. However, Chatterjee proved it false since the plaintiff lived in Calcutta in 1926 and had stopped wearing the outfit and hair of the sadhu since 1924. Eventually, De accepted meeting Chandra Sekhar Banerjee in 1923 and the plaintiff in Calcutta in 1924.

He also agreed about his interaction with Sarajubala Devi in 1925 in Calcutta. She had informed him about identifying the plaintiff as her brother-in-law.

Mohini Mohan Chakrabarty, the man who drafted the report on behalf of Needham to send it to Lindsay, opined the sadhu couldn't answer multiple questions related to Kumar. He had interacted with the man before the sadhu declared his identity and was surprised to see Jyotirmayee Devi supporting him. "Jogen Babu and I were sure the man bore no resemblance to our late Mejo Kumar. I couldn't fathom why Jyotirmayee Devi backed his claims. The sadhu was aware of the songs and ballads about Bibhabati Devi, Satya Babu, and Dr Ashutosh, assassinating their characters. He didn't object but Mejo Kumar would have put an end to such baseless allegations."

Soon, Chatterjee highlighted how Mohini Babu, had initially accepted the sadhu as Kumar. But his thoughts were influenced by his employer and the authorities. Since they labelled the sadhu an imposter, Mohini changed his stand. But Mohini refused, stating he formed his opinion the day he drafted his first report for Needham. Mohini wasn't aware whether his opinion would benefit or harm the sadhu. It was evident Mohini's views aligned with his superiors, possibly more out of duty than what he genuinely felt.

Chapter 35
Exposing Jogen Banerjee

In 1934, Chaudhuri presented witnesses from the defence counsel's side while Satya Babu and Ashu doctor met to discuss the proceedings. Mohini Babu had finished testifying. Jogendra Nath Banerjee, more popularly known as Jogen Banerjee, was next. Jogen Babu began his career as a private secretary to the Kumars before his promotion to a crucial position in the administration. The authorities bestowed him with the title of Rai Sahib, but things fell off between him and Gobinda Banerjee. It turned Jogen Babu against the sadhu.

Satya Babu's worry lines stretched across his forehead. "Do you think Jogen Babu's health condition will permit him to appear as a witness?"

Ashutosh nodded. "He doesn't have an option. He's lucky his son Rabindra was sentenced to fourteen years imprisonment and not awarded a death sentence like the other chap who was a part of the conspiracy to kill the Governor, Sir John Anderson. They took turns in taking a shot at the Governor. You employed Jogen Babu as an advisor to Mejo Rani after the Court of Wards fired him for his son's misdeeds, thus helping him lead a normal life. I'm sure he's going to return the favour."

Satyen thought of the time he consulted with Chaudhuri and made Jogen the principal organiser for the defendants in the case. Jogen Babu knew the functioning of the estate, the Kumars, and the Bhawal Raj family inside out.

When Jogen Babu appeared in court, he produced a letter from his doctor. It stated they couldn't examine him beyond two hours at a stretch because of his ill health. Despite his physical state, his appearance had a grim determination that became obvious as he stated his version. "I heard of Kumar's death on a Sunday night while returning from my trip to Barisal. It wasn't a Saturday night like some people mentioned. Based on Boro Kumar's orders, I went to fetch Mejo Rani and the group that had accompanied Mejo Kumar to Darjeeling. I met the sadhu at Jyotirmayee Devi's house with Mohini Babu and spent some time alone with him. Later, whenever I visited him, I saw him surrounded by a group whose modus operandi seemed to demean Mejo Rani, Satya Babu, Ashu doctor, me, and every employee loyal to the real Mejo Kumar. I was certain this sadhu couldn't be our Mejo Kumar."

When Chatterjee cross-examined him about his relations with his brother Sagar Babu, who had identified the sadhu as Kumar, Jogen wrinkled his nose. "He is blind and oblivious to the truth."

"It is also alleged you tried to influence the thoughts of the people supporting the sadhu?"

When Jogen Babu shook his head in disagreement, Chatterjee presented a piece of paper. It held a specimen statement where the witnesses said they knew all three Kumars well and had interacted with Mejo Kumar. They had found no similarities between the Hindi-speaking sadhu and the Bengali-speaking Kumar. As per Jogen Babu's instructions, the statement needed modification for each group of witnesses who would utter their personalised version in court. Jogen Babu didn't have an option but to accept that he tried to influence the witnesses.

When Suren Banerjee met the plaintiff a couple of days later, the latter asked, "If they had to tutor all the tenants who testified against me to say the same lines, does it mean they feel different about my identity? Isn't it evident the need for coaching arose because they recognised me as Ramendra Narayan?"

Banerjee couldn't agree more. The previous day, Chatterjee had highlighted how all the witnesses spoke the same lines in the court. Over four hundred witnesses had appeared on behalf of the defence counsel. Out of this, almost three hundred witnesses possessing the sample statement of Jogen Babu were tenants and employees.

"Chaudhuri realised the fallacy of Jogen Babu's action. Jogen Babu's people emphasised no resemblance between you and Kumar, a line prominent in the specimen statement. When Judge Basu pointed it out, Chaudhuri changed his line of argument and mentioned the dissimilarities observed were in the facial features or the hair colour. However, Judge Sahib wasn't convinced. We presented hundreds of witnesses certifying you as Mejo Kumar, who could observe the similarities easily. If Chaudhuri still considered them liars, what could have convinced them to appear at the court and speak in your favour?"

"And what did that blasted man say?"

"Now, he has moved away from the aspect of utter dissimilarity. He says your vague resemblance with the Kumar could deceive people merely acquainted with you. But those who knew you well didn't find it difficult to identify the differences."

The sadhu sighed. They had a long discussion about the implications of Jogen Babu's specimen statement and his testimony in court. When it was time for him to leave, Banerjee shifted in his chair. Chatterjee had asked him to meet the sadhu with a purpose.

"Is there anything else you want to discuss?" The sadhu waited since he could sense the restlessness in Banerjee.

"Rani Bibhabati will appear in court next. She's already reached the town, and Chaudhuri Sahib has been training her to face the trial."

Though his body stiffened, the sadhu uttered, "Oh! I see."

Banerjee knew why Chatterjee sent him. The ambiance grew uncomfortable. He wished he could blurt out the words and vanish into thin air. "While she'll present her version of the events guided by the defence counsel, we will cross-examine her as a part of the procedure. While we'll try to be respectful towards Mejo Rani, the questions might get personal and unpleasant because of the circumstances."

The sadhu stopped Banerjee with a hand gesture. "It's okay. You are doing your duty, and I'm fulfilling my responsibilities towards my estate and subjects. Whatever path you take to ensure justice is delivered is your choice. I have no desire to interfere. I've made numerous attempts to arrive at a compromise and maintain dignity. But if the other party refuses to cooperate and plays dirty, we don't have an option."

The sadhu returned to his room. He had been dreading this day for years. As much as he felt exhausted, he still looked forward to the next session in court with a ray of hope. But Bibhabati's appearance meant washing dirty linen in public. Initially, he worried about her respect and honour. But he soon realised those qualities were least significant to the Second Rani. Her sole focus was to save her brother. Her next priority was the income she earned through the estate. Was there someone else she was trying to protect, someone she liked? Probably, she never cared for him. The social status she enjoyed made her stay when he was the Mejo Kumar of Bhawal.

After his presumed death, it didn't take her long to claim the insurance and seek income from rent while handing over her portion of the property to the Court of Wards. She had left for a comfortable life with her brother in Calcutta. Jyotirmayee felt convinced about her role in his death.

While the plaintiff was patient with Bibhabati's obstinate stand and her instigating the tenants against him, people close to him realised how drastically Mejo Rani had changed. He didn't want to take the legal route initially to safeguard his family's reputation, including his wife's. As Bibhabati's apathy and vile attitude gained prominence, the sadhu's concern turned to indifference and anger. Now, he only cared about retrieving everything that belonged to him.

Chapter 36
Bibhabati in the Witness Box

Bibhabati looked like a ghost in her white saree, standing in the dark corridor. Why was she nervous about the following day, despite learning to handle the barrage of questions over the last few days? It was already March 1935. She had been preparing herself for the day with her lawyers, Satyen, and a select few people who supported her stance.

Yet, she could feel butterflies in her stomach. What if she became tongue-tied and failed to respond? Worse still was the thought her statement would mess up things for them. Satyen had boosted her morale. "No one knows the truth more than you. Just state the facts as they happened."

Chaudhuri's team guided her about what to speak and how to keep calm. He assured Bibhabati of objecting if the plaintiff's counsel went below the belt. Yet, she had felt restless the whole day and could barely eat or rest.

A maid had placed a bowl of fruits and a glass of sherbet on the table. It stayed untouched even after hours. She thought of the one who started it all. If Jyotirmayee hadn't insisted on validating the sadhu's identity or been so persistent about the public declaration, the man would've possibly retired to his past life. But Mejo Didi fuelled the thoughts about the return of Mejo Kumar by accepting the sadhu as Raja Ramendra Narayan Roy. Jyotirmayee was protecting her interests. It was ironic how

Jyotirmayee considered Bibhabati's behaviour prejudiced when Mejo Didi and the Bhawal family made their biased perspective obvious.

The cool breeze brought her back to the present. She had stood her ground, braving all attempts of a forced reconciliation. The next day, she would hold her head high and face the judgmental world. Bibhabati saw Satyen approaching in the light from the candles on the stands.

"I've been looking for you." He spoke in a soothing voice.

"I was watching the sky and enjoying the breeze. The weather was hot and humid during the day, but it's pleasant now."

"Same as the situation in our lives. It feels tiring and drains our energy, but things will get better. Tomorrow is a big day for us."

Bibhabati clasped her hands as she felt a shiver run down her spine.

"Bibha, I can sense your anxiety. I don't mean to burden you with unnecessary responsibilities. I would gladly take them on my shoulder and ease out your troubles. Unfortunately, I don't have the right to do so in a court case. You're going to set an example for the future generations as a lady of steel who didn't give in to an imposter's devious plans." Satyen gave an assuring smile. Bibhabati sighed.

Her lips quivered as she spoke. "What if I fumble or mess it up…."

Satyen didn't allow her to finish. "The question doesn't even arise. Why would you fumble about things you have experienced first-hand or seen with your eyes? Yes! It happened decades ago, but you were around when Mejo Kumar died. Bibha, you saw everything. Is there anything you don't know about what happened in Darjeeling? You only need to recollect them as they had occurred and present your version to the judge."

"Yes, yes! I have seen it with my eyes or heard it from you."

"*You saw it all except the cremation. Am I clear*?" he spoke through clenched teeth in a sharp voice.

Bibhabati took a step back on an impulse and nodded.

"Great! Sleep well. You need adequate rest to keep your brain cool."

He smiled.

She felt her cheeks flush; she held on to the wall to steady herself. "Yes, I shall retire to bed now."

Satyen's eyebrows furrowed as he saw her walk to her room. Bibhabati knew how to maintain her dignity amidst all the chaos, but she was equally clear about her priorities. Satyen spoke about her resolution to Chaudhuri when the latter had warned him of Chatterjee's probable tactics to unnerve her in the court. As the defence counsel guided Mejo Rani about her approach and behaviour in court, her intelligence and gentle yet firm nature impressed him.

On the morning Bibhabati was due to appear in court, she prayed hard to God to give her the strength she needed. At the same time, Jyotirmayee sat in her pooja chamber and prayed for her brother's well-being.

The defence counsel asked Bibhabati to describe her life after marriage until the commencement of the Darjeeling trip. The lawyers asked her about events that transpired at the time of Kumar's death and the cremation process. They flung questions about her stand related to the sadhu; she gracefully handled them.

It was Chatterjee's turn to cross-question Bibhabati. He asked a couple of things about her marital life in Jaidebpur. Bibhabati appeared calm, though her heart paced.

"Tell us what happened to Kumar after you reached Darjeeling."

"His health started deteriorating after a few days. So, we got the best doctor available in the town. Dr Calvert agreed to treat him, though he wasn't the only one."

She mentioned all the doctors who treated Kumar at various points. "But my husband wouldn't listen to their advice. For instance, he refused to take the injection the doctor thought was critical at that juncture."

"The prescriptions mention gallstones. But people don't die of gallstones. They don't get bloody stools or other critical symptoms that Kumar suffered in Darjeeling. What is your opinion of this?"

"None of us thought there was a remote possibility of losing him. The trip was to help him recover."

"Did it occur to you that the cause of his death could be something else?"

"No! Why should I think so?"

"Do you know about arsenic poisoning? Are you aware Dr Ashutosh Dasgupta prescribed arsenic to your husband? It's known to cause bloody stools."

"No! No! I have no clue about arsenic, and I don't think it could be the reason for his death."

"But you have known Dr Dasgupta for a long time?"

"Yes! Ever since my marriage. His father was our family doctor."

"Do you think he had a part to play in Kumar's death?"

"That's outrageous!"

"He might have his reasons."

Chaudhuri objected.

"What is your opinion of Dr Dasgupta?"

"He's a good and sincere man. As a doctor, he was dutiful towards my husband."

"I heard you weren't allowed to see Kumar on his deathbed, and your brother even asked you to stay away from his dead body."

"That's a lie! I was with my husband till his last moment. I sat through the night, grieving and guarding his dead body on the bed until they brought it downstairs in the morning."

"What time did they bring down?"

"I think between 7 to 7:30 a.m. though I can't tell you the exact time."

Chatterjee asked her a couple of more questions related to the cremation. Her answers corroborated what the defence counsel witnesses had stated. Bibhabati's testimony spread across days as Chatterjee questioned her about the sadhu next.

Chapter 37

Questioning her Morals

Bibhabati stayed calm whenever Chatterjee tried to poke her with information to trigger a reaction. He began with her stand against the sadhu. "Why are you so reluctant to meet the plaintiff?"

"Because he's an imposter. My husband is long dead."

"But don't you think there's a possibility of you making a mistake? Numerous people have identified him and given him the respect of Mejo Kumar. So, why couldn't you check the similarities or dissimilarities and validate personally?"

"I don't see any similarities. Besides, I've repeated umpteen times my husband's demise and cremation happened in Darjeeling."

"What about Satyabhama Devi? She identified him and sent a letter to the district collector to the same effect. I believe she sent you a correspondence but never heard from you."

"I returned it without reading. Satyabhama Devi was an elderly, fragile woman. She didn't personally check and validate the sadhu as Mejo Kumar. The sadhu's supporters would have influenced her thoughts. As much as I respect her, nothing she said could change my mind. So, I didn't accept the letter."

"Do you think his supporters are influencing his close family members?"

"Did anyone from his family in Jaidebpur think the sadhu could be Kumar immediately on meeting him or with conviction? It was only after he publicly declared his identity that they informed me about the sadhu and that too through an official intimation. If my sister-in-law had identified him the moment she saw the sadhu, she would have informed me without delay."

Chatterjee sighed. The lady was a tough nut to crack, and Chaudhuri had prepared her well. "You saw the plaintiff on multiple occasions, arranged by Buddhu Babu after the first spotting from the verandah of your Lansdowne home."

"It happened by chance. We planned nothing, and Buddhu had no role to play in such chance encounters."

"But you were taken aback when you saw him for the first time? Did it ever occur to you that it could be him?"

"No! I saw no similarities with my late husband."

"You could've forgotten how he looked. That's why you failed to see the resemblance."

"Impossible! Can a wife ever forget her husband's face?" She fumed.

Chatterjee was glad to draw a reaction out of the unusually composed woman. He hit the iron while it was still hot. He addressed the court. "I feel such by-chance meetings can occur once but not on multiple occasions. The sightings happened with Rani's consent and through someone's help. It could be possible Mejo Rani wanted to see the sadhu from a distance because she felt he was similar to Kumar or had recognised him as her husband."

He changed the topic after she refused to comment further. "The sadhu has mentioned three different identification marks on your body. Your big toe is longer than the other toes, a lump of flesh sits near the corner of your eye, and there's a mark on your body in an area that can only be known to your husband. What do you have to say about this?" Chatterjee noticed Rani's cheeks turn red.

She took a deep breath and replied, "The first identification mark is hardly unusual or unique. The second point is true and is noticeable if observed minutely. As far as the third mark is concerned, it's a lie." She paused for a second before proceeding with a resolute tone. "If the court wishes, I'm ready to be examined for the mark."

A round of murmur rose in the court at Rani's bold statement, but Judge Basu dismissed the idea because it was outrageous.

When Bibhabati assumed Chatterjee was about to finish analysing her statements and probing for details, the man threw a googly. "Is it true that you were pregnant? Your lawyers claim you mentioned it to them."

"I said my periods stopped for three months. I had informed the same to the doctor treating me in Calcutta."

The lawyers from the defence counsel's side had raved about how Rani Bilasmani was thrilled about Bibhabati's pregnancy and had announced that Bibhabati would bear a son, the successor of the Bhawal Raj family. Chatterjee didn't want to let go of the opportunity to press upon the fact the pregnancy news never reached Rani Bilasmani or Ramendra's family because Bibhabati hushed it up in Calcutta with the help of the same doctor she mentioned a while ago.

"What are you saying? If there was such news to share, would I ever keep it a secret? I knew it would bring immense joy to my marital family." Bibhabati feigned surprise.

"Any wife would want to hush up the truth if she didn't want her husband to discover he wasn't the child's father. It would be too scandalous to handle."

Even before Chatterjee could finish his statement, there was a furor in the court as the defendant's lawyers raised objections to the implications of Chatterjee's statements. Bibhabati stood like a statue as the opposition's claims of an apology from Chatterjee grew louder. It took Judge Basu a long time to control the chaos and bring order to the proceedings. He admonished Chatterjee for the unnecessary line of questioning.

When Bibhabati returned home, she felt shaken by Chatterjee's thoughts and questions. It wasn't the first time she faced allegations for her assumed behaviour and actions. After her husband's death, the rumours of her link-up and betrayal grew stronger behind her back. She was aware of the names they associated her with, but no one dared to utter them to her face. Eventually, when she shifted to Calcutta, the rumours died, or she was so far away that they failed to reach her. But standing at the court, she felt humiliated and traumatised. Her only solace was Chaudhuri's words, which Satyen conveyed. "Tell Mejo Rani she was an epitome of poise and grace today. She maintained her demeanor and stood bravely amidst the mudslinging battle of words."

Before going to bed, she couldn't stop thinking if the news had reached Ashutosh and how he was dealing with it.

Chapter 38

Ananda Kumari

Ashutosh knew the pointed questions Bibhabati faced ever since she was in the witness box. She handled them graciously, giving no advantage to the opposition. But things had been different that day. The plaintiff's counsel embarked on an attacking mode and displayed the audacity to question Bibhabati's character.

It wasn't the first time people linked his name with Mejo Rani, her assumed pregnancy, and Kumar's death in Darjeeling. And it would not be the last time. It irked him. He had met Satyen in the evening, who seemed disgusted at how Bibhabati's testimony ended.

"We can't do anything until they prove the sadhu a fraud. They have an opportunity to throw brick-bats at us now. Kumar's sisters and their families are encouraging it. Soon, our chance will come, and we won't spare anyone." His nostrils flared up.

Ashutosh changed the topic and asked him who he expected in the witness box next.

"Ananda Kumari – the youngest Rani, widow of Rabindra Narayan Roy."

"She's the third defendant in the case. So, she'll look out for her son's interest, but why would she support the second Rani?"

Satyen smiled. "Remember the conflict in the family when Choto Rani decided to adopt a son?"

Of course, the doctor could recollect it vividly. None in the Bhawal family had supported the young widow, especially the sisters.

Jyotirmayee was vocal against Ananda Kumari's decision. Jyotirmayee and her sisters birthed many children. If Ananda Kumari wished to shower her affection on a child, she was free to adopt any of them. But the young Rani was a headstrong woman. Ananda Kumari went against the family's wishes and adopted a boy, her brother's son, a few years after the Court of Wards took over the estate.

"Didn't Sarajubala Devi and Bibhabati support Jyotirmayee Devi against Ananda Kumari?" The doctor felt confused.

"Bibha supported Jyotirmayee initially. Later on, she realised her sister-in-law's true intentions. So, she chose to support Ananda Kumari in the adoption process. Now, it's Choto Rani's turn to show solidarity with Bibha. Also, she's smart enough to understand if the fraud gains a share of the property, it means probable complications for her adopted son."

"Ah! I get it. So, she hasn't recognised him as well?"

"No, she's certain the man's not Mejo Kumar." Satyen looked away.

"I hope the plaintiff's lawyers aren't as harsh to her as they were with Mejo Rani."

"Chaudhuri Sahib will ensure that," Satyen assured.

The doctor was glad Satyen didn't mention the assumed pregnancy or Bibhabati's rumoured link-up with him. With time, he understood Satyen better. The man's priorities were clear, and he could go to any length to protect his interests. The rest didn't matter as long as it didn't create any hurdles in his plans. Ashutosh couldn't help but wonder if Satyen would have been equally invested in Bibhabati's life if she wasn't married into the wealthy Bhawal Raj family. When Ashutosh went to bed, his mind was a mess as various chaotic thoughts ran loose.

Ananda Kumari Devi looked quite plain compared to the charming Bibhabati. But she was a mother on a mission to safeguard her son's future. Ananda Kumari married the fat and short, fair-complexioned Rabindra in 1904. Six years after the Court of Wards took over their estate, she adopted a boy. Even before Rabindra passed away, Indumayee had built her house, and Jyotirmayee's house was under construction. Ananda Kumari resented how the sisters didn't step into Raj Bari or Nalgola palace after their youngest brother's death. Though she left Dhaka after the Court of Wards took over, she eventually returned and settled down in Dhaka.

When the lawyers questioned Choto Rani about the educational qualification of the three Kumars, she confidently mentioned seeing them speak in English and write in Bengali in the past. Irrespective of not having any degree, she was aware of her husband's ability to write letters in Bengali, just like Mejo Kumar.

Ananda Kumari identified the letters as written by Ramendra Narayan to his wife. She denied hearing any rumours about the botched-up cremation. She claimed the telegram about Kumar's death read by her husband mentioned Ramendra Narayan passed away at midnight the previous day.

"Did you meet the sadhu?"

"Twice. And I see no similarities between the man and Mejo Kumar, even now in the court." She looked at the sadhu straight.

Chaudhuri brought up Jyotirmayee's severe opposition to the young widow's desire for adoption. "Do you think Jyotirmayee was worried that after you adopt a child, your son will become the legal heir and her son or her sister's sons would lose all possibilities of inheriting the property?"

Ananda Kumari paused before muttering, "Quite possible!"

When it was Chatterjee's turn to cross-question, he mentioned how Bibhabati had initially opposed the adoption. He believed Ananda Kumari was scared that if she didn't support Bibhabati in court, they would overturn the adoption, making her son lose all rights. "She's hiding the truth to save her son's future. I sympathise with the heart of a mother, but I must mention the family's reasons for opposing the adoption process. Rani Ananda Kumari was known to be a woman with no moral character. Her philandering nature led the family to decide that she didn't deserve to inherit the property or adopt a son. I would want to reopen the ...."

But Judge Basu intervened quickly. He wasn't willing to let the court witness another attempt at assassinating a woman's character.

"Ananda Kumari's decision to adopt, and the subsequent protests by the Bhawal family, are both inconsequential to this case." He ruled out Chatterjee's plea. Basu dismissed the court for the day.

Later that week, when Jyotirmayee expressed shock at the answers Ananda Kumari gave in court, the plaintiff nodded in agreement. "She spoke blatant lies to save her and Ram Narayan's future."

Chapter 39
Expert Analyses

The plaintiff's counsel presented a group of experts to identify the sadhu as Kumar through the recognition criteria. The defendants, following suit, brought another set of experts who assessed the same parameters to conclude a mismatch between the sadhu and Ramendra Narayan.

The handwriting expert consulted by Chatterjee ruled his opinion in favour of the sadhu. "Keeping in mind both signatures have a gap of twenty years between them, it's clear that the same man has done them. However, the signatures on the letters seem like a forced attempt to replicate the original." The same set of signatures, when analysed by the expert on behalf of the defence counsel, led him to believe they belonged to two different people.

The counsels turned to expert photographers next. The vice principal of the Government Art College in Calcutta pointed out semblances in physical traits between the sadhu and Kumar, especially the peculiarity of their ears. He believed the plaintiff's and Kumar's pictures were of the same person in different stages of life. He also compared Jyotirmayee Devi's photo with that of Ramendra Narayan and the sadhu and found them to share common traits. The principal of the same Art college dismissed any similarities. He claimed the plaintiff's nose was wider as compared to Kumar's. The plaintiff's ear lobes were stuck out while Kumar's were pendants.

Another foreign-born photographer running the photography shop named Edna Lorenze Studio in Calcutta mentioned the similarities he observed between the two, considering the age difference. He highlighted the striking likeness of the ears. Only the hair had thinned due to age, though the curls were the same. However, the managing partner of Bourne and Shepherd didn't think the photographs were of the same person.

In December 1934, much before the expert panel arrived for identification, Chatterjee's team had discovered a piece of evidence about the plaintiff's identity. When Mejo Kumar signed a life insurance proposal on the 25th of March, 1905, he underwent medical tests at the Calcutta Medical College on the 2nd of April, 1905. Dr Andrew Caddy had noted his observations. The Board of Revenue sought the same paper from the insurance company in 1921, along with the death certificate. However, they didn't present it while submitting other documents related to his insurance.

"Dr Caddy mentioned the height of 21-year-old Ramendra Narayan as 5 ft 5 inches, his hair colour as brown, his eyes as grey, and his moustache as fair. The manager, Kali Prasanna Babu, evidenced the same when Bibhabati submitted her claim to the insurance company after Kumar's death. No wonder Chaudhuri and Ghosh didn't want to bring it to the court's notice." Chatterjee spoke after getting the document in hand. His team had connected with the insurance company's office in Edinburgh to retrieve it.

"The sadhu's height is 5 ft 6 inches." The defendant's counsel reminded him. A doctor appearing on behalf of the plaintiff explained how growth occurred till the twenty-fifth year for an Indian man. So, it wasn't unusual for the plaintiff's height to grow by one inch. Another doctor validated the same.

Chatterjee mentioned the identification marks highlighted by Jyotirmayee on Ramendra's body – a tiger claw mark on his right arm, rough skin near his ankles, an injury mark on the left ankle caused by a carriage wheel, a broken tooth, and an operation mark. The plaintiff's body visibly bore all these identification marks. The defendants had previously argued no carriage wheel leaving a mark had run over Kumar's ankle. Jyotirmayee was misleading the court by stating those marks visible on the sadhu's body as the marks on Kumar. There was no evidence of such scars on Kumar's body.

Until the presentation of Dr Caddy's document, the defendants stuck to their point of no mark. However, the report by Dr Caddy mentioned a scar on the left ankle, though the defendant's doctors argued it was a skin condition.

Chatterjee presented his case. "Why wasn't this document submitted when it was in the custody of the Board of Revenue for so many years? It proves the similarities and can cause inconvenience for the defendants."

A panel of three doctors examined the sadhu for checking the identification marks as consequences of Kumar's syphilis. His nasal bridge had a swelling that the doctors, on behalf of the defendants, claimed to be a result of an injury or blow. However, Dr Chatterjee, the doctor on behalf of the plaintiff, was confident it was a syphilitic node. The plaintiff's behaviour and physical responses were in tandem with that of a man with syphilis in the past.

The following morning, the plaintiff dragged his feet toward the verandah. He had spent the previous evening in Billu Babu's company while discussing the confusion related to the rains on the night of the attempted cremation in Darjeeling.

"I fail to understand the issue. Many people stated it rained that night. Because of the rain and storm, they sought shelter. That's when Darshandas saved me from the cremation."

Billu nodded. "Well, Chaudhuri Sahib says they have proof it didn't rain that night."

"Oh, yes! Chatterjee Babu mentioned the *Calcutta Gazette* paper, which published no rainfall on the 8th, 9th, and 10th May 1909 in Darjeeling."

"Yes! But some other documents and experts corroborate the same. Whatever documents are available in our favour, someone has tampered with them."

"Well, if tampering is evident, isn't it obvious they are trying to hide the truth?"

"While we understand the intention, the court will accept only facts with proof." Billu sighed.

The sadhu pondered over the conversation. He had spent enough time with Chatterjee to understand Ukil Babu, and his team wouldn't give up on any aspect of the case without giving a tough fight.

While the sadhu sat on the verandah, Chatterjee was already toiling away with the tampered evidence collected from the Darjeeling Planter's Club. The club maintained a register with the rainfall readings quite meticulously. However, the entries after May 3rd, 1909, were missing. The next available date in the record book was May 13th, 1909. The Club's Head Clerk had appeared in the court years ago and stated how two gentlemen came for the register of 1909. Most likely, they tore away the data entries from the 4th till the 12th of May since it validated the sadhu's statement of rainfall on the 8th night.

The rainfall register maintained by the Botanical Garden was of no use since the entries were haphazard and poorly maintained, making it an unreliable source of information.

While Chatterjee struggled to prove the occurrence of rains, Chaudhuri had multiple sources to conclude the dry spell in weather during that period. Besides the *Calcutta Gazette,* he produced a witness connected with the Meteorological Department of St. Joseph's College. The witness showed the records from the 4th to the 11th of May of no rainfall. He dismissed the theory that it could rain in isolated places in Darjeeling. St. Paul's Darjeeling also had a routine of recording the weather and publishing it in the Government gazette. Their records showed no rainfall between 8 a.m. on 4th May to 4 a.m. on 12th May.

Chaudhuri said these documents made Lindsay believe the sadhu was an imposter.

It didn't take Chatterjee long to figure out the primary intention of the defendant's counsel was to dismiss the idea of the missing body and prove the cremation took place the following morning. It would rule out the possibility of the return of Ramendra Narayan. But he also knew though it was vital, it wasn't the only proof. The evidence of tampering on the Planter's club records gave him a ray of hope.

Chapter 40
A Maid Gossips

The Lansdowne House bore a deserted look as the trial proceeded. Bibhabati mostly stayed in Jaidebpur, and Satyen travelled to Dhaka as and when required. His wife stayed back to look after the children and maintain a facade of normalcy. The maids and servants found surplus time in hand compared to before.

A maid from the Banerjee household passed her afternoon chatting with her friend, employed by a wealthy but aging family in the neighbourhood. They spoke about their work, abusive husbands, and the pain of not bearing a child. Both were in their late forties. Soon, the topic veered to the Banerjee household, and her friend was curious about the case.

"Is it true she's unwilling to meet her husband?"

"She says the sadhu isn't her husband. He died in a hill station; I forget the place's name. But they burnt him there."

"But my Sahib was telling Memsahib the other day how it's in the papers that the man looks like her husband."

"I don't know what's the truth. Some say the brother killed her husband with the help of a doctor, and she was aware of the plan."

"What?" the friend gasped.

"Don't tell anyone. If the master finds out I've been talking about it, he'll send me back to my village."

"No, no! You can trust me. Is it true she and the doctor?"

"Where did you hear it? Has it appeared in the papers, too?"

Her friend blushed. She didn't know if it was in the papers or her employer's conclusion about the loose moral character of Bibhabati.

"I haven't seen her give any special attention to the doctor," Bibhabati's maid stated.

"Oh! Then it must be gossip. But what if he's her husband, and she's refusing to meet him because she doesn't want to live with him any longer?"

The maid pondered if she should speak about the secrets of the household. But it was just a harmless gossip session.

"I don't think he was a bad man, though he was a womaniser. I heard he had many mistresses. During a heated conversation, she blurted it out to her sister-in-law. But it's not the only time. The servants know it better since the master makes no bones about expressing his displeasure at the fate his sister suffered."

"*Bapre!* You have such an interesting time in the house."

"Too thrilling for my taste. I don't know if I should say this to you because it's a secret."

"You can trust me. After all, you're the only one I speak to." She touched her friend's arm.

Though the maid knew her friend might flip, she was worried her tummy would burst if she hid the gossip any longer. "The head servant's assistant has relatives in Dhaka. He visits them once a year. Recently, when he went to meet them, he travelled to Jaidebpur to get a pulse of the case. He saw how some people perceived Rani's relationship with her brother. It's evil..." The maid bit her lips.

"What about it? I mean, it's well understood her brother is way too protective and possibly doesn't know where to draw the line. He should've stayed away from her affairs after she got married, but he got involved even when things turned messy."

"No, not that. It's like... umm.... how do I explain... means they don't consider the brother-sister relationship pure."

"Eh? What does that mean? Why are you speaking in riddles?"

"Uff, people say she had an illegitimate affair with her brother and was pregnant with his child. She came to Calcutta to get an abortion!"

"That's shocking! Someone wishes to malign her character and her brother's life by spreading such lies!" Her friend put her hands over her ears.

"Of course, I don't trust it. I have worked long enough in the house to know the truth. It's obvious how much the master cares about his sister and how dedicated she's to her brother. I just shared it with you because it affected my sanity," the maid justified her actions.

As both women sat discussing other things, their minds wandered off to the unspoken thoughts about Bibhabati and Satyen. They were unaware it wasn't the only time people suggested an incestuous relationship.

Several pamphlets had reached Satyen, where some unidentified supporters questioned if Kumar's wife's behaviour with Satya Babu aligned with how a sister behaved with her brother. They hinted at a steamy affair between the duo, portrayed Ramendra as the victim, and claimed their urgent need to hide the truth led them to murder Kumar.

"Why would a married woman leave her husband's home after losing him? A good Hindu wife always wants to spend her life in a place full of her husband's memories.

The questions got dirty and suggestive with every passing paragraph.

Some ballads, poems, and stories spoke about a disloyal wife who took to her lover's arms and helped the man kill her husband. There were similar stories of a brother-sister duo unable to control their attraction toward each other. They ended up killing the sister's husband. Some stories ended on a tragic note where the sister committed suicide out of guilt. The stories had a victim husband and a scheming wife though none mentioned Satyen's name or his profession directly.

Chapter 41
Arsenic in Medicines

Throughout the case, Chaudhuri raised doubts about the plaintiff's statement of memory loss and its subsequent revival. He made it evident the theory felt far-fetched. A reputed clinical psychiatrist and the superintendent of the Ranchi Mental Hospital, Col Berkeley-Hill, appeared as an expert witness. He stated the sadhu could be speaking the truth since a memory lapse was possible without affecting his reflexes and physiology.

He wasn't shocked that the sadhu could recollect his past life even after eleven years since Berkeley-Hill had read about a case where the subject's memory loss lasted for seventeen years. The sadhu suffered from amnesia and had picked up a foreign language like Hindi during this period. Though he spoke in his native language Bengali now, it wasn't unusual to observe a Hindi accent in his speech.

"There could be physical and mental causes for amnesia. A brain injury might be a physical cause, while the fear of death would be a mental cause," he elaborated.

However, the doctors, on behalf of the defendants, found inconsistency in the sadhu's statements. His behaviour resembled a state of regression. On the other hand, he seemed dissociated. Both mental states were quite different and couldn't co-exist in an individual with memory loss.

Almost every point validated by an expert from the plaintiff's side was counter-argued and nullified by a specialist of the opposition.

Dr Henry Calvert was a vital witness in this case. While he was one of the first witnesses contacted for a statement in London, his version of the events underwent specific changes as the case proceeded and the questions dug deeper. Before Chatterjee cross-questioned Calvert, the plaintiff's lawyer recollected what the doctor mentioned in his statement.

"Dr Calvert said he attended to the patient with the late Dr Nibaran Sen for fourteen days when Kumar's health deteriorated in Darjeeling. They treated him for biliary colic and gallstones. Kumar's condition worsened after he refused a morphine injection, and he died in the night in Calvert's presence. The doctor left sometime after his demise. Kumar neither had pneumonia nor did the doctor suspect arsenic poisoning. The way the events took a sudden turn was unexpected, even for them."

The first question was about the prescribed medicines. Dr Calvert couldn't recollect many aspects of his treatment with precision because of the long gap between Kumar's demise and the ongoing case. But he was confident about the timing of the death at 11:45 p.m. and had mentioned the same in the insurance papers for the claim. The case impacted him greatly. That's why he remembered Kumar died around midnight. The doctor also stated the nature of the medicines prescribed was the second-best alternative to the morphine injection Kumar had rejected.

When Chatterjee showed him the prescription for 8th May, the day Kumar passed away, Calvert mentioned Kumar suffered from diarrhoea and had passed blood-stained stools. But there was no watery stool and blood discharge.

Chatterjee focussed on the doctor's presence at the time of Kumar's death. He wanted to know if Lindsay had asked him the same question and the doctor's response to it. The doctor couldn't recollect if he answered such a question. The lawyer prodded the doctor for an answer for the same question now. Calvert looked confused for a split second but quickly gathered composure.

"Did Lindsay ask you if you'd seen the body after death?"

"No!"

Chatterjee told the court. "Dr Calvert sent a letter to Mr Lindsay in response to the latter's queries about Kumar's death. I suggest the letter be produced in the court to corroborate Dr Calvert's statements."

His statement met resistance from the lawyers on behalf of the Court of Wards.

Chatterjee highlighted a particular statement of Dr Calvert where he mentioned he wasn't sure whether he was present at the time of death. Chatterjee's voice boomed in the court. "The witness, in his statement, while he was in London, clearly stated he was present at the time of Kumar's death in Darjeeling. His letter carries a contradictory statement. Isn't this an instance of deliberate lying by Dr Calvert? The opposition was aware of the mess and knew it could raise questions about the authenticity of the doctor's statements. Now it's clear why they didn't want to produce the letter in court and rely on what the witness says here. But it also makes me question if the rest of the details about Kumar's sickness, his treatment, and his death are genuine or if there's some discrepancy in these aspects."

Chatterjee consulted the highly qualified and respected Lieutenant Colonel MacGilchrist. He was a medical expert, clinical practitioner, and research scientist. When Dr MacGilchrist saw the prescriptions, the doctor believed most medicines weren't related to the treatment of biliary colic. He went through the treatment details for 6th, 7th, and 8th May and pointed out the purpose of each. From indigestion, diarrhoea, muscle cramps, and pain in the stomach, the medicines catered to all but not biliary colic or gallstones. Some suggested remedies made it evident the patient was suffering from severe cramps, which could have resulted due to loss of fluid from the body owing to diarrhoea or arsenic poisoning.

Chatterjee presented Dr Ashutosh Dasgupta's prescription next. Dr MacGilchrist saw it as a remedy for malaria, though the dosage seemed to be high, raising fear of purging. His medicines seemed to contradict Dr Calvert's treatment and could cause stomach irritation. None of the prescribed remedies aligned with biliary colic treatment.

Chaudhuri cross-questioned MacGilchrist on the number of pills. But MacGilchrist clarified his stance. He was unaware of the plaintiff consuming twelve arsenic-laden medicines. The doctor had never mentioned deliberate poisoning using arsenic since he believed it could have been an accident. MacGilchrist backed the arsenic poisoning theory because of the dosage, but he didn't want to get into unnecessary trouble by going against a colleague.

Dr Bradley came in next on behalf of the plaintiff. He was clear about an overdose of arsenic based on the mentioned symptoms and Dr Dasgupta's prescription. Dr Bradley also noted daily consumption of three such arsenic pills could be fatal considering Kumar's health at that point. Bradley toned it down, stating Calvert's memory could've tricked him since chances of the latter making a mistake were rare. He felt Kumar's symptoms were of biliary colic when Dr Calvert started treating him. Calvert had continued his prescriptions on the same line, unaware of the external interference. It was already late when Dr Calvert realised the symptoms were acute. Bradley assumed Dr Calvert was unaware of things going on behind his back. Dr Dasgupta took advantage of it. By the time Calvert figured out the mess, Kumar was already on his deathbed.

The doctor duo of Col Denham-White and Major Thomas appeared on behalf of the defendants for the second time. They agreed with Calvert's treatment. They felt Dr Dasgupta's prescriptions suggested arsenic within acceptable limits and wouldn't have caused poisoning if the intake was as per the prescription. The doctors opined Dr Dasgupta had suggested a remedy for malaria based on the possibility of the patient contracting the disease.

While cross-questioning the doctors, Chatterjee queried about the effect of twelve pills on a patient in such a complicated state of health. The doctor rubbished all possibilities of any sane individual agreeing to intake twelve pills together. Even if the doctor administered them after dissolving the medicines in a liquid, the patient would immediately throw up. Eventually, they concluded Mejo Kumar suffered from dysentery, though the suggested remedies were far from its treatment.

Chapter 42
Dharamdas Reappears

When the defendants were producing witnesses, Dharamdas was back at the scene again. He had finally agreed to testify in court. In the third week of September 1935, people thronged outside the court to see him. Dharamdas was a tall man with a gigantic build. His testimony was critical for the defendants

Chaudhuri initiated the questions, and Dharamdas introduced himself. Major Patney, superintendent of Dhaka Central Jail, was appointed as an interpreter since the witness didn't understand any language except Punjabi. When Chaudhuri showed him the plaintiff's picture, Dharamdas identified him as Sundardas, his disciple. Sundardas was earlier known as Mal Singh, who only spoke Punjabi. Chaudhuri asked him to look at the plaintiff in the court.

Dharamdas took a long look. "It's him, Sundardas!"

"But he claims you and other sanyasis saved him from cremation in Darjeeling."

"I have never been to Darjeeling. Nor have I saved anyone."

"What about Darshandas, Pritamdas, and Lokdas? Darshandas, earlier known as Gopaldas, in his statement, mentioned their roles in saving the plaintiff."

"I've heard of Gopaldas, though I doubt whether he was known as Darshandas later. I'm not acquainted with the other names."

Suddenly, the court buzzed with voices. A section believed the man to be a game-changer for the defendants. However, for the majority, he was a cheater.

"How do we know he isn't some fake Dharamdas Naga?" the voices in unison boomed outside the court.

"First, ask him to prove he's the same Dharamdas who the sadhu considers his Guru. The opposition employed this fake Guru to prove the sadhu wrong." The voices kept rising, and suddenly, a commotion broke outside.

Basu adjourned the court for the day and announced the next date. The situation was volatile. The judge couldn't risk continuing the proceedings lest people grew violent and harmed the witness and other parties. He ordered police protection on the date when Dharamdas was to appear in court again.

However, Basu received a request for a private court in the house where the witness was staying. A medical certificate accompanying the letter stated Dharamdas had a high fever, rendering him incapable of visiting the court. Basu agreed to personally visit and check on the witness before considering the petition; Chatterjee believed the witness was evading public gatherings. The doctor attending to Dharamdas deemed the witness unfit to be at the court. Chatterjee wanted Dharamdas to appear at the court and was ready to wait. Chaudhuri had anticipated the same reaction. But the lawyer wanted to proceed with Dharamdas' testimony before the court closed for the puja holidays.

Chatterjee began questioning the man. Major Patney continued his role as an interpreter. Soon, Chatterjee stopped and spoke to the judge, "Major Patney is leading the witness through his statements under the pretext of translation. Also, I just heard he met the witness over the weekend with the defendant's lawyers. I refuse to proceed unless the interpreter is changed."

Chatterjee and Chaudhuri locked horns over the interpreter's issue. Basu intervened and changed the interpreter. Chatterjee began cross-examination, but the witness fell sick again, leading to the court's dismissal.

The next day, Chatterjee, armed with facts and evidence, questioned the witness. "Feeling better today?"

The witness nodded. Chatterjee proceeded, "How much has your physical appearance changed over the last fifteen years?"

"I look the same."

"What's your age now?"

"Sixty."

Chatterjee probed him about his clothes and sandals since he belonged to the clan of *udasis,* who didn't wear such things. He also poked the witness about a recent swelling on his abdomen that the clothes supposedly hid. But Dharamdas claimed the condition existed for years.

"Who's paying for your expenses?"

"Arjun Singh Pardesi. He met me at Nankhana and told me why it was essential to come to Dhaka."

"Do you know on whose behalf you are appearing as a witness?"

"I've no idea. I'm here to share the truth since I know the sadhu's history."

"So, did Mal Singh become Sundardas, your disciple at Aujla, his hometown?"

"No, I initiated him at Nankana Sahib when he was twenty-two."

"How did Mal Singh look like?"

"He was thin."

"Thin? His village people said he was a fat man."

"They must have confused him with his namesake, a fat man from the same village."

"Since you mentioned making a statement fifteen years ago, you must have been forty-five then. Who did you meet?"

"I met a Bengali man. He came with a police inspector, and they recorded my statement in front of a magistrate."

"Do you know the Bengali babu noted your age as fifty-five?"

"No, I'm not aware of it."

"You identified the plaintiff through his picture in court a few days back. Was it the same picture this Bengali Babu gave you for identification fifteen years ago?"

"Yes, both were the same."

Chatterjee produced the report by Surendra Kumar Chakrabarty, the Bengali Babu who had met Dharamdas. "It states Mal Singh, a fat man, was initiated at fifteen by Dharamdas in Aujla, and the former became Sundardas henceforth. Surendra met the fifty-five-year-old and dark-complexioned Dharamdas, who had a *jata* on his head and a beard at that time. The latter identified the plaintiff through a picture in which the sadhu was standing."

Almost everyone in the house could sense a change in the environment as Chatterjee concluded the contradictions between the witness' statement in the court and the one he gave fifteen years ago.

"Dharamdas just claimed both photographs are the same. However, the photograph shown to him in the court had the plaintiff in a sitting pose, unlike the previous photograph where he was standing. Mal Singh's age, body type, and place of initiation don't tally between the old report and Dharamdas' latest statement. When I consider all the points of discord in unison, I wonder if the sixty-year-old witness in front of us is the same fifty-five-year-old Dharamdas from the past. Well, the age of the witness doesn't match up too. Who's the real Dharamdas then?"

Before the court closed for puja holidays, Chatterjee's argument created confusion and suspicion about the identity of Dharamdas. However, after the break, Sasanka Ghosh submitted the statement Dharamdas made in front of the magistrate fifteen years back. Strangely, it neither had any signature nor fingerprint evidence; Chatterjee argued there was no proof it was Dharamdas' statement.

The defendant's counsel presented a magistrate as a witness in the court. The magistrate, a zamindar, confirmed the statement produced in the court was indeed given by Dharamdas to Surendra Babu and recorded by him in Urdu in 1921. In it, the forty-five-year-old Dharamdas mentioned how Mal Singh of Aujla became his disciple at twenty in Nankana and was named Sundardas. The cat-eyed and fair-skinned Mal came with his relatives to Dharamdas eleven years ago, though he left Dharamdas six years back. Dharamdas had seen his disciple once at Prayag four years ago but didn't meet him again. He confirmed the man in the picture was Sundardas.

Mamtazuddin Talukdar, the police inspector who accompanied Surendra Chakrabarty also turned up to testify. He narrated how, armed with a photograph and some cash, the duo travelled to faraway places like Lucknow, Benares, and Haridwar before some sadhus directed them toward Punjab after recognising the man in the photograph as Sundardas and mentioning Dharamdas as his guru. When the inspector spotted Dharamdas in a Gurdwara near Amritsar, the latter identified Sundardas from the picture and agreed to record his statement with the magistrate. The inspector informed the court Surendra Babu wasn't present during this session. The inspector also reaffirmed the identity of the guru.

However, when Chatterjee cross-examined the inspector, some contradictory points came up. For instance, the inspector confirmed they hadn't done background checks about Dharamdas, though Surendra's report claimed otherwise. As per the same report, Dharamdas had a dark complexion, though the inspector stated a fair complexion.

When Surendra appeared in court, he took full responsibility for the mistakes in the ages of Dharamdas and Sundardas, wrongly mentioned as fifty-five and thirty, respectively. However, he agreed to the authenticity of other parameters in the report, like the brown beard and moustache, and Dharamdas identifying the standing sadhu in the photograph as Sundardas. Surendra Babu validated that the Dharamdas he met fifteen years ago was the same man who testified in the court.

A few more witnesses from Aujla corroborated that Mal Singh, a poor man, left home at sixteen and eventually became a sadhu. The witnesses saw a picture of the plaintiff after they were contacted in Aujla first, and they identified the man as Mal Singh.

Chapter 43

Discovering a Diary and Ashutosh's Testimony

Suren Banerjee came across the mention of a diary through a document the plaintiff's team received from the insurance company. They were probing Bibhabati's claim after Kumar's death. Suren believed it could give them an insight into the actual events.

When Suren mentioned the diary, the sadhu pondered before responding. "I don't remember seeing Satya write or note anything. I could be wrong, or he might've written in private."

Suren looked thoughtful. "We need to retrieve it. If we ask him to present it at the court, he might deny its existence."

"Dharamdas Naga's identity validation will take some more time. Chaudhuri will call Ashu doctor next in the box, followed by Satyen. Before that, we need to find the diary. Why don't you talk to Birendra Banerjee?" Chatterjee remarked.

Suren subtly got an associate to dig information out of Birendra. Unfortunately, Birendra wasn't aware of Satyen's habit of writing a diary, though he mentioned the stealth of some vital documents from Jaidebpur.

Suren consulted with Chatterjee about the next move. "Do you remember the man who gave us insider information and documents because of his past proximity to Mejo Rani? We need to reach out to him."

Suren met the man in the wee hours of the morning the following day. The man seemed reluctant to converse.

"You have been extremely cooperative. Also, I appreciate your sentiments. People shouldn't bully and force you to go against your will. But a couple of weeks ago, I came across the mention of a diary in some official documents. Further investigation led me to believe it belonged to Satyen Babu. But it went missing years ago. Would you have any idea what happened to the diary?"

"How should I know?"

"You're an intelligent man of the world. I'm sure very few things escape your observant eyes and sharp ears."

"Is it an important document?"

"Oh, it could be. I can't confirm until I see the content with my own eyes. But if Satyen had noted the details related to Kumar's death, it could be a game-changer for us."

What transpired between the two for the next half an hour was a secret, but Suren left the house with a wide grin and a journal in red cloth.

When Suren handed over the diary to Chatterjee, they hadn't expected a tieasure trove. The lawyers managed to keep the document a secret until they had a chance to go through the writing and conclude its implications.

Chatterjee finished reading the diary soon after the Aujla witnesses wrapped up their testimonies in court. He called Suren, "No one can keep a record of things so precisely as Satya Babu has done about Ramendra Narayan's sickness and treatment. Do you understand what it hints at?"

Suren thought for a while before nodding his head. "Insurance claims and Bibhabati's share."

"Yes! When one is certain the patient won't survive the illness and knows the nominee would need to furnish details about the death, he notes the sequence. So, Kumar's death was not only expected but pre-decided. Now, my question is, did Bibhabati Devi know about it?"

"Do you think the records could be a way to ensure they don't make a mistake in the dosage or in portraying to the world how Kumar's treatment was in full swing?"

"Highly possible. It points to a greater conspiracy theory. So, Satya indeed plotted Kumar's death, and he couldn't have done it without the help of a medical expert. Ashu doctor must be his partner in crime."

"Yet, we don't have a way to prove it."

"But we have evidence to change the perspective of people. Also, certain discrepancies in the treatment are noticeable between the records and previous statements. We need to address these loopholes. We must keep this diary a secret."

Dr Ashutosh was next to appear in the witness box in September 1935. He was already famous for the defamation suit he had filed and won because of the Government's intervention. The possibility of Kumar's death due to arsenic poisoning cast doubts on the doctor and his actions.

Chatterjee asked Dr Ashutosh Dasgupta about the timing of Kumar's death.

"He passed away around midnight. Dr Calvert and Dr Nibaran Sen were around him. All three of us, including me, checked before confirming his death."

"Was Dr B.B. Sarkar also available then?"

"No! He wasn't with us at that time."

"Why did you decide on a midnight cremation?"

"Why would there be a midnight cremation when Kumar had just passed away minutes before? His cremation took place the following morning."

"Were you at the funeral?"

"Yes! I saw them put the dead body on the funeral pyre and carry out all the necessary rituals related to Hindu death. I was there until the body turned into ashes. Birendra lit the pyre as we witnessed the tragic end."

"Well, you were with him throughout his stay in Darjeeling. He trusted you with the medication and treatment prescribed by Dr Calbert and Dr Sen. Yet, isn't it true you altered the medicines and their dosages so much that even Kumar questioned you on what you gave him since he wasn't getting better? Earlier, you stated you hadn't prescribed any medicine but followed orders from the senior doctors. However, the prescription shows otherwise. Did you add arsenic to the mixture on 7th May or before it? Are you aware Dr Calvert said he would never suggest arsenic considering Kumar's health condition?"

Ashutosh looked flustered by the constant bombarding of questions. "I never made a prescription on my own for Kumar but wrote it under the guidance of the senior doctors attending to him. Though I don't remember who suggested arsenic between Dr Calvert and Dr Sen, it was one of them. I only followed their instructions."

"You must be aware the expert doctors who studied the case and suggested medication for Kumar have concluded arsenic recommendation for a patient with biliary colic was unjustified."

"If Kumar had diarrhoea on the 7th, I wouldn't have suggested it. If a patient has diarrhoea, arsenic raises the possibility of aggravating his condition. But with biliary colic, it wouldn't harm the patient." Ashutosh stuck to his points.

"In the defamation suit you filed, your statements about the timings of Kumar's illness and the visit of various doctors don't tally with the details you gave in this case."

Ashutosh blamed the long gap between Kumar's death and the defamation suit. It made his recollections flawed and his memory weak. After he went through the documents, prescriptions, and other details for this case, he correlated them with the actual events. "I apologise for the unintentional mistakes I made previously, but assure you that what

I say in the court now is the absolute truth. Please ignore my statements in the previous case wherever they don't match my present statements."

Basu felt irritated with Dr Ashutosh. He saw through the gimmick and concluded the doctor was a habitual liar. Basu was sure neither Dr Calvert nor Dr Sen had come on 7th May to Step Aside. Mostly no one had sent for the doctors, unlike what Ashutosh claimed.

A few days before Bibhabati had appeared in the witness box, Barrister R.N. Banerjee, popularly referred to as Bebul, appeared as a witness from the defendant's side. The honourable professional with a royal lineage was a ray of hope for Satyen and Chaudhuri.

"My brother and I carried the dead body in the morning in our coats and trousers to the new cremation ground. We saw the body turn into ashes before leaving the ground," Bebul declared.

No Hindu man who knew the funeral rituals would walk in the funeral procession wearing such clothes, Basu thought. But Chaudhuri justified the barrister's London returned lifestyle as the reason. When probed further about the old cremation ground being the obvious choice since the new cremation area was still not ready, Bebul stuck to his statement about Kumar's cremation.

If he had stopped, Bebul's testimony might have still become food for thought to the court. However, Bebul went ahead and claimed to have met Bibhabati on the morning of 9th May.

"Where did you meet the widow?" An amused Chatterjee prodded.

"Of course, at Step Aside. She couldn't have come with us to the funeral." Bebul sounded exasperated at the silliness of the question.

"Our esteemed witness, after returning from abroad, has possibly forgotten how the purdah system works. It seems farfetched that Bibhabati Devi would immediately meet a stranger of the opposite gender after becoming a widow," Chatterjee concluded.

While announcing his judgment, Basu rejected Bebul as an unreliable witness.

Even Gita Devi, whose police officer husband was acquainted with Satyen, couldn't save the situation. Her statements came too hurriedly. Basu felt someone had trained her to blurt them out, though she involuntarily gave away moments of truth.

Chapter 44
Satyen's Version

Everyone was eagerly waiting for Satyen's turn at the witness box. While people resented Bibhabati for her stand against the sadhu, many sympathised with her situation for she had seen the hardships of life as a widow. Almost everyone reserved their anger and hatred for Satyen. His involvement in Kumar's death went undisputed.

Satyendra Nath Banerjee was an advocate at the Calcutta High Court and a first-class honorary magistrate. He knew the Bhawal Raj family well through Bibhabati's marriage to Ramendra Narayan. In the court in December 1935, Satyen confirmed all three Kumars were literate and knew how to speak English. He had heard Mejo Kumar interact with the foreign officials and their spouses in English. He identified Ramendra's signature on the letters.

When questioned about his role in Kumar's death, Satyen answered in a firm tone. "I heard I'm responsible for Kumar's demise. I supposedly plotted his death with the help of Dr Ashutosh Dasgupta. To say that's rubbish and offensive to my reputation is an understatement. I don't understand why people are still harping about a non-existent angle of my role in his death."

Satyen stated Kumar had a fever and biliary colic before he went to Darjeeling. He wasn't keeping well for a while. Chatterjee considered it ridiculous since Kumar had gone about his usual schedule of *sikhar* and official work. Satyen detailed Kumar's sickness, followed by his death at midnight, the funeral procession in the morning, and cremation in the day attended by many people. His sister Bibhabati Devi was with Kumar until his death and guarded his dead body until the morning. All claims of Satyen not allowing her to see her husband were rubbish.

"Do you think any married Hindu woman would tolerate such disrespectful behaviour towards her husband? She spent every minute with him until we took his body away for cremation. Of course, it devastated us. Never even in our wildest dreams did the probability of his demise occur. He was unwell, and his health started deteriorating, but we were hopeful he would bounce back."

Chatterjee cross-questioned him on his possession of documents and about the communication sent after Kumar's death.

"I saw the telegrams only after the appearance of the sadhu since they were in the custody of Sarajubala Devi's brother. We figured out Boro Rani's brother had the ones where we mentioned Kumar's illness. But the telegram we sent to tell them about his sudden demise was missing. We asked around, but no one knew."

"Why didn't you let Dr Pran Kishore Acharya see the body after Kumar's death?"

"I don't know who called Dr Acharya. Or did he come by himself? We already had two experts, Dr Calvert and Dr Sen, treating Kumar. It made little sense to call another doctor to examine a dead body. However, I can't recollect the doctor or the incident."

Satyen was still in the dark about the diary reaching Chatterjee's hands. He had never mentioned it to Chaudhuri or anyone else. On multiple occasions in the past, Satyen had considered burning it. Yet, he preserved it as a long-cherished secret. Years before the sadhu turned up, Satyen figured someone had stolen it.

A couple of days before he was to appear as a witness, the news of the plaintiff's lawyers laying their hands on Satya Babu's diary started doing the rounds. The news reached Chaudhuri, who was furious. Chaudhuri needed to prepare his witness for cross-examination. When he met Satyen the same evening, he spoke angrily.

"Why didn't you mention the diary to me? The opposition has possibly caught hold of it."

"I don't have it in my custody since 1912. I saw it the last time before the Court of Wards took over the estate. Someone stole it along with other important papers of the estate. The set has been missing since then."

"Satya Babu, I must know the truth, or I won't be able to modify my line of questioning. Please give me an overview of the entries you recorded there."

Satyen didn't argue further but gave a filtered perspective of why he noted what he had written.

"Is there anyone you suspect?"

Satyen hesitated before replying. "I would lay my bet on Manamohan Bhattacharyya. That man is an opportunist. He had access to both Bibha and Ramendra Narayan and their documents. He handed over Kumar's horoscope to the imposter's lawyers. I won't be surprised if he flicked my diary and then gave it to Chatterjee or his associates. I'm sure he was rewarded handsomely for shifting loyalties. Bibha appointed him as her clerk. Look how he returned the favour by back-stabbing her." The bitterness in his tone was unmissable.

Chapter 45

Satyen's Controversial Diary

Chatterjee requested the court's permission to produce an important document the following morning. "This is Rai Bahadur Satyendra Nath Banerjee's diary, where he recorded every detail ever since Mejo Kumar fell sick in Darjeeling. Satyen Babu, I hope you recognise your handwriting." Chatterjee smirked.

"Where did you get it?" Satyen held his tongue. He didn't want to make it evident the diary was crucial.

There were murmurs in the court. Looking at Chatterjee holding the journal in his hand, people went berserk as they tried to guess its contents. Chaudhuri began questioning Satyen about the need to keep a diary.

Satyen mentioned his thoughts as a brother, trying to protect his sister's interests. "Kumar's health deteriorated despite our best efforts. I didn't write the diary while we were in Darjeeling. We were too engrossed in finding ways to save him. When we returned to Jaidebpur, I could sense a change in the attitude of the Raj Parivar toward my sister. I heard speculations of Bibhabati giving up her shares in the estate in return for a monthly allowance. Plans for executing a deed of management on similar lines went around. I didn't want them to hand her a raw deal. I could sense a greater ploy to deprive her of her financial rights. That's when I worried about her future and decided to record the critical events. Though my memory was sharp enough to recollect incidents from Darjeeling, I knew it wouldn't stay so vivid always. I noted details since the day Kumar fell critically ill, with his health spiralling downwards. While it looks like I started recording the incidents from 7th May onwards, I wrote my first entry about the Darjeeling incidents on 20th May."

"Why wasn't this diary mentioned until now?"

"Well, the diary wasn't in my possession for decades. I saw it last in 1912, after which it went missing. I believe someone stole it just before the Court of Wards took over the estate."

"Do you suspect anyone who could be involved in this theft?"

"It has to be someone with access to Bibhabati and Mejo Kumar." Satyen didn't mention he doubted Manamohan because he lacked evidence.

When it was Chatterjee's turn to cross-examine, he asked Satyen about the sequence of events in Darjeeling after Kumar's death.

"Along with Dr Ashutosh, Dr Sen and Dr Calvert were attending to Mejo Kumar at the moment of his demise."

Chatterjee interrupted him. "Did Dr B.B. Sarkar also attend to him?"

"My Sejo Mama, Surya Babu was in Darjeeling during that period. He had called Dr Sarkar, but the doctor left before Kumar passed away. He didn't attend to Mejo Kumar."

"What was Bibhabati Devi's condition after losing her husband?"

"She was devastated but maintained a strong demeanor in the face of adversity."

"So, you didn't have to take her to a different room because she had fits?"

"No! She stayed with the dead body until the morning."

"Right! Did you send anyone to the sanitorium that night to take out the dead body?"

"Someone might have gone to the sanitorium to inform the gentlemen staying there of Kumar's death. But there was no question of taking the body out for the funeral."

"Now I would like to draw your attention to the same events as noted by Satyen Babu in his diary. As per his writing, four doctors attended to Kumar when he expired at midnight – Dr Dasgupta, Dr Sen, Dr Calvert, and Dr Sarkar. Kumar's last words to Satya Babu were to tell Ashu doctor that he had difficulty in breathing. Satya Babu writes Bibha had fits. The doctors went away, though the nurses remained. He mentions sending a man to get his Sejo Mama around 3 a.m. They sent messages to Jaidebpur and Uttarpara about Kumar's death. And the last line states he sent his man to the sanitorium to get other men for taking the dead body out for cremation."

But Satyen was unfazed. "I made a mistake. Dr Sarkar wasn't there at the time of Kumar's death. I was running up and down. Bibhabati was in a dazed state after losing her husband unexpectedly. That's what the word fits means here. I'm not saying the professors at the sanitorium are lying, but I didn't send anyone to deliver the message that the body was to be taken out for a funeral that night. Kumar died at midnight, so how's it possible to inform them about his death in the evening? It must have happened the next evening."

Chatterjee opened a different page in the diary. "There's something else I wish to ask. Your diary tells me after you returned to Jaidebpur from Darjeeling, you spent many sleepless nights because you were scared. You had nightmares. Were you scared of Kumar's ghost returning to haunt you? There's a popular superstition if you don't cremate a dead Brahmin as per rituals, he returns as a *brahmadaitya* to haunt his surviving relatives."

"See, I'm a superstitious man. I am not just scared of ghosts and *brahmadaityas* but also of anything that seems eerie to me. It could be a slight noise or a sudden movement, especially at night. It has nothing to do with Kumar's death."

Chatterjee shifted to the current situation. "Were you querying the European tailors in Calcutta about the size of clothes and shoes of Kumar?"

"Well, we were trying to find whether Kumar's and sadhu's measurements and shoe sizes were the same. I thought the plaintiff had larger feet as compared to Kumar."

"And did you find out both Kumar's and the plaintiff's shoe sizes are six?"

"I wasn't aware."

"You were personally involved in these inquiries."

"Yes! I knew Kumar well enough to validate or negate certain identification parameters."

"So, did you know Kumar had a scar mark from a carriage wheel on his left ankle?"

"I never heard of it."

"You must see the report then."

After hearing Chatterjee read out the details from the report, Satyen mumbled. "How's it possible?"

In his concluding question, Chatterjee asked Satyen about an entry in his diary, which mentioned a fight between the Ranis. "On this page, you write the quarrel is a positive sign. Can you explain what you mean by this statement?"

"I don't recollect writing it. I must have meant how these small quarrels between family members show they care about each other."

"Not how you could manipulate the situation to your advantage and play them against each other." Chatterjee raised his eyebrows.

"Of course not!" Satyen's nostrils flared.

Satyen was the defence counsel's last witness. Until then, it was a deliberate attempt from the defendant's witness to prove that Kumar was a better-looking aristocrat, fond of the European lifestyle compared to the rustic plaintiff.

Months before Dharamdas appeared in the court, the defence counsel presented Phani Bhushan Banerjee, a cousin of Kumar's, as a witness. The cousin maintained a lesson book. He noted the English terms which Mejo Kumar supposedly knew, his traits, and his daily routine. During the investigation, Chatterjee discovered the idea was to assist Phani Babu with information supplied by the authorities. A defendant's pleader wrote some entries. It acted as a guidebook for his testimony against the plaintiff with word descriptions of billiards, polo, sweater, soup, menu, and cupboard among others.

Initially, he didn't admit to the plaintiff's presence in his son's upanayana ceremony at his father-in-law's house in Dhaka. He also negated Elokeshi's existence in Kumar's life. But he confessed to both after Chatterjee provided evidence.

Eventually, Chatterjee disclosed how the authorities rewarded Phani Babu for his devotion to the estate. "Other than some withdrawn suits, Phani Babu's due interest in rent arrears has been reduced." Initially, Phani was reluctant to admit the truth, but he gave in to the claims of the withdrawn suit and 6000 rupees as remission. However, he stuck to the point it had nothing to do with testifying against the sadhu. The same was true of most defendant's witnesses, who seemed to be tutored or appeared in the court with a vested interest.

Between Chatterjee and Chaudhuri, the counsels had presented over fifteen hundred witnesses within less than two years. It included six hundred and eight days of the court hearing. Both counsels took six weeks each to present their concluding statements based on proofs and testimonies. Chaudhuri closed his argument by stating the plaintiff was not Kumar Ramendra Narayan Roy. Chatterjee concluded all shreds of evidence pointed towards the fact that the sadhu and Mejo Kumar were the same. 20th May 1936, was the last day of the court.

Chapter 46

Discussion of the Proceedings

It was yet another morning at Jyotirmayee's house. The plaintiff, now referred to as Mejo Kumar by most of his family members and subjects, sat out in the verandah. A couple of talukdars were about to arrive for a discussion on rent collection. The case had turned out to be financially exhausting. Of late, he completely stopped thinking about Bibhabati.

After hearing Chatterjee read out certain portions from Satyen's diary, his heart sank. *"His last words to me – tell Ashu I feel difficulty in breathing. Shariff Khan went mad. Sent a man to the sanitorium for men to get the corpse removed for the funeral."* Chatterjee emphasised these sentences. Satyen's record added suspicion to Kumar's mysterious death and hushed-up cremation attempt. His attempts at justification didn't sound convincing to the plaintiff, but it almost made him certain Bibhabati knew the truth of his death. Whether she was an accomplice like Ashutosh was yet to be known, but Satyen couldn't have proceeded with his plan after returning to Jaidebpur without earning her trust. The brother-sister duo seemed concerned about Bibhabati's shares only.

"I lived with an unfaithful woman who stayed married for my wealth," he muttered to himself.

"What did you say?"

"Oh, it's you." The sadhu spun around to see Jyotirmayee.

"You looked lost in thoughts."

Jyotirmayee sat in the adjacent chair.

"I didn't see you since morning. Were you out somewhere?"

"I went for a walk." The plaintiff smiled.

"It's been a long time since we spent some weeks at home. For the last couple of years, you have been in the court or at Ukil Babu's office."

"Chatterjee Babu told me Judge Sahib is going through the statements and pieces of evidence. He'll conclude after analysing the arguments and counter-arguments. I believe he's typing it out personally."

"Hmmm ..." Jyotirmayee only hoped that Justice Basu would rule the judgment in their favour.

"Lindsay Sahib always disliked you because he was Rankin's friend, and we hated Rankin for the way he took away our mother's rights by labelling her incapable of managing the estate. You vowed to seek revenge. Later on, when we got the rights back, Rankin left with a bruised ego. That's why Lindsay Sahib never wanted to hear our story. In his mind, you were a cheater, and he wanted to prove the same to the world," Jyotirmayee reminisced.

"All these firangis are like that. When grandmother wrote a letter to the district collector, he ignored her appeal and didn't even have the courtesy to reply. But how do I criticise these officials when Bibhabati meted out the same treatment to Choto Thakurma by returning her letter?"

"Do you remember the day when she came here as your bride for the first time?"

The man didn't reply. Their marriage happened in Jaidebpur, and he hadn't waited beyond three days to return to Elokeshi.

"She wasn't worthy enough to become your wife. I wonder if she came with such a corrupt mind in our family, or was it her brother's influence all along? I could never imagine the unemployed youth who spent most of his time at his sister's home harbouring such dangerous thoughts."

Like every devoted sister, Jyotirmayee overlooked her brother's flaws.

As kids, the three Kumars were barely interested in studies. Satyabhama gave indulgence to the undisciplined boys. Except for Ranendra, the younger Kumars Ramendra and Rabindra weren't even keen on fulfilling their duties towards the estate. Ramendra's passion lay in women, merry-making, and hunting. But those traits befitted a zamindar of that era.

Jyotirmayee never considered Ramendra's indifference towards Bibhabati and his flirtatious relationships with other women as factors responsible for the crack in their marriage.

For the plaintiff, though he regretted some decisions from his past, he had moved on and embraced the new life. For most people, he had become Ramendra Narayan the day he lit Satyabhama's funeral pyre. But it rarely occurred to him that he could've also wronged his wife in the past. Instead, he saw it as a man's way of living and expected his wife to adjust.

"They'll rot in hell for what they did to an innocent man like you," Jyotirmayee cursed Bibhabati. "The drama she created after returning to Jaidebpur was only to draw sympathy since she knew what her brother had done to you."

The man sat in silence. He wondered if Bibhabati was also having a similar conversation with Satyen.

Calcutta

Bibhabati didn't get out of bed at the first sign of the sun. After weeks, she didn't have to wake up with a sinking feeling of dealing with a court case. She slept well the previous night, knowing they had done their best. Now it was up to the judge to decide. Chaudhuri Sahib sounded confident about the judgment in their favour, Satyen had informed her. They waited for the official announcement. As much as she tried, Bibhabati couldn't get over the questions from the plaintiff's lawyer in court.

"Did you and Mejo Kumar sleep in the same bed?"

"Was yours a happy and satisfying marriage?"

"Was Kumar affectionate towards you?"

"Were you aware of his philandering ways?"

"Did your mother get involved in saving your marriage? Did she send letters asking you to ensure that he shares the bed with you only, not other women?"

"Were you brothers-in-law men of loose moral character?"

While she maintained a dignified silence on questions that sounded intrusive and displayed the royal family in poor light, she limited her answers to no.

Bibhabati turned out to be a hard nut to crack; Chatterjee changed his line of questioning.

"Are you saying your husband was very fond of you?"

"Did he shower you with affection?"

"Did your husband want you around him always?"

"Was your husband a domestic man?"

Bibhabati's response was the same – no or maybe. At times, she refused to comment. She told the court they had a marriage like any other husband and wife – blissful and peaceful. Bibhabati couldn't bring herself to divulge that her husband rarely called her into his room. Instead, she told them how he frequented her room upstairs, to paint a picture of a happy marriage.

She felt a shiver run down her spine as she reconstructed her past in her mind. During her tenure as Ramendra's wife, she received no affection or gift from her husband. His syphilis, followed by his stubbornness in not adhering to the doctor's suggestions, made it difficult for her to contemplate starting a family with him.

She had wept inconsolably after losing her husband as the other women took out her conch shell and iron bangles to break them. When she moved to Calcutta to live with Satyen, she often wondered if the sobs came out of the grief of losing her husband or the fear of losing her social privilege and status. Was there anything for Bibhabati to look forward to in her married life in Jaidebpur? Yet, when Kumar passed away, her demeanor was like a mourning widow. When she heard witnesses recounting her heartbroken state after losing Mejo Kumar, Bibhabati knew her emotions felt genuine.

Satyen had mentioned Shariff Khan to her the previous night. "The idiot triggered the idea of an attempted late-night funeral, a missing body, and a botched-up cremation. He suggested our involvement in foul play related to Kumar's death. What a bunch of lies!"

Bibhabati wondered how Khan had arrived at such a strange conclusion. She knew Khan also told the court how Satyen hadn't let her stay near her husband in his last hours. Another witness stated Satyen took Bibhabati away after she started having fits. They wanted to prove Bibhabati wasn't around and was thus unaware of what Satyen and Ashutosh might have done to Kumar. During the trial, the plaintiff's team often slandered her name as an opportunist, a selfish wife who only cared about her husband's property, and a woman with questionable morals. She wasn't new to the last part, having heard of her supposed liaison with Ashutosh. Recently, she heard worse. It was beyond her dignity to understand how people nurtured such disgusting thoughts about the pure bond of a brother and a sister.

The judgment was bound to be a slap on her haters' faces. She was looking forward to getting back to her peaceful life in Calcutta. Irrespective of whether the imposter sadhu stayed or left after the judgment, Bibhabati knew the chances of a cordial relationship with those who supported the fraud were dim. Even her relatives from Uttarpara hadn't rejected the sadhu publicly. Some even went to the court to testify in his favour. She was sure that her aunt Sarojini Devi did it deliberately. It was her way to get even with Bibhabati, whom she hated. Little did Bibhabati know that the next few years would force her to face bigger turbulences in life.

Chapter 47
Basu's Methodology

Pannalal Basu had spent uncountable hours listening to the case for two years. When both sides finished their arguments, it was left to him to arrive at a decision. Basu refused police protection and a typist in his home as he started working on the judgment. Over the months, he had seen how wealth and power could change witnesses and make them modify or withdraw their statements. Basu didn't want to be influenced by anything except facts and evidence. He took it upon himself to go through each aspect and write his opinion. Later, he typed out the detailed statement, stored the papers safely, and slept with the key under his pillow after locking his study room.

Basu wasn't initially aware of a police officer in plain clothes hovering around his house daily since 8 in the morning. It was a high-profile and sensitive case. The authorities didn't want to risk Basu's safety. Basu visited the Raj Bari a few times to understand the royal family's way of living. He noticed how the servants kept the rooms on the ground floor of the residential quarters clean and lit incense sticks at dusk in memory of the Kumars. He noticed two staircases, each leading close to a room of Mejo and Choto Kumar, respectively, known as *baithak khanas.* The *baithak khanas* were adjacent to their bedrooms. Basu realised the Ranis came through these stairs to their husband's rooms when the Kumars sent for their wives.

Basu contemplated the various aspects and facts presented by both parties before writing down his conclusion. The Kumars lived like rich

Bengali bhadralok, bothered little about education, and had questionable morals. Elokeshi's statement proved how Ramendra continued his affair with his mistress even after marrying Bibhabati. Bibhabati's marriage to Ramendra was neither blissful nor satisfying.

Basu recollected the servants' statements where they mentioned how Kumar would rarely send for his wife through an aide. No one remembered seeing him visit Bibhabati in her quarters.

Bibhabati had received nineteen lakhs of rupees from the estate until that year. Yet, she didn't have a bank account to keep the money. Satyen's constant presence in her life and his inability to provide a statement of income made Basu doubt if he was the one supervising her sister's income. Bibhabati claimed to have locked the money inside an iron chest with the key in her custody. Despite Basu's prodding, Bibhabati couldn't provide records or statements of the money she earned, which convinced him she wasn't handling the money herself. It made Basu suspicious that Satyen controlled his sister's life as much as he owned her income. From what he had heard and learned, Satyen seemed like a shrewd and scheming man.

Basu noted how witnesses mentioned an upset Bibhabati refusing to acknowledge or talk to Satyen when they returned to Jaidebpur after Kumar's death. And when she spoke, she cried about becoming a beggar from a queen only because of her brother. Many people thought it hinted at Satyen's involvement in Kumar's death and how even Bibhabati had guessed about the foul play. However, Basu wondered if it could've been a mere figure of speech.

Basu found it strange the defence stuck to the theory of the sadhu being a Punjabi medicine man who cured people of sterility. That's how he supposedly landed at Jyotirmayee's house in Jaidebpur. The argument felt ridiculous considering the time period of just three days to hatch a conspiracy of such magnitude.

Basu analysed Jyotirmayee's reaction to the sadhu's presence. The then forty-year-old widow, who followed every rule and ritual meant for Hindu widows, didn't think twice before coming out of the purdah to cater to the sadhu who had fainted on her verandah.

What resolve it must have taken for Jyotirmayee to get the sadhu indoors as her brother Ramendra Narayan and keep him with her family members, including women. They hadn't established the sadhu's lineage or his identity then. She not only overlooked any dissimilarities due to the time gap or the sadhu's lifestyle as a monk, but stuck to her conviction of the sadhu being her brother through thick and thin over the years. She left her house on 7th June with her brother after the authorities prohibited him from entering Jaidebpur. If it was a conspiracy she hatched, it was too risky. To catch hold of a stranger, a Punjabi man, and try to establish him as her brother felt far-fetched. Even when it came to the theory that Jyotirmayee opposed Ananda Kumari's desire to adopt a boy because she was worried about her sons losing claim to the property, Basu didn't feel convinced that Jyotirmayee would decide to adopt a stranger as her brother as a countermeasure.

Basu noted, 'Jyotirmayee Devi took the stance only because she was sure it was her brother who returned as the sadhu. I'm trying to decipher whether her faith rose from genuine recognition or mere emotions. But I can't disregard the presence of many other people, including members of the Bhawal Raj in Jyotirmayee's house at that moment, who identified the plaintiff as Mejo Kumar. Even Jogen Banerjee accepted he was a believer initially. It is a matter of debate if Jyotirmayee's conviction influenced his belief. However, Jogen Babu claimed to have rejected the plaintiff as Kumar later since he couldn't find any similarities. When Jogen Babu and Mohini Mohan Chakraborty met the sadhu at Jyotirmayee's house, he answered many questions correctly, especially the one whose correct answer was not even known to Dr Ashutosh. However, by then, the employees were aware of the Court of Wards' opinion about the sadhu, and thus, they highlighted the questions the sadhu failed to answer. They intended to prove what the Court of Wards already believed.'

Basu stayed unfazed by public opinion in the sadhu's favour. But he couldn't stop thinking whether the tenants would have accepted the sadhu as Mejo Kumar, or paid him *nazars* and rent, if they had found no resemblance to Ramendra Narayan.

Chaudhuri questioned why the sadhu didn't claim his property after retrieval of his memory. He would have behaved with the same royalty and sophistication if he were a prince. Basu was aware of the visit of Ananda Chandra Roy, the famous lawyer from Dhaka, who possibly gave all the alternatives available for the plaintiff to seek legal recourse. But no one could imagine what the sadhu did next, and Basu considered it courageous. The sadhu went to the collector's office and spoke to him directly.

As per Basu, one of the turning points in the case was – 'Satyabhama's reaction and perspective of the plaintiff. She accepted him as her second grandson. Satyabhama, who lived all her life in a palace, didn't hesitate to leave her luxury behind and stay with the plaintiff in his rented house in Dhaka since July 1922. She was an illiterate lady but instructed her attendant what to write in the letter to Bibhabati. Satyabhama brought the seal and put it herself before sending it to Mejo Rani. When she passed away, the plaintiff conducted her funeral rituals without any objection from the onlookers and family.'

When Basu analysed the witness' recognition of the plaintiff, he found that most friends, relatives, and family members identified the sadhu as Kumar. However, hundreds of tenants claimed to have recognised him as Kumar, though they couldn't specify which trait convinced them about the similarities. Ramendra was a man who had left an impact on those who met him. He was often seen in the market, in the field, in the jungle, and in multiple places. Almost every day, he was at the stables, looking after the horses or at *pilkhana*, tending to the elephants. So, Chaudhuri's theory that the tenants rarely had the opportunity to see or know Kumar well, didn't hold ground.

Even though the defence side had produced a substantial number of witnesses who claimed to find nothing similar between the sadhu and Mejo Kumar, Chatterjee had already established Jogen Banerjee's sample instruction sent to the tenants to give testimony against the sadhu. Basu suspected a chunk of the witnesses was forced into giving testimony against the sadhu. He thought of Mukunda Guin, the murdered secretary. He wondered about the man's role in Darjeeling, which made the authorities pick him for a police job.

Chapter 48
Basu's Analysis

Other than the plaintiff's family members, like Jyotirmayee Devi and Sarajubala Devi, many relatives of Bibhabati's family also turned up as witnesses in favour of the sadhu. In comparison, only a handful of her relatives testified in Bibhabati's favour. Most of Kumar's friends validated the sadhu's identity. Those incidents were known only to Kumar and his specific friends, and they shared the same in detail, even if scandalous.

Most officials who spoke against the sadhu felt prejudiced against Kumar and some against Indians. Be it Rankin, who testified despite not seeing Kumar for over two decades, or Lindsay, who had a preconceived notion the sadhu was an imposter.

Basu heard about Bibhabati spotting Ramendra on various occasions in Calcutta accidentally. But he couldn't agree with Chatterjee's argument that the arrangement of the meetings happened with Rani's permission. 'It could have been a mere case of curiosity from Bibhabati's side. It was equally possible the plaintiff had arranged these sightings to be better prepared about Rani's looks when asked in court. These incidents don't lead to any conclusive inference,' he noted.

The Court of Wards and the defence counsel brought up the comparison of measurements and shoe sizes of Kumar with the plaintiff. After he heard both wore shoe size six, Chaudhuri could barely hide his disappointment. Chaudhuri highlighted the plaintiff's body was much fatter than Kumar's. But Basu considered it unimportant since

Chaudhuri compared Kumar's body when he was twenty-five to the plaintiff's body at fifty-two. Even the slight increase in height was considered normal since the height measured as per documents was at Kumar's twenty-one years, and people usually grew until they turned twenty-two or twenty-three.

His fair skin, reddish brown hair, and cat's eyes resembling the brown colour were Kumar's prominent traits. Basu observed the same in Jyotirmayee Devi. He also figured out that the third Kumar and Buddhu had similar features. These could be called family traits. He had peculiar pierced ears; the lobes didn't join with the cheeks. When the opposition couldn't prominently observe the same in the plaintiff, Basu blamed it on his fatty cheeks.

Basu wrote, 'The scar on Kumar's left ankle was an aftereffect of Kumar's accident with a carriage wheel. Bibhabati remembered the accident and mentioned Kumar walking with crutches, but she rejected the presence of a scar. Dr Caddy's medical report for the insurance papers mentioned the scars. A letter from Bibhabati's sister Malina written in 1904, was also produced in the court, where Malina expressed relief about the speedy recovery of Kumar's legs three weeks after Rabindra's wedding. The question of Bibhabati not knowing about the scar doesn't hold good.'

When they brought up the scaly feet topic and asked Phani about it, he rejected the idea that Kumar had scaly feet and that the skin condition ran in Kumar's family. By then, Basu was skeptical about the authenticity of Phani's statement. Phani's purpose seemed to oppose things that went in the plaintiff's favour. But Basu had observed how most members of Kumar's family suffered from this typical skin problem. Besides, Phani's sister's son-in-law was an estate employee, and Basu knew it could be a crucial reason for his stand against Kumar.

Syphilis wasn't prominent in the sadhu, but the expert doctors who examined the plaintiff had a different opinion. Some couldn't detect syphilis, while a few doctors could identify the syphilitic node on the right side of his nasal partition. Other identification marks on the plaintiff, like two moles on his penis, a claw mark on his arm, and a broken tooth, were evidenced in Kumar, stated by his family, old servants, and mistress Elokeshi. Even the operation mark on his abdomen was the same as on Kumar's. The plaintiff claimed syphilis started as a sore in his penis area, followed by abdominal swelling, and then spread to other body parts. A certain Dr Elahi had operated on his abdomen.

Chaudhuri intended to prove the plaintiff was an ordinary, uneducated man with below-average intellect in contrast to Ramendra Narayan Roy, the son of a king. Ramendra was supposed to be an aristocrat with a decent command of English and western cultures. When the sadhu couldn't understand and reply about the technical terms associated with sports that Mejo Kumar liked, the defence stated Kumar seemed well versed with such terminologies. They tried to make it obvious the plaintiff was a bloated non-Bengali *palawan*. But Basu felt convinced that Kumar was as illiterate as the plaintiff came across to him. Besides, he didn't deem it necessary for any sports person to know the game's technicalities. The plaintiff couldn't reply to questions related to games like polo, making it evident that Kumar's family or lawyers hadn't tutored him.

Basu found it ridiculous how the defence wanted to portray Kumar as an educated royal man. Yet, the conspirators hadn't taken cognizance of his literacy status and found an illiterate Punjabi to play his role as part of the hatched conspiracy. The defence could prove his educated status only through a couple of signatures and unconvincing letters. Even though old servants saw him in the company of Britishers, the wealthy zamindars could be a part of such gatherings without even knowing or conversing in English.

Seeing the nine letters Kumar supposedly wrote to Bibhabati produced in the court, Basu noted, 'The topics are limited to Kumar meeting the commissioner or the district magistrate. It strikes me as odd that a man of twenty-one wrote such formal letters to his newly married wife, who had just entered her teens. There is no expression of love or familiarity. Though Bibhabati claims to possess some more letters from her husband, she refuses to show them to the court because they are silly and personal. Some dates and incidents in the letters don't tally. For instance, Kumar was in Calcutta on a certain date, but the letter states he met some officials in Dhaka on the same day.'

Next, the signatures came. The handwriting expert, on behalf of the plaintiff, concluded the signatures by Kumar and the plaintiff were of the same person. The defendant's handwriting expert mentioned striking similarities, though he couldn't give a conclusion. He noticed the English writing of Kumar and the plaintiff were similar, but the Bengali writing looked like it was by a different person. The defendant's team sought another handwriting expert's opinion, who concluded the writings by two people.

Basu had already deduced that the physical and mental identification parameters highlighted the plaintiff and Kumar as the same person. He inspected each trait individually and compared it with the evidence obtained. It was left to the defendants to prove that Mejo Kumar died in Darjeeling, or that the plaintiff was the Punjabi Mal Singh of Aujla and not a Bengali.

Basu was satisfied since his concluding statements had reasoning and evidence to justify his stand. When he locked the study room on the night he wrote about the tallying identification traits, Basu sensed relief.

Chapter 49
Basu's Conclusion

Basu went through Dr Calvert's medical certificate and the prescriptions of the doctors who attended to Kumar in Darjeeling. From the preliminary observations, it was clear the initial medication prescribed by Dr Calvert had nothing to do with biliary colic. Basu observed Kumar's age mentioned as twenty-seven on the certificate. At the time of his death, Ramendra wasn't even twenty-five. While going through Satyen's diary, he found Satyen trying to figure out Kumar's age through various sources and means. Calvert's certificate hinted at the possibility of Satyen giving the age of Kumar as twenty-seven since Satyen was unsure about Kumar's exact age. It made the judge suspicious about other details and wondered how much of the information came from Satyen and the level of involvement of Dr Calvert in the case.

As mentioned in the court, the eldest Kumar wanted to probe into Kumar's sudden death, especially after he received anonymous letters stating Mejo Kumar was alive. But Satyen had presented these certificates and put an end to speculations.

Calvert's first prescription on 6th May had no suggested remedy for biliary colic treatment. Even Dr Dasgupta's medicines for 7th May were generic and meant for any patient suffering from malaria. Kumar didn't display any symptoms of malaria. However, it was noteworthy that this prescription suggested arsenic, a probable cause of his diarrhoea. Dr Ashutosh mentioned writing it under the guidance of one of the senior doctors attending to Kumar. He couldn't remember whether it was Dr

Sen or Dr Calvert. Since Dr Calvert denied having to do anything with this prescription and Dr Sen was long dead, it couldn't be verified.

Basu was confident none of the senior doctors had suggested the prescription since one of them would have signed on it. Dr Dasgupta didn't even attempt to prove Kumar had malaria. He kept shifting the responsibilities toward the senior doctors. Dr Ashutosh was an unworthy witness in Basu's mind.

Irrespective of Dr Calvert's repeated statements on Kumar's on-and-off pain, the judge noted the doctor had attended to Kumar first on 6th May and not before that day.

The lawyers presented five prescriptions written on 8th May. The expert panel of doctors, keeping the serial numbers of the prescriptions in mind, concluded the following sequence of illnesses that Kumar suffered from – dyspepsia, collapse, profuse diarrhoea, and cramps and pain in the stomach. Kumar collapsed due to acute diarrhoea. Biliary colic wasn't mentioned anywhere in any prescriptions or even in the telegrams.

On 10th May, Dr Calvert mentioned colic in his condolence letter to Boro Kumar. Basu noted with surprise, 'What made Dr Calvert write a certificate confirming he attended to Kumar's biliary colic for fourteen days, a sickness he claimed Kumar suffered from on and off? Strangely, the defendant's version makes it evident the doctor saw the first symptom of biliary colic only on 7th May and supposedly prescribed arsenic for it. But there's confusion since it's evident Calvert wasn't even around Kumar during this period. It baffles me how a doctor who had never seen a case of arsenic poisoning accepted the reason for Kumar's death as biliary colic so easily, wrote it out in the condolence letter, and mentioned it even in the affidavit handed over to Satyen or Dr Ashutosh. Biliary colic sounds more like an illness created to cover up the actual reason for Kumar's death. That's why the word 'colic' appears for the first time in the condolence letter written by Calvert to Ramendra Kumar.'

After hearing the expert panel of doctors, Basu derived that an irritant had been administered to Kumar's body, leading to bloody stools. Since arsenic was the only irritant discovered in the prescription and Dr Ashutosh was the one attending to Kumar on 7th May, Basu pinned his suspicion on Dr Ashutosh.

Basu proceeded to derive the timing of Kumar's death. Bibhabati told the court that Dr Calvert arrived around 2 p.m. and stayed there until midnight. In his letter to Lindsay, Calvert stated he couldn't recollect whether he was present at the time of Kumar's death. However, he said the opposite in the court in 1931. Basu didn't think it made sense for the doctor to sit and wait until midnight at Step Aside on 8th May. There were no more prescriptions, thus confirming Basu's suspicion that the Kumar possibly expired between 7 to 8 p.m. Dr Sarkar's statement validated the same. Dr Sarkar claimed the absence of a doctor when he went to see Kumar at Surya Babu's request. Dr Sarkar wasn't as reputed as Dr Calvert or Dr Sen. So, the absence of the other two doctors justified his presence. Basu had the testimony of Ram Singh Subba, who claimed to have seen Dr Sarkar with Kumar's dead body around 7:30 p.m.

What was equally mysterious was the missing telegram announcing the death of Kumar. The witness from the plaintiff's side remembered the words as 'died in the evening,' but the one from the defendant's side stated 'died at midnight.' Lindsay had retrieved all the other telegrams from Sarajubala Devi. But it was strange how he never insisted on the last telegram. Basu wondered if it was because the telegram was already in their custody.

Basu couldn't ignore how numerous witnesses remembered hearing about Kumar's death around 8 p.m., including the professors at the sanitorium. It was possible only if he died before 8. From his previous deductions, Basu felt the prince had died between 7 to 8 p.m. The judge doubted Bibhabati's statement about being with Kumar until midnight when there were reports of her having fits. Again, the fact that Satyen and

Dr Ashutosh claimed the presence of Dr Calvert and Dr Sen during this period made it improbable for Bibhabati or any woman to be present in the same room. There were no prescriptions from this phase. Despite Dr Ashutosh's claim of injecting Kumar, the doctor couldn't recollect which medicine he had administered.

As Basu analysed the timing of Kumar's death, he was well aware of the beliefs and superstitions harboured by a Bengali Hindu household. He wrote, 'Usually, people prefer not to keep the corpse overnight since there's a superstition associated with a stale dead body, though there are notable exceptions. But this aspect also makes it more convincing that there was an attempt to cremate Kumar's dead body at night.'

The cremation was to happen at the old grounds, which didn't have a shed. Basu had a hazy opinion on the rains since no records could prove it rained that night.

The defendants claimed Kumar's morning cremation. Bibhabati stated she guarded the body until the funeral procession began. However, many witnesses disclosed seeing the body in a covered state at Step Aside and while burning. Some people suspected the replacement of Kumar's dead body with another corpse, making it necessary for the defendants to cover it.

There were two versions related to Bibhabati's actions after the cremation. The defendants claimed Bibhabati was with Mahendra Babu's wife, Kasiswasi Devi, who helped her remove her jewellery and change into a white saree. However, the other version stated Surya Babu bought Bibhabati from Step Aside to Kasiswasi's house. Bibhabati had already changed into a white saree and wore no jewellery. Kasiswasi had asked why she removed the ornaments before the men returned from the cremation grounds. Basu felt sure that Bibhabati had no female company at Step Aside on the day of Kumar's cremation. That's why Surya Babu took her to be with the other women in his house.

Jagat Mohini, the nurse with a dubious identity, was an unreliable witness too. Basu doubted her statement of being asked to carry the holy water and sacred thread to the cremation ground. There were stories of members of Kumar's entourage playing the role of a priest and chanting the hymns. Since Birendra Banerjee accepted about not taking a bath before putting fire to the funeral pyre, Basu understood the cremation happened in a hurry.

Two people had come forward and given the same evidence. Khetra Nath Mukherjee, also known as Swami Onkaranand, was an employee of Darjeeling municipality. He responded to Jagat Mohini's call and was present when the body, covered in white cloth, was taken out in the morning and burnt without the usual rituals. Basanta Kumar Mukherjee, Superintendent, Deputy Commissioner's office made his way to Step Aside at the behest of Jagat Mohini. It shocked him that no one offered a *pinda* before burning the dead body on the pyre. None of them saw the nurse at the new cremation ground.

Basu believed the morning cremation was a fake one. Those who took part in the process were scared or embarrassed to accept they failed in protecting Kumar or even his corpse. However, not all had managed to keep it a secret. Murmurs and hushed voices led to rumours reaching the royal family.

Satyen had visited Darjeeling within ten days of the sadhu declaring his identity. Only a man who feared the exposure of his past acts would do so, as per Basu. It was almost evident that something had not gone right with the cremation. The defendant's experts dismissed the sadhu's memory loss since regression and dissociation weren't simultaneously possible. But the judge didn't think the plaintiff's mental condition matched with the co-existence of both states.

For years, the defendants claimed the plaintiff to be Mal Singh of Aujla, yet they never asked him questions about Mal Singh. Basu found it strange. Even though Dharamdas had come forward to state that the plaintiff was Mal Singh, the judge had reservations about the authenticity of the man who posed as Dharamdas.

Basu concluded, 'The photograph shown to Dharamdas fifteen years ago was different, or the man who testified as Dharamdas the Guru then wasn't the one who stood in the court claiming to be the Guru. The man who appeared as Dharamdas in 1921 without a swell in the abdomen differed from the one who appeared now. As per Surendra Chakrabarty's report, Mal Singh had black hair, whereas the plaintiff had brown hair. Lindsay noted the colour as golden brown when he met the sadhu for the first time.' It was a case of deliberate cheating, and the judge condemned the action.

Chapter 50
Basu's Verdict

With the passing months, people grew restless, waiting for judgment. However, the plaintiff and the defendants were not just the concerned parties. The authorities were equally worried about the outcome. They had utilised a chunk of the revenue for expenses related to the case. In between, Sasanka Ghose requested a raise in his fees, but the estate had to turn it down since they had already overshot their budget. Even Chaudhuri claimed not to have received his due of almost one lakh and ninety thousand rupees.

Meanwhile, Sasanka Ghose sent a note to the Court of Wards to raise at least seventy thousand rupees to meet the cost of filing an appeal, in case the plaintiff won.

"While a bank loan is an option, I would suggest mortgaging the share of the third Rani's adopted son to raise the money. Please note the property would eventually come to him if the plaintiff loses the case. I recommend having a plan in place beforehand in case of a sudden turn of events."

Though the new estate manager didn't entertain such an idea, Sasanka's statement raised many eyebrows since it hinted at the possibility of the case going in the plaintiff's favour. Words reached Dr Ashutosh, and he immediately informed Satyen about Sasanka's idea.

Satyen was outraged at the thought of a re-appeal after facing so much emotional turmoil and financial challenges. He didn't even want to entertain the idea of a loss. But it wasn't the first time Satyen heard about things not working in their favour, despite assurance from Chaudhuri.

"I heard from a reliable source that Justice Basu isn't letting anyone near his work area. He refused police protection and declined to hire an assistant. Do you think his judgment will go against the public sympathy?" a well-wisher had commented.

"He's a morally upright man who doesn't let others influence him. If he thinks someone is a victim, he won't spare the culprit from punishment," another friend remarked.

Satyen wrinkled his nose. "So the judgment should surely be in Bibha's favour. After all, we have faced mental torture by an imposter and his supporters."

However, the majority didn't echo the sentiment. Most people felt strongly for the plaintiff, who had suffered for nearly two decades, was betrayed by his wife, and was still struggling to prove his existence. Their sentiments for the widow Bibhabati transformed with her denial to give the man a chance, and because of her brother's cunning moves. Chatterjee was equally optimistic.

The authorities received a proposal to raise a bank loan. However, the commissioner responded they were waiting for the judgment, due in a few days.

Basu finished typing five hundred and twenty-five pages of the report. Before concluding, the judge considered every aspect, statement, and piece of evidence, from both the plaintiff's and defendant's sides. Finally, the day everyone was waiting for, was about to arrive.

On 24th August, 1936, Judge Basu was to deliver his judgment. The newspapers went into a frenzy. Most had a representative assigned to the court so that they could report the updates on an ongoing basis through the telegraph. Almost the entire population of Dhaka assembled in front of the court to witness the landmark judgment. The excitement in the crowd was palpable, and people thronged the streets in huge numbers.

In Jaidebpur, the Raj Bari and estate offices were assigned police protection because of the volatile situation. Chatterjee and Chaudhuri sat on their respective seats, each confident of the outcome in their favour. The plaintiff looked visibly exhausted, while Satyen acted indifferently.

Basu's conclusions were sharp and to the point. He had considered the aspect of identity as the first parameter. Based on the evidence from both sides, including Bibhabati's relatives, he believed the plaintiff wasn't an imposter. Well-respected men, elderly women, and educated people comprised the lot who asserted the plaintiff was a genuine man. Even Jogen Banerjee, the man who organised witnesses on the defendant's side, had agreed to an authentic reaction of identity from people who saw the plaintiff as a sadhu on the day he declared his identity.

Besides, the identification marks which tallied were unique to Kumar and the plaintiff. He dismissed the conspiracy theory since the plaintiff never tried to hide his identity. If anything, he knocked at the collector's door proactively to establish who he was. He collected rent. Yet, the authorities didn't question him until he came forward with his claims.

"After the plaintiff declared his identity, Satyen Banerjee told the Government to safeguard the evidence related to Kumar's death. He rushed to Darjeeling the following week to locate the witnesses present during the cremation. What were the defendants so afraid of that they didn't mention the doctor's report about identification marks noted for insurance in court for the longest time? They should have presented the document and destroyed the claims of the plaintiff, who Lindsay had already declared an imposter. Instead, the plaintiff sought this particular document as evidence to prove he was Kumar.

"The plaintiff requested the Government an inquiry into his identity immediately after his declaration. His family members wrote to the authorities before that. When they were so keen on facing the questions and being examined, the narrative of hiding the plaintiff and grooming him for the role of Kumar doesn't fit.

"I declare the plaintiff is Ramendra Narayan Roy, second son of the late King Rajendra Narayan Roy of Bhawal. Since there is no evidence to prove that the plaintiff was initiated to sanyas and had renounced the world, he should be given possession of one-third of the properties in the suit, the same share enjoyed by the first defendant now. The plaintiff will get his costs from the defendants at an interest of six percent per annum."

As Judge Basu concluded his judgment, the crowd burst into cheers. Satyen's face turned ashen, realizing the impact of this judgment on his prospects and monetary status. The streets were filled with people, screaming, 'Jai Madhyam Kumar er r jai! Jai Mejo Kumar er jai!'

B.C. Chatterjee, Suren Banerjee, and Arabinda Guha had become messiahs for the people of Jaidebpur. The procession moved towards 4, Armanitola – Jyotirmayee's rented house near the Armenian Church.

Jyotirmayee had spent hours inside her puja room anticipating the outcome while holding on to her faith in the Almighty. A maid came running inside after the news of the judgment reached the house. She updated the family members, who rushed outside to welcome the plaintiff, now established as Ramendra Narayan Roy.

"Ma Thakrun, Judge Sahib has returned our Kumar to Bhawal."

Jyotirmayee couldn't see who spoke the words as the realization of winning the case hit her. Tears streamed down her eyes as she held on to the walls to steady herself. She was the first to believe the sadhu; she had spent years looking out for Ramendra, trusting he was alive. Her love and dedication towards her brother won over every theory of conspiracy, cheating, and death. Even after losing her son Buddhu and incurring heavy financial debts, she didn't give up. After years of struggle, her persistence and faith triumphed. She cried her heart out. Before she could regain her composure, she saw darkness ahead of her eyes and fell hard with a thud.

When Jyotirmayee opened her eyes, she lay on the cot, surrounded by female relatives. She tried sitting up when her sister Tarinmayee held her by the shoulder to help.

"We won, Mejo Didi. Our trust won. Truth triumphed over evil," Tarinmayee whispered. Her voice broke.

"Where is Mejo?"

"He has been checking on your health frequently. You fainted on hearing the news."

An hour later, Jyotirmayee called out to the servants. "Light the lamps, blow the conch shells, and ask the women to give *ullukar*. Bring all the sweets in the town. It's time for celebrations."

Ramendra smiled at the enthusiasm his sister displayed. It was as much her battle as his. He was grateful for her unwavering faith and support in every aspect.

The evening saw crowds assemble in front of Jyotirmayee's house for one glance at Kumar. People thronged the streets of Jaidebpur, singing praises of Kumar and the Bhawal family.

Chapter 51
Bibhabati Reappeals

Dr Ashutosh Dasgupta couldn't be at the court because of his professional commitments. But his mind was restless throughout the day. His worst fears came true when he heard about the judgment.

Ashutosh hurried indoors and quickly closed the doors and windows of his house, scared of an unruly mob. He could feel his heart racing as he wiped the sweat from his forehead. A servant came to his room with a jug of water when the doctor had a blurry vision before tripping on the floor. As the servant rushed to hold him, the doctor passed out.

Dr Ashutosh wasn't the only one impacted by the shock of the court proceedings. Bibhabati sat like a rock behind closed doors. Satyen's wife and son knocked on the door, asking her to respond, but she was oblivious to their pleadings as anger, frustration, and shock manifested in tears that refused to stop. Where was Satyen, she worried. Bibhabati wondered if the court had ordered her to return to the Raj Bari and live with the man now established as Ramendra Narayan. She could feel the chills as she imagined her marital family forcing her to return to her old room. Bibhabati hid her face inside the pillow to stifle her sobs.

Satyen left the moment people started cheering for Kumar outside the court. He feared for his life. He didn't have the time or desire to look at the face of the plaintiff, though he noticed the disbelief plastered across the defence counsel's face.

He went home and locked himself in his study. Annoyance, frustration, and helplessness made him pace back and forth inside the room, punching random items. He used the choicest expletives in his mind for Basu, the plaintiff, Kumar's sisters, and lawyers. His diary had validated several claims; Satyen bit his lower lip. There were so many lapses, despite his proactive endeavours to hand over the evidences to the authorities and maintain records of events. But he wasn't the kind to lose hope or money.

"I'm the invincible Satya Banerjee. Today's temporary setback will never break my spirit. The game isn't over until I get the desired outcome." He racked his brain to find the next alternative in fighting the plaintiff.

Bibhabati felt more concerned about her brother than what could happen to her after the judgment. In his study, Satyen sat etching the next steps in his new plan. Of course, he remembered Bibhabati as and when she fit into his course of action. But her anxiety wasn't his priority.

While Bibhabati and Satyen grappled with the consequences of the court case, it baffled the authorities equally. The case involved the Court of Wards, and they expected the judgment in their favour. They desperately needed to win, not just to keep control but also to meet their financial requirements. The court case had drained them of a large sum, and multiple payments were still pending. The commissioner of Dhaka released a notice stating the plaintiff's one-third share would be in the custody of the Court of Wards until the completion of legal procedures for the handover. It allowed them to collect rent.

When the plaintiff didn't receive his share after a month, he lost his patience. He spoke to Arabinda Guha.

"What is taking them so long to finish the formalities when the court passed the judgment a month ago? Don't they realise it's their responsibility to hand over my one-third share?"

Even Guha was confused about the scenario. He decided not to delay it further and wrote to the commissioner, enquiring about the status. He reminded them of the court's orders and requested speeding up the process of the release of the one-third share that belonged to Ramendra Narayan.

The Government was in no mood to entertain the court's judgment. Instead, they appealed against Basu's judgment in the Calcutta High Court. Bibhabati Devi, Ananda Kumari, and her adopted son Ram Narayan Roy challenged the verdict through the manager of the Bhawal estate. They filed a case against Ramendra Narayan Roy and Sarajubala Devi since the latter had supported the plaintiff. Though the property now belonged to the plaintiff as per Basu's judgment, the expenses of the new case were to be borne from his one-third share since it was still in the Court of Ward's custody. The arrangement sounded ridiculous.

The re-appeal didn't stop the plaintiff from visiting Jaidebpur and his estate in April 1938. It was 1909 when Kumar last ruled over Jaidebpur in the capacity of Ramendra Narayan Roy, Mejo Kumar of Bhawal estate. Though he had visited Jaidebpur as the sadhu before the authorities barred him from entering the town, it wasn't in his official capacity as the Bhawal prince. When the subjects met their prince, they felt overwhelmed with emotion.

While the prince was getting a warm welcome, people's attitude towards Bibhabati underwent a massive transformation. From gaining sympathy as the widow of the late Mejo Kumar earlier, she was now the woman who betrayed her husband and refused to acknowledge him. They loathed the brother-sister duo responsible for wreaking havoc on the estate. For years, Bibhabati became an example to young girls about the monstrous wife they shouldn't become.

While Bibhabati and Ramendra geared up for another legal tussle, Justice Basu chose to shift away from his legal profession. During the Bhawal case, which was already famous for being one of the longest-running cases in history, Basu had fathomed the consequences of his verdict. When he had finished typing out his analysis and preparing the judgment, he sought his wife. "I have decided to let the Bhawal case be my last."

His wife had known Basu for a long enough time to understand the decision hadn't been easy for her husband. Basu was a morally upright man. If he had acted as per the desires of those in power, they wouldn't still be living in a rented house. But she respected his choices.

On the day he announced the verdict, Basu knew he had rubbed the influential the wrong way. Continuing his work in the legal domain would become challenging since things would get complicated because of the same people. They wouldn't forget his stance on the Government's involvement in a case between two private parties. Neither would they let Basu forget his refusal to budge from his stand. He returned home and announced his decision to retire, despite having many years of service left. It was the most respectful way to quit a profession that had earned him a name and reputation.

At night, his wife asked him what Basu thought would happen to the plaintiff after he gained back possession of his share of the property.

Basu smiled at his wife. "Do you think the authorities will let go of control so easily? That estate earns them high revenue. Forgoing one-third share means losing out on rent and revenue till Ramendra Narayan is alive. They can't afford it. Nor do they have any intent to do so. I feel they'll re-appeal against my verdict at the High Court. Chaudhuri will argue I didn't analyse the case in depth and held a biased perspective toward the plaintiff because of public sympathy. They'll try to prove my judgment is flawed so that the jury takes a fresh look at the evidence. I haven't seen a more scheming man than Satyen Banerjee in my career. Irrespective of Bibhabati Devi's wishes, he'll keep the gun on her shoulder and make her agree to a re-appeal. He has much to lose if Bibhabati's finances dry up."

"What kind of man plays with his sister's future?"

"A shrewd and cunning man, whose only motive is to secure his future and enjoy the fruits of someone else's labour with no shame."

"That sounds disgusting." Mrs Basu always wanted to know what her husband felt about Bibhabati's role in Kumar's death, and whether he considered Mejo Rani loyal or adulterous. But years of marriage had taught Mrs Basu how her husband wouldn't appreciate the intrusion.

A year later, Basu was relieved from his position after finishing the formalities. By then, Bibhabati, represented by the manager of the Bhawal estate, had re-appealed against Basu's judgment just like he predicted. Two years later, Basu moved away from the city to take up new responsibilities as the manager of the Panchet estate. He wanted to be far away from the drama unfolding in the Calcutta High Court related to the Bhawal case.

On the way to their new destination, Mrs Basu asked, "Why do you think the subjects prefer a prince to the authorities? Is it because people feel he is one of their own?"

Basu mused over the topic. It wasn't the first time he thought about the mass public sympathy toward the plaintiff.

Basu smiled, "Because they felt the authorities who oppress the subjects in the name of law and order had wronged him. But the same law became flexible when it came to the white people. Though Kumar wasn't involved in the day-to-day functioning of the estate, he was a warm and benevolent man. Many people received help from him. I heard he even went against the authorities for his subjects."

Mrs Basu nodded.

Chapter 52

The Case Begins at High Court

As Basu began a new inning in his career, little did he know that his landmark judgment on the Bhawal case would earn him a permanent place in the history of the country's legal system. At times, Mrs Basu sat in the compound of her new residence and gazed at the surroundings. Some days, she thought of Bibhabati and the women in the Bhawal Raj family.

Bibhabati and her sister Malina knew how to read and write, and grew up in a progressive household, since their mother, Phulkumari, emphasised the importance of education. In comparison, the women of the Raj Parivar received primary education at their father's behest. After Raja Rajendra Narayan's death, Rani Bilasmani refused to educate her daughters further. The Rani believed a knowledgeable woman was a misfit and created unnecessary problems for her family. It didn't matter whether the girls wanted to study further. No one sought their opinion. Like most royal households, sarees, jewellery, and ways to keep their husbands happy, engulfed their existence. How Bibhabati adjusted to such a change of ambiance was a curious topic for Mrs Basu.

Ramendra Narayan had no peace despite his win at the lower court. Until now, he was trying to convince the authorities to hand over his share to him. But now, Bibhabati, supported by the Board of Revenue, had dragged him to the High Court. Yet, he wasn't willing to give up without a fight. Jyotirmayee didn't share the same enthusiasm but Sarajubala stepped in to support the plaintiff, morally and financially.

Satyen heard about Sarajubala backing the plaintiff through his lawyer friend Phani Bhushan Chakrabarti, who was also a part of Chaudhuri's team at the High Court. Satyen smirked. "Why am I not surprised? Boro Rani was always unusually fond of her second brother-in-law. What kind of understanding do they have? Ask the cooks and servants, and they'll divulge the scandalous secret."

P.B. Chakrabarti responded, "Are you hinting at a special bonding here?"

"You, my friend, pick up cues quite fast. I don't need to state the implied association. People aren't fools." Satyen ran his fingers through his head.

When Chatterjee and Guha discussed the case over the last few months, Guha mentioned a statement about Satyen Banerjee. "I can't get over Justice Basu's comment on Satyen Banerjee's character. 'Scheming man' is the term he used for that leech, and I couldn't agree more. What kind of a human manipulates the status, wealth, and power he gets to enjoy because of his association with a prince and then returns the favour by plotting his death?"

"Leech is the apt term for a man like him. Imagine living off your sister's husband's money and then murdering him! No remorse, no guilt. He spent the rest of his life living off his sister's income and ensured he had full control over her share by coaxing her to live with him. The way he ran to Darjeeling on hearing about the sadhu makes me confident about his hand in Kumar's death."

"At times, I feel Bibhabati was equally involved in her husband's death. It's impossible that she didn't know about her brother's ploy. If she wanted to save her husband, she wouldn't have taken him to Darjeeling. Worse still, she could've alerted someone in the family or anyone close to her. Instead, she witnessed everything in silence or actively helped Satyen to accomplish his plan."

Chatterjee had stared at Guha. It's not that the thought hadn't crossed his mind, but he still found it hard to believe a woman could be so despicable.

"Throughout the proceedings, I wondered why a woman wouldn't want her husband to return alive. The only plausible reason could be because she wanted him dead." Arabinda continued. "It's ridiculous how she cried foul about her husband's character. How's it possible for her or her family not to be aware of his mistresses or his wild lifestyle before marriage? Yet, she married him for luxury, power, and status. When she secured her financial standing, she didn't even think twice before becoming a part of the conspiracy to kill her husband. Now, she stands in court, claiming they wronged her. Outrageous!"

Chatterjee didn't comment. Guha took a deep breath and said, "I hope she and her brother pay for their sins and never get a penny from the estate."

A few weeks later, the Chief Justice of the Calcutta High Court asked for detailed evidence related to the case, including photographs and reports collected to date. They printed the evidence in multiple volumes. The jury comprised three esteemed men. First was a barrister from London, Sir Leonard or L.W.J. Costello. The second member was an ICS officer with no legal background, R.F. Lodge. The third was an exceptional lawyer, who was locally educated and built his career in the country, Charu Chandra or C.C. Biswas.

Chatterjee and Chaudhuri led their respective counsels, though their teams now included many prominent bar members. Two years after filing the re-appeal, the hearing began on 14th November 1938. Chaudhuri took the line of argument as predicted by Basu about how flawed Basu's judgment was because of his erroneous methods of deduction.

The validation of identity didn't answer pertinent questions related to the Darjeeling incident. Since Basu felt convinced about the plaintiff's identity as Kumar, he accepted the plaintiff's version of events in Darjeeling. Chaudhuri highlighted the records which showed no rainfall on the 8th and 9th of May, thus ruling out the possibility of people seeking shelter from storms. However, Basu had accepted the same.

Next, the defence presented multiple witnesses to prove the time of Kumar's death was midnight. Bibhabati's evidence was crucial in establishing the fact. However, Basu had ignored the obvious and stuck to the timing of death between 7 to 8 in the evening due to his reverse deduction that the plaintiff was Kumar, whose body wasn't thus cremated.

Even his story of getting saved by the Naga sanyasis sounded more like the work of a creative mind, with very little connection to reality. The similarity in physical traits proved nothing, as per Chaudhuri. Tenants and close relatives, including Jyotirmayee, identified the plaintiff. It was direct evidence, and she would benefit by establishing the imposter as Mejo Kumar. But Chaudhuri doubted the credibility of the tenants' statements. The plaintiff's ignorance and inability to respond to topics like sports, Kumar's domain of expertise, was baffling.

Chatterjee had expected the same line of debate from Chaudhuri. Basu had upset the defendant's plans by negating most of their statements. When Chatterjee rose to defend Basu's judgment, he stated, "If the allegations of the defence counsel were true, then Judge Basu wouldn't have spent so much time analysing the evidence before concluding. He would have immediately decided in my client's favour instead."

Chatterjee justified how Basu had arrived at the point of identity not only by depending on the evidence of one witness (Jyotirmayee Devi), or the aspect of identification parameters only. He explained the holistic approach in Basu's understanding of the issue. He spoke about the plaintiff's speech impediment due to the cyst under his tongue. Specific types of poison led to such cysts. It gave way to a strong suspicion that someone had poisoned Ramendra Narayan.

Satyen's diary was a bone of contention for both parties. Chaudhuri claimed there were missing pages from the diary, which the plaintiff and his team had deliberately hidden. Chatterjee felt amused that the defence counsel was complaining about the missing pages. Chaudhuri hadn't even bothered to present the diary to the court.

Chatterjee argued that even the Darjeeling events couldn't negate the parameters that determined the plaintiff's identity. The judge had arrived at the timing of death through elimination and not just based on probability. Chatterjee concluded his statement with a request to dismiss the appeal and uphold Basu's detailed judgment.

Chapter 53
Justice Biswas' Analysis

As the hearing continued, Justice Biswas, Justice Lodge, and Justice Costello discussed the proceedings among themselves on individual aspects highlighted by the lawyers from both sides. Though Biswas and Lodge shared their honest opinion, Costello rarely disclosed his stand about the plaintiff and defendants.

In August 1939, when the hearing concluded, Justice Costello applied for two weeks' leave in addition to the vacation duration of the court. He informed the same to Justice Biswas and Justice Lodge. "I intend to visit England and hope to return by November. We can announce the judgment soon after. Until then, let's individually analyse the case and write our opinion."

Biswas fidgeted. "But we need to discuss our perspectives before concluding."

Justice Costello agreed. "Let's do it immediately after I return to Calcutta." Having assured his colleagues, he sailed towards his destination.

Unfortunately, things didn't stay as hopeful and cheerful. World War II broke out as Costello travelled back to his country. A year passed, and the restlessness grew among the plaintiff's and defendants' sides. Things turned for the worse as the battle became violent; chances of Costello's return looked dim.

Back in his country, Costello had anticipated the grim situation based on the devastating circumstances over the past few months.

Lodge and Biswas had sent him their judgment on the case. He decided to send them his written judgment in a sealed envelope. Justice Biswas and Justice Lodge met to decide on the course of action.

"I suggest we wait no longer. The current situation deems it impossible for Justice Costello to make the journey back to Calcutta. Let's pronounce our judgments and read his verdict in court," Justice Lodge suggested. After a detailed discussion and on certain conditions, Biswas gave in.

Biswas was to announce his judgment on 20th August 1940. He appraised the gathering about Costello's position and the sealed packet. Biswas voiced his perspective on the case first. He assured the assembled crowd about reading Costello's verdict at the end. Biswas was cautious enough to mention the rule which permitted a High Court judge to read out the signed judgment of another High Court judge, if the latter was absent from the court because of unavoidable circumstances. As a final precautionary measure, he also clarified that neither Justice Lodge nor he had any idea about Costello's decision until then.

Biswas followed Basu's methodology of writing a long and detailed judgment. When Justice Biswas analysed the statements from both sides and Basu's verdict, he felt a connection with his fellow countryman from the same profession. Chaudhuri and the Court of Wards were hell-bent on proving how Basu had formed a biased opinion. That's why Basu dismissed most of the defendant's theories and witnesses' statements. However, Biswas thought otherwise.

According to Biswas, the defendants failed to provide conclusive evidence in multiple instances. He stated the example of the attempted cremation in Darjeeling. If they took out the body for cremation in the evening and arranged a second funeral procession in the morning, it wouldn't be possible without a replacement body. Biswas focussed on how no one claimed to have found Kumar's body and brought it back. The plaintiff's responsibility was to prove the attempted evening cremation. It justified the remaining sequence of events. However, the defendants needed to establish the morning cremation of Kumar's body. The defendants had massively failed to prove it was Mejo Kumar's body.

Biswas altered the analysis sequence after Chaudhuri claimed Basu's judgment had fallen into a pattern once he believed the sadhu was Ramendra Narayan Roy. He analysed Jyotirmayee Devi's role since the defendants were keen on a conspiracy theory, which she supposedly hatched to establish an imposter as her second brother.

Biswas stated, "The defendants failed to prove any bad blood between Jyotirmayee and Bibhabati for the former to plant a stranger as the latter's dead husband reincarnated. Until the plaintiff's appearance, the women shared a relationship of mutual admiration and respect. Jyotirmayee or her son had nothing to gain if the plaintiff was identified as Mejo Kumar since the claim to property would eventually pass on to the adopted heir of Ananda Kumari."

It was also noteworthy how she met the sadhu only after numerous people saw and interacted with him at Buckland Bund. She verified the physical and mental parameters before validating his identity. The plaintiff was more than willing to be questioned by various people to establish his claims. He considered it ridiculous how Chaudhuri insisted on the spontaneity of recognition, while the methodology followed in establishing the plaintiff's identity was far more elaborate and scientific.

Bibhabati Devi was an important witness who refused to recognise the plaintiff. However, Biswas believed her stubbornness stemmed from her belief that Ramendra had died, and they had cremated him in Darjeeling.

Biswas observed Satyen Banerjee's urgency to prove Ramendra Narayan's death. It didn't escape his notice how Satyen collected evidence, visited Darjeeling, and supplied official documents to the Board of Revenue immediately after the sadhu declared his identity.

Bibhabati's brother got Calvert's death certificate from the life insurance company and accompanied Sasanka Ghose to Darjeeling to meet Lees before 15th May.

Satyen's influence tainted Lindsay's perspective. Biswas believed, Lindsay, even before he met the man, had labelled him an imposter in his mind. Lindsay wasn't sure of the many statements he recorded. Even for the imposter notice, he seemed to have based his viewpoint on the death certificate and the evidence of no rainfall. Strangely, the plaintiff didn't even speak about rain on the night of cremation until then. It was evident Satyen Banerjee had voluntarily fed information to the authorities.

Biswas found the authorities' unwillingness to share official documents with the court offensive. Even the diary would have stayed in oblivion if the plaintiff's counsel hadn't retrieved it. Biswas stayed up many nights wondering about the need to record Mejo Kumar's treatment sequence in the diary. He believed it was the human psyche to record such things when there was an intent to twist facts.

Biswas felt intrigued by the purpose of the condolence letter Dr Calvert sent to Boro Kumar. Mukunda Guin had sought it. It seemed more like an avenue to give a clean chit to those who accompanied Ramendra to Darjeeling about their roles in Kumar's treatment. It was also a ploy to stop further investigation into his death. Mukunda's employment with the police after Kumar's death made Biswas suspicious of the secretary's intentions.

Dr Ashutosh was labelled an unreliable witness after he changed his statement multiple times. He had introduced arsenic in the prescription and tried to shift the responsibility on the late Dr Nibaran Sen. Chaudhuri claimed the plaintiff wanted to justify his speech impediment. So, the plaintiff's counsel brought up the aspect of arsenic poisoning, though there was no substantial evidence. But Biswas didn't find the theory convincing.

Calvert's statements about biliary colic and blood in stools didn't match because the symptoms and prescriptions didn't tally. Since Satyen followed the same line of justification, Biswas thought one was lying or influencing the other's opinion. However, Calvert's letter to Lindsay about his inability to recollect his presence at the time of Kumar's death irked Biswas since Calvert had stated otherwise in his official statement. None of the telegrams except the one sent on the morning of Kumar's death mentioned the criticality of his sickness. Thus, the illness that Kumar suffered from and was treated for, remained a mystery.

Chapter 54
Justice Biswas' Judgment

Chatterjee had once mentioned the misuse of power by the official authorities to Arabinda Guha. "Dr Crawford, the commissioner of Darjeeling, doesn't remember who asked for Kumar's death certificate, or under what circumstances he wrote it. Dr Calvert mentions biliary colic as the reason for death in the insurance claim. No one questioned him about why his treatment didn't seem aligned with the sickness. I'm glad it didn't escape Judge Basu's observation."

Biswas was vocal about how the officials randomly chose who to support and whom to dismiss from a sense of superiority.

While Justice Biswas delivered his judgment, the analysis of the tampered register of the Darjeeling Municipality rainfall arrived from Scotland Yard. It suggested that the number 6 was erased and replaced by 13, but it could've been 8 or 9. They tampered with the date to such an extent that a hole formed in the paper. Biswas was flabbergasted by how the defendants hadn't presented the record in court. The plaintiff had submitted the evidence, though it wasn't in his favour. It led to the same question of why the defendants were so keen on hiding records and evidence.

Biswas analysed Dr Pran Krishna Acharya's statement. The Brahmo Dr Acharya mentioned the body covered from the face to the foot. Dr Acharya's presence was supposed to act as evidence about the existence of Kumar's body in the morning. But Dr Acharya's stand eventually turned out to be a case against the defendants after he insisted on seeing the body.

The nurse, Jagat Mohini, was no saint either. Biswas noted her desperate attempts to prove herself as a Brahmin widow. She claimed to see the body taken out for a funeral in the morning. But most evidence quashed her statements; she was deliberately misleading the court.

Even Bebul Banerjee's statements of carrying the body to the new cremation ground and meeting Bibhabati at Step Aside were fabricated lies woven by the defendants to justify their theory. Since Satyen hadn't mentioned Bebul attending the funeral in his diary, it raised questions about the latter's presence. Later, Chatterjee proved Bebul wasn't even present in Darjeeling that day, but was attending a funeral elsewhere. Gita Devi had also given contrasting statements, thus making the court believe there was a discrepancy in what she saw and spoke.

Biswas pointed out a few observations concerning the dead body. "Why would Birendra Banerjee do the cremation instead of the Second Rani, who had undisputed rights to perform the rites? Even Satyen Banerjee stepping in for the funeral rituals would make more sense. Was it a deliberate attempt to keep the Rani away from the cremation? There was a body, and there's no doubt about it. But they covered it from head to toe. The funeral procession's grandeur makes it evident that the intent was to ensure people remember a funeral was taking place. But Satyen's diary entries gave away the rushed cremation details where they barely adhered to any Hindu rituals. They didn't bathe the body nor rub ghee into it. They didn't put new clothes on it or offer *pindas* before *mukhagni*."

Biswas found no reason to doubt Darshandas and his rescue story. He believed the group of sanyasis had saved Kumar, thus quashing the cremation of Kumar's dead body theory. The plaintiff's memory loss justified his nomadic life of traveling with the sanyasis. However, he reserved his doubts about the man who turned up as Dharamdas.

More often than not, Biswas fumed at Chaudhuri's mockery of Basu as the judge of a mofussil court. His foreign degree made Chaudhuri belittle another countryman from the same profession and ridicule him for his choice of words and Bengali accent. Chaudhuri faced Biswas' wrath on the former's ridiculous stand of not cross-examining the plaintiff based on his belief the sadhu was tutored and was an imposter.

While preparing his judgment, Biswas couldn't help the causticity in his thoughts about the English-speaking barrister leading the lifestyle of a Sahib. Chaudhuri's bias and high opinion of himself made him overlook the thorough procedures and methodology followed by Basu in judging the case.

When Biswas concluded his perspective, he boldly voiced his concurrence with Basu's judgment. He expressed his admiration for the trial judge's error-free analysis in such a short duration. While Chatterjee glowed, Chaudhuri's face darkened as Biswas pronounced his verdict.

Later in the evening, Chaudhuri sat with his high-society friends in the club.

"What else do you expect from such low lives? Bloody desis! Uncouth fellow!" Chaudhuri gulped down his drink in one go.

He was upset at Biswas's judgment. The judge's audacity to admonish him stunned Chaudhuri.

"But we needn't worry. I have full faith in Lodge. Our man knows Lindsay well. Lodge has done his research on the fraud sadhu and his modus operandi. I'm sure he won't let the cheater get away so easily."

Chapter 55
Justice Lodge's Opinion

When it was Lodge's turn to state his perspective, he couldn't help but think of the multiple sessions over drinks with his social circle discussing the Bhawal sanyasi case. He knew Lindsay, and held a tinge of admiration for the man in his heart.

Lodge mentioned the unnecessary crowding at the court premises by the plaintiff's supporters, which led to unusual tension in the ambiance of the court proceedings during the initial trial. He hinted at Basu feeling the pressure due to the highly emotionally charged state of the crowd. From the beginning, Lodge seemed to side with the defendants and their witnesses, who he felt were subjected to humiliation and character slandering by the plaintiff's supporters. He also extended his support to the Court of Wards, for punishing those employees and tenants, who sided with a man labelled as an imposter by the authorities. Lodge observed Basu treated witnesses differently, with the trial judge bestowing compassion and trust on the plaintiff's side.

Lodge defended Lindsay's record of the statement during his first interaction with the plaintiff. He also supported Dr Calvert and dismissed all claims of distortion of the truth or the twisted intent of his condolence letter. He found the theory of arsenic poisoning ridiculous. Lodge gave Dr Ashutosh Dasgupta a clean chit on prescribing arsenic since it was within permissible limits. The word 'inexperienced' summed up Dr Dasgupta's mistakes, if any.

Lodge stated he couldn't spot any evidence of intent to murder. A wide smile spread across Chaudhuri's face. He had been waiting for this statement. It absolved his client and her brother of the deadly crime. Lodge highlighted that inconsistency in Basu's thought process made the trial court judge doubt Dr Calvert's treatment and prescriptions for biliary colic. There was no conclusive evidence of any foul play, thus clearing Dr Calvert and Dr Dasgupta of all allegations.

Dr Calvert noted the timing of Kumar's death as 11:45 p.m. on the death certificate. So, the word evening or its casual mention anywhere else was attributed to an involuntary oversight. Chaudhuri beamed, while Chatterjee bore a sunken look. Lodge dismantled the cremation theory at 8 p.m. by calling the witness unreliable.

Dr B.B. Sarkar's presence, which Satyen noted in his diary, was insignificant. The plaintiff, possessing the journal, magnified the incident to twist the doctor's visit to his benefit, and prove that Dr Calvert and Dr Sen had already left by then. Basu upheld many witnesses' statements while concluding. But to Lodge, they were just silly people.

Lodge opined, "If a telegram announcing Kumar's death had reached in the night, the telegram office staff wouldn't have held it back under the pretext of not wanting to convey the bad news to the family at night."

The professor's group, especially Prof Maitra, were portrayed as upright and honest people. They wouldn't lie about the news of Kumar's death received at the sanitorium in the evening. In an unexpected move, Lodge agreed with the character analysis of this group and blamed the erroneous version of the events on the professor's memory playing tricks on him. The rest of the group, influenced by Maitra, ensured their statements aligned with his. Basu had argued the professors had no interest in the case or in Kumar's property. Thus, there was no reason to doubt the genuineness of their testimonies. Lodge grabbed the 'no interest' bit and stated how it allowed the group to be liberal in stating supposed facts.

Like most things, Lodge considered the theory of the evening cremation silly. Only stupid people would go to the old cremation ground when the new place was ready and nearby. Besides, the statements about people seeking shelter in nearby huts without its residents' knowledge and returning to find a missing body, sounded improbable to him. The rainfall records proved the lack of rains or storms on the designated dates, thus ruling out all stories of running from natural calamities.

He found it ridiculous that a substitute body was arranged overnight and cremated the next morning. Also, Ramendra had spent some days in Darjeeling, where people knew who he was and how he looked. It was risky to even replace his body with someone else's. Even if there was a remote possibility of a duplicate body, there was no chance of bringing it back at Step Aside instead of cremating it. Also, the family would've never allowed strangers to join the procession of a substitute body.

While Basu considered Darshandas a reliable witness whose story of recusing Ramendra Narayan stayed consistent even under pressure, Lodge labelled it an effect of tutored lies. To him, the plaintiff's rescue story had two different versions, as stated to Lindsay and in court. There was no evidence of a cave, and he thought if the sanyasis needed shelter, they would have gone to the new cremation ground with a shed. Darshandas' statement of not trying to figure out any details about the man he rescued and not meeting the plaintiff, despite visiting Dhaka as Gopaldas, sounded like fiction. Lodge rejected his testimony.

The judge spoke in favour of the morning cremation, but refused to believe what Dr Acharya stated because the doctor's answers had glaring contradictions in what he told Lindsay and later spoke in the court. While he favoured the witnesses from the defendant's side and treated them with exceptions, Lodge's attitude towards witnesses from the plaintiff's side seemed orthodox. The contradictions in the statements of the defendant's witness, like Bebul Banerjee, were acceptable, but any disparity in the testimonies from the plaintiff's side was immediately rejected.

Lodge thought it natural that the defendants took out Kumar's funeral procession with pomp and glory because the Bhawal prince deserved the grandeur. Irrespective of some deviations that might have occurred, Lodge believed they had fulfilled all the necessary rituals.

For Gita Devi and her statement related to how Bibhabati had removed the jewellery before the family returned from the funeral, Lodge felt the customs varied based on how an individual behaved under certain circumstances. The grief-stricken Bibhabati might not be aware of what she was doing in the absence of an elderly female relative to guide her.

Lodge mentioned the plaintiff's claim of memory loss was a convenient way to avoid probing about the decade gap in his return to Jaidebpur. Why didn't he try to get in touch with his family? He waited for someone to identify him, which is what Jyotirmayee did, to convince the subjects about the return of their Mejo Kumar. Besides, the plaintiff was an unreliable witness, according to Lodge. He had given different statements in the memorial, to Lindsay, and in the witness box.

Chapter 56
Justice Lodge's Verdict

With every passing sentence from Lodge, Chatterjee's face became grimmer. Lodge's judgment sided with every point the defendant's counsel had contested in Basu's verdict. Lodge gave a clean chit to those whose actions Basu had questioned. Yet, Chatterjee kept the faith Lodge wouldn't favour Satyen. Unfortunately, his hopes were only short-lived as Lodge defended Satyen Babu's decision to move Bibhabati away from Jaidebpur.

Lodge stated, "The elder and younger princes of Bhawal were drunkards with no moral character. Satyen Babu smelt a conspiracy against his sister once she returned a widow. A woman, without her husband and any successor, was helpless and powerless in the royal family. So, it isn't surprising Satyen Babu decided to take charge, secure her future financially, and move her to Calcutta."

While it was clear that he handled her money, Lodge thought it was imperative. As a woman, Bibhabati lacked the skills to deal with the matters of the world. Besides, no one could prove that Satyen forced Bibhabati to shift or he took her wealth without her consent. So, why did the opposition make a villain of a man who was only trying to protect his sister?

His diary entries were mundane reactions of a man whose sister wasn't treated well after Ramendra's death by her marital family. When Satyen rushed to the Board of Revenue secretary to supply them with evidence, it showed his responsible mindset in trying to keep the cheater at bay.

Lodge believed the rumours of Ramendra Narayan being alive had been floating around for a long time. It was easy to convince the natives about his miraculous return. Yet, when the plaintiff submitted his memorial to the Board of Revenue, he gave a version different from what he stated in court later. Lodge thought the plaintiff's claim that he didn't know what his lawyers had written in the memorial was ridiculous.

In Lodge's eyes, Jyotirmayee Devi was a conspirator who led people to believe the sadhu was her brother. Jyotirmayee didn't spontaneously recognise the plaintiff as Ramendra when she met him. The same logic applied to other relatives and witnesses who couldn't identify him instantly, but had to seek evidence to validate it. Lodge believed recognition needed spontaneity, while the trial judge and Biswas favoured evidence supporting the identity.

As per Lodge, none knew what arrangements Jyotirmayee might have entered into with the plaintiff. Lodge felt she had assembled the naïve natives so the plaintiff could declare his identity in front of them. The sadhu claimed he had renounced worldly pleasures and would utilise his share of wealth for the benefit of the local people. So, people paid rent to the imposter instead of giving it to the Board of Revenue. Lodge's perspective felt biased. He conveniently stereotyped Bengali women through his opinion on Jyotirmayee's reaction to meeting the sadhu.

While the plaintiff performed Satyabhama Devi's last rites with no objection from the family, Lodge thought Jyotirmayee had no option but to let him continue. Stopping him would lead to suspicion about the sadhu's identity. Lodge labelled Jyotirmayee untruthful, whose opinion couldn't be trusted.

Chatterjee found Lodge's statement contradictory. He insisted on spontaneity in recognition as a primary parameter for identity. Thus, he didn't consider Jyotirmayee or those witnesses' testimonies valuable who had validated the plaintiff's identity through verification tests. However, multiple witnesses like Jogen Banerjee, identified the sadhu as

Ramendra Narayan on their first sighting. Some of them retracted their statements and declared the sadhu fake. If spontaneity was the criteria, their initial recognition should've held good. Chatterjee was shocked to hear Lodge state how they must have realised their mistake after analysing why the sadhu couldn't be their Mejo Kumar.

For the witnesses from the plaintiff's side, Lodge's approach was to read extracts of their statements, and opine the witness met the plaintiff under the assumption the latter was the Second Kumar. Thus, the witness' opinion was unconvincing. It was strange how he dismissed most of the plaintiff's relatives' testimonies because they sided with the sadhu. The judge rejected most statements of the plaintiff's friends and acquaintances due to a lack of spontaneity in the first recognition.

N.K. Nag's testimony was crucial for Basu to conclude the plaintiff's identity. But for Lodge, it was an exaggerated testimony where the secret story the friends shared, was conveyed to the plaintiff by someone else. Lodge expected the plaintiff's friends to recognise the man the moment they saw him. The same didn't apply to the defendant's witnesses. There was no conclusive proof the plaintiff wasn't Ramendra Narayan Roy through their testimonies. But Lodge believed it was the plaintiff's responsibility to prove who he claimed to be. The onus didn't lie with the defendants to discard the claim.

He rejected Ram Singh Subba's testimony about seeing the dead body and labelled him a liar. The body was neither in the room mentioned by the munshi, nor was Dr Sarkar's presence an indication of the absence of Dr Calvert and Dr Sen.

For the physical and mental similarities in traits between the plaintiff and Ramendra Narayan, Lodge thought the period through which the witnesses saw the plaintiff played a crucial role. The witnesses remembered the look of a man from decades ago. Since they kept seeing the plaintiff for a while, their memory of what Ramendra Narayan looked like was replaced by how the plaintiff looked. But those who saw him under the assumption he wasn't Ramendra continued highlighting the points of no resemblance.

For Lodge, the plaintiff's eyes were brown compared to Jyotirmayee's and Ramendra's hazel eyes. His nose differed from that of Ramendra. His scars near the ankle were circumstantial. Alternatively, the plaintiff could've created them to establish himself as Mejo Kumar. Minimum marks on the plaintiff's body due to syphilis as compared to Kumar, who was in the tertiary stage of the disease, proved the former was a different man. Only the parameter of the scaly foot matched, but the differences outweighed one similarity.

The plaintiff's inability to speak Bengali without a Hindi accent even after a decade, his ability to state the numbers while the prince didn't know how to count, and his ignorance of the technical terms related to shooting – a sport in which Kumar excelled, went against him. Lodge couldn't spot any similarities in the signatures of the plaintiff and Kumar. However, he also mentioned the little resemblance observed by the experts was because his circle had tutored the man.

In Lodge's opinion, the man who appeared in the court as Dharamdas was genuine, though his testimony wasn't quite reliable. Based on the evidence, he felt the plaintiff was a Punjabi man, though no one had proved that he was Mal Singh of Aujla. With that, he recommended the dismissal of the judgment of the trial court.

Lodge made it clear the plaintiff wasn't Ramendra Narayan Roy, but an imposter supported by Jyotirmayee Devi and other family members.

A tie happened between Biswas and Lodge's judgment in Costello's physical absence. Only the third judge's verdict could decide the outcome.

Chapter 57
Justice Costello's Judgment

Chatterjee sounded slightly concerned when he met the plaintiff next. Considering the third judge wasn't an Indian, he wondered if they had a chance to win. Besides, Costello wasn't coming back and didn't possess the bulk of evidence analysed by Biswas and Lodge.

The plaintiff observed the creases on Chatterjee's forehead as the conversation began. "I didn't expect Justice Lodge to be so bluntly biased. He mentioned almost all our witnesses as unreliable. He labelled Jyotirmayee Devi as the chief conspirator. There was no rationality in his reasons for rejecting Basu's judgment."

"But the other judge spoke in our favour," the plaintiff stated. He usually let the team of lawyers deal with the situation, but Jyotirmayee was in a fragile state of health. Neither was he getting any younger. There was an urgency to reach a decision.

"The score's 1-1 now. Only Justice Costello's decision can change the situation."

"Is it allowed? He's not even here. So, how will he understand and analyse such vital information?"

"As Justice Biswas mentioned, a new rule allows Biswas and Lodge to read Costello's letter containing his confidential verdict. Until now, Lodge and Biswas sent their opinion to Costello through letters. Ideally, the trio should have got an opportunity to discuss the pointers and decisions before pronouncing them to the world. But now it doesn't look feasible."

"And how will that affect us?"

"Well, if Costello's verdict is in our favour, we win. But if it goes in the defendant's favour, they win. There's a finality in the verdict once they read his judgment."

"Is there nothing we can do?" The plaintiff looked at Chatterjee with helpless eyes.

"If Biswas and Lodge agree not to read out Costello's opinion due to distance, their verdict will stay, making the final decision inconclusive. In that case, the trial judge's decision stays valid, and the judgment is in our favour."

"For that, both the esteemed judges need to agree on dismissing the letter by Costello. If they have such diametrically opposite opinions, do you think they will see eye to eye on this aspect?"

Chatterjee shrugged. It was his only hope, though he couldn't shake away the discomfort in his heart.

Chaudhuri, delighted with Lodge's decision, didn't nurture any negative thoughts about the outcome.

"Don't worry! Why would Justice Costello, sitting thousands of miles away, give his judgment in favour of an illiterate imposter?" he assured Satyen Banerjee.

"I told you Lodge is a sensible man. I'm glad he took an objective view of reality instead of getting swayed away by emotions. Costello will not disappoint us, either. The only thing I'm wary about is Biswas trying to convince Lodge about not reading Costello's verdict in court." Earlier, Chaudhuri had explained to Satyen why Costello's absence could become important in the final verdict.

"We can't lose again. Everyone knows the plaintiff is an imposter, and his sister is the brain behind this trap. Bibhabati and I are suffering from mental trauma and heavy financial losses."

"Do you think you are the only ones who have incurred financial burden? So much is at stake and can only be brought back to normal when the Court of Wards retains control of the Bhawal estate." Chaudhuri didn't mention the pending fees of many lawyers.

On the following day, as predicted, Biswas tried to convince Lodge not to consider Costello's judgment. But Lodge disagreed. He believed Costello had enough resources and opportunity to understand the case. If Costello had sent a letter with his judgment, it meant he was equipped with adequate information to conclude. The judges couldn't judge his verdict or reject it. Irrespective of the depth of discussions, they were duty-bound to read it as a valid judgment.

Chapter 58

The High Court's Judgment

Biswas was assigned the duty of reading out Costello's analysis. Costello noted the pressure created by the Court of Wards on the witnesses from the plaintiff's side, the defendants withholding critical documents, and the circulation of a fake photograph. But he also couldn't overlook how the plaintiff's side slyly got hold of the defendants' diary. Costello was critical of the court allowing lawyers from both sides to cross the line at times, resulting in unnecessary character assassination. However, he praised Judge Basu for his methodical, stepwise, logical, and exhaustive approach to the case. He rebuked Chaudhuri for picking out selective portions of the judgment and twisting the implied meaning to suit his purpose.

For Costello, the story was consistent and fit into places, even if it sounded improbable. Similarly, if a chunk of witnesses held a similar opinion, it wasn't justified to dismiss them based on their credibility otherwise. He decided to analyse the case from the Darjeeling events. Costello agreed with Basu that Kumar didn't suffer from biliary colic, and arsenic aggravated his situation. The judge also believed the death occurred around 7 p.m. based on the evidence from the Prof Maitra's group at the sanitorium. So, a night cremation was feasible. Besides, he couldn't rule out claims of multiple witnesses about taking shelter.

He also criticised Crawford's certificate and Calvert's strange condolence letter to Kumar's elder brother. Since the evening cremation was evident, the truth about the morning cremation was questionable.

Costello felt the defendants arranged a replacement body to establish Kumar's cremation in the morning. Since they brought it in through one of the rooms, they kept it covered downstairs. Some testimonies gave the truth away when the witnesses mentioned they were on the verandah downstairs, and noticed Kumar's aides bringing the body out of the adjacent room. He considered Bebul Banerjee's testimony unreliable while accepting Ram Singh Subba's statement. Costello noted how Subba's evidence and the testimony of Kamal Kamini Devi hinted at the possibility that Bibhabati was locked in her room and not allowed to see her husband.

Costello didn't see any reason to doubt Darshandas' testimony. Automatically, the rescue story became authentic. The accompanying people took Kumar for cremation while he was unconscious. Later, the Naga sanyasis rescued him.

Costello didn't believe Jyotirmayee Devi hatched a conspiracy in three days. He didn't think that the plaintiff's inability to answer questions related to racing and shooting went against him. Costello stated if Jyotirmayee or his lawyers had tutored the plaintiff, the man could've come up with perfect answers. But he did what the illiterate Ramendra, after his loss of memory and wandering in the forest for more than a decade, would have done.

Also, the defendant's witnesses claimed no similarities between the plaintiff and Mejo Kumar, which dismissed all conspiracy theories against Jyotirmayee, automatically. He found it genuine how Jyotirmayee Devi went from belief to conviction about the sadhu being her brother by testing his identity before validating it. Her approach would've been flawless if she had set it up.

Besides Phani Banerjee, not a single relative from Kumar's side testified against the plaintiff. It made Costello believe they had indeed recognised him as Mejo Kumar. He also found the idea of Phani Babu's lesson book preposterous. It was ridiculous to suggest all relatives supported Kumar for personal interests. N.K. Nag's story established the plaintiff's credibility, since the witness seemed authentic, even to Lodge.

Costello didn't believe that Bibhabati refused to give the plaintiff a chance to prove his identity because of any ill motive. However, he understood and empathised with her marital state before the Darjeeling events. Ramendra wasn't a man of character. Because of his wild lifestyle and the company of multiple women, he also contracted an undesirable disease. Though widowhood was a painful phase for any married woman, Costello had an objective view of Bibhabati's living conditions in Calcutta. She had adjusted to a comfortable life. To return to her previous lifestyle would be a nightmare for the young widow. Besides, one couldn't deny Satyen's influence. The circumstances justified her denial of the plaintiff being her husband.

Costello accepted all the four parameters of physical similarities – hazel eyes, scaly feet (a family trait), scar on the ankle, and the specialist doctor's recommendation that the plaintiff had once suffered from syphilis. Costello agreed with Basu's view of mental parameters that proved the plaintiff was Ramendra, and not Mal Singh of Aujla. He condemned the fake photograph and the false testimony of fake Dharamdas trying to prove otherwise. Costello argued if the plaintiff was a Punjabi man, who couldn't speak Bengali, he wouldn't have risked declaring his identity publicly.

In his concluding statement, Costello reasoned the need for their judgment to be unbiased, and free from prejudices. It was essential for the jury to keep an open mind. Costello criticised the defendants and their behaviour in creating false narratives. He didn't spare the administration for their stand of waiting and watching the defendants and plaintiff at loggerheads.

Costello appreciated Biswas' analysis and declared his thoughts aligned with the judge. His closing statement said,

"Nothing, in my opinion, can displace the identity, unless it appears that the Second Kumar died in Darjeeling, or that the plaintiff is Mal Singh of Aujla, or not a Bengali."

Costello ordered for dismissal of the appeal. Whether Costello's judgment was valid was decided two months later when the High Court opened after renovation. Since Biswas and Lodge's previous stands on the validity of Costello's verdict were in tandem, the High Court dismissed the appeal with costs in February 1941.

While reading out Costello's perspective, Biswas felt their meeting before Costello left India had possibly influenced the judge's thoughts and made him look at the case from a neutral perspective. Lodge wondered what made Costello believe in Basu's judgment. When he met Costello the last time before the judge sailed away, Costello seemed convinced by Lodge. Later on, when Biswas assessed the magnitude of Costello's statement, he felt Costello appreciated Basu spending countless hours listening to witnesses and their testimonies, analyzing every minute detail before concluding. On the other hand, the jury only judged his verdict and reasoning, to agree with or dismiss the points.

It was true the authorities stayed indifferent during 1921-30 and interfered only when the plaintiff declared his identity. They let suspicion ahead of evidence and failed to hold a neutral perspective about the plaintiff.

Sitting far away in a foreign country, Costello had deduced a crucial aspect of this case. He knew that evidence could disprove the plaintiff as Mejo Kumar, but no evidence was sufficient to prove beyond doubt that the plaintiff was Ramendra Narayan Roy.

Chapter 59

The Consequences of the Verdict

Chaudhuri couldn't believe how the case slipped away from his grip. He was almost certain Costello's verdict would be aligned with that of Lodge. When Biswas read out Costello's verdict, Chaudhuri slumped into the chair.

The day the High Court judges declared Costello's judgment valid and dismissed the appeal, Chaudhuri drove to the ghats of the Ganga, and flung his bag into the river. Later, he locked himself in his study.

"I didn't expect it to go on for so long since I believed it would be child's play to prove the man an imposter. But it became complicated as the trial proceeded. Of course, Basu's verdict disappointed me. But what can one expect from a trial court judge?" Chaudhuri had confided in Sasanka Ghose when they filed for an appeal against Basu's judgment. Chaudhuri didn't explicitly state how he didn't consider Basu a colleague of equal rank since the latter never secured a foreign degree. He found it weird that Basu didn't even ask the plaintiff's lawyers to explain how the theory of cremating a substitute body held ground. Lodge stated it to be a ridiculous assumption that someone could arrange another body within a couple of hours. Who had hatched the plan, and how did they do it? Why did no one from the supposed evening cremation turn up for the morning cremation? According to Chaudhuri, Basu hadn't bothered to question these loopholes. The high-profile case became a blotch on his impeccable career trajectory. It made Chaudhuri famous for the wrong reasons.

Chaudhuri could hear the familiar voices of his associates. But he was in no mood for further discussion on the Bhawal estate and its Mejo Kumar. Chaudhuri decided to take a break and move out of the country immediately, though he experienced random guilt pangs for letting the defendants down.

Chatterjee was flooded with congratulatory wishes as a lawyer remarked how the esteemed counsel had secured a permanent position in the people's minds with his win in the High Court. Jyotirmayee Devi had once commented from behind the screen, "Ukil Babu, you'll go down the pages of history for your decision to stand with the truth." It was coming true as he heard a crowd chanting his name outside, along with praises of Mejo Kumar.

Over the last couple of weeks, whenever he sat alone in his study, Chatterjee visualised the faces of people associated with the case. The fair complexioned plaintiff with a round face and helpless cat's eyes, the plain-faced widow Jyotirmayee with pleading brownish eyes, the pale-faced widow Bibhabati with beautiful but apathetic eyes, the rough-looking Satya Babu with scheming eyes and cunning glances, and the lean-faced Ashu doctor with flippant eyes and a perpetual smirk. Is that how they were or was it his perspective of their nature? Chatterjee reflected.

Later that evening, he sat with Arabinda Guha as the duo discussed how the plaintiff had looked happy, but his expressions of joy seemed restrained, unlike his reaction to the trial court's judgment. "He's possibly worried this is not the end."

"Even we don't know if Satyen Babu will stop here or influence his sister to go to the London Privy Council. Since they have already spent so much money, time, and effort, now their target will possibly be to try the last option. They wouldn't want our client to enjoy his success and wealth." Chatterjee tapped on the table.

"I always thought Chaudhuri's decision of not cross-examining the plaintiff worked against him. It amuses me how the defendants' lawyers claimed there was no point in such a task since the plaintiff appeared coached by Jyotirmayee Devi, his relatives, and..." Guha smiled before stating the obvious. "Us."

"Well, Amiya Babu's thoughts were severely inspired by the proceedings of the Tichborne case. He based his moves on the belief the plaintiff was a fraud. But he overlooked how so many people, and not just Kumar's relatives, found striking similarities upfront. They should've focused on the finer details of similarities instead of strengthening their baseless argument of utter dissimilarity. Again, their refusal to cross-examine the plaintiff made people suspect the defendants were scared the plaintiff would easily prove himself as Ramendra Narayan. Then, they should've succeeded in proving him to be Mal Singh of Aujla. The case turned complicated for the defendants with the replaced photograph and fake Dharamdas." Chatterjee laughed. "Imagine claiming Jyotirmayee Devi as the chief conspirator, but failing to prove how she conspired in three days before declaring a fraud Punjabi as her brother. It's a delusional theory."

"Also, note the huge number of people supposedly a part of this conspiracy because they identified the plaintiff. The defendant's counsel never answered how these witnesses benefited by testifying in the plaintiff's favour." Guha chimed in.

While the plaintiff's lawyers celebrated their success, Satyen spoke to Bibhabati in his room. "These people are delusional. I knocked on so many doors of the authorities to convince them why the trial court judge shouldn't be an Indian. Look at how the first biased judgment turned the case in favour of the imposter."

The trial court judgment made him sad and frustrated. But the High Court's verdict annoyed him. It almost looked like they would finally win it when Costello's letter dashed their hopes.

"Just because they failed to prove the sadhu is an imposter doesn't mean he's Mejo Kumar. We still have a way to fight his claims." Bibhabati spoke in an unusually stern tone.

"What do you mean?"

"I heard you speak with a lawyer from Chaudhuri Babu's team months ago about the London Privy Council. We must appeal to them." Satyen stared at his sister, who seemed to have aged by ten years in a day. Yet, there was a sense of maturity in the reclusive woman who had rendered her unwavering support to her brother.

"I don't know if it's a good idea. Neither do I have the zeal to go through or to make you bear the torture anymore."

For the next couple of months, Satyen shut himself from the world. He barely spoke or ventured out of his room. Every time he saw Bibhabati, he remembered the hopelessness of the situation. Dr Ashutosh saw him losing grip and struggling to cope with the harsh realities. On a fateful night in the same year, Satyen suffered a massive heart attack, leaving Bibhabati to face the last leg of the battle by herself.

Bibhabati wailed like a child. Satyen's last words haunted her for days. "I failed to protect you against these manipulative people."

While Bibhabati felt the pain of their defeat, Satyen took it to heart and never recovered from its effects. The rest of the world's sympathy lay with the plaintiff, now established as Ramendra Narayan Roy. They never failed to make Bibhabati feel like a social outcast. As the case took a nasty turn in court, Satyen and Bibhabati were at the receiving end of taunts and jibes. The press wrote scathing articles. Random people turned up near their house, singing ballads about an unfaithful wife. The plaintiff's supporters staged plays, portraying her and Satyen as murderers who poisoned a wealthy prince. At social gatherings, she could feel people's eyes on her

Satyen stayed indifferent, boosting her confidence. Nowhere in his mind lay a faint possibility of losing the case. Chaudhuri Sahib had seemed buoyant about a favorable outcome. The trial court judgment affected them, but she trusted Satyen when he spoke about Basu's biasedness because of public sympathy for the plaintiff. They believed the High Court jury would see through the ploy.

Chaudhuri Sahib celebrated Lodge's judgment and commented on how he could see a disappointing future for the plaintiff. Bibhabati had let her dreams of a peaceful and comfortable life float again. Costello's verdict crashed their aspirations and hopes. Satyen failed to cope with the grim situation as he sunk deeper into depression.

But a section of their circle of acquaintances supported them. P.B. Chakrabarti was one such friend, like the honourable zamindar Saradindu Mukherjee. Mukherjee took the bold step of getting his daughter married to Satyen's son. He refused to pay heed to his so-called well-wishers, who warned him of the consequences of such a drastic step.

Till he was around, Bibhabati depended on Satyen for all the major decisions of her life. He led the way, and she followed his orders. But Satyen's death created a vacuum in her life, forcing her to take charge.

She spoke to P.B. Chakrabarti. "I don't want to give up. My brother wouldn't have wanted it. You speak to Boro Ukil Babu and let me know how we can appeal to the authorities."

Chakrabarti had already done his homework before coming to the Lansdowne house. The Board of Revenue incurred huge losses after the judgment went in the plaintiff's favour. The Court of Wards wasn't keen on a re-appeal.

Chaudhuri had washed his hands off the case. He refused to discuss any possibilities of a re-appeal or be associated with this case. "It's gracious of Bibhabati Devi to seek me again, but I'm not in a position to continue as her lawyer." Chaudhuri had turned down the offer without a second thought.

But Chakrabarti was willing to give it another chance since he thought they could reverse the judgment. Bibhabati appointed him as her lawyer to appeal for leave at the London Privy Council.

After the trial court's judgment, Dr Ashutosh visited Bibhabati on and off, to check on the family. Both had passed the age and stage where their rumoured affair could affect their camaraderie.

To some, it seemed like an unrequited affair that settled into a comfortable domain of friendship.

Chapter 60

The Last Leg of the Battle

World War II was wreaking havoc everywhere, and its effects reached Calcutta when the High Court announced its judgment. People started leaving the city for safety as the British fought tooth and nail against the Japanese. Things got chaotic with rampant bombings, loot in shops, and berserk attacks in December 1941.

Earlier that year, after the High Court judgment, the plaintiff gained possession of one-third of his share in the estate. But the authorities coaxed him to sign a power of attorney, whereby the estate manager could run the property on his behalf. The plaintiff moved to Benares in 1942.

Sarajubala, who was fond of and kind to the man, accompanied him. She also took along her brother's family. Sarajubala knew how to handle things with the hand of steel. Boro Rani always felt convinced that the plaintiff was her brother-in-law. Over time, her attitude towards Bibhabati transformed from sympathy to disgust. She failed to understand why a married woman would refuse her husband, and continue living like a widow, when the High Court had upheld the judgment. It should've changed her mindset.

Sarajubala had financed the plaintiff's case when Bibhabati appealed in the High Court. Jyotirmayee was frail and old; Sarajubala took charge of the plaintiff's life.

"You need a wife, a woman who would take care of you, and make you her universe. Not some vile female who would marry you for vested interests. I have found such a girl for you – Dhara Mukherjee. Her family is respectable and comes from Calcutta. Like us, they are here to escape the effects of the war. I will not take no for an answer. The difference between your ages is as desired, and Dhara's maturity will ensure your marital life is blissful."

Sarajubala made it evident that the return door to the plaintiff's life was closed for Bibhabati. But she also knew Mejo Rani was too headstrong to bite the dust and accept that she was wrong. A Hindu man could have more than one wife, and Sarajubala didn't want her brother-in-law to wait any further.

The plaintiff married the twenty-nine-year-old Dhara Devi in Benares the following year. It wasn't any low-key affair, for it was the marriage of the prince of Bhawal. People spoke about the grandeur of celebrations even weeks after the wedding. The news reached the Lansdowne House, but Bibhabati stayed unaffected. Her husband Ramendra Narayan Roy was dead in Darjeeling, and she clutched onto this truth as she focused on her last hope of a win.

After the Japanese retreated, the plaintiff returned to Calcutta to a house on Vivekananda Road owned by Sarajubala Devi. It was expected Chatterjee would lead the case for the plaintiff. In an unfortunate turn of events, the lawyer passed away.

Things had started looking up for Bibhabati after she applied for special leave to appeal to the London Privy Council. Chakrabarti was due to leave for England soon. However, she was unprepared for the unprecedented events that followed. On the evening Chakrabarti came to meet her, he struggled to keep his emotions under check.

"I have been appointed a judge at the High Court." Bibhabati sensed a tinge of pride in his voice. After the usual congratulations, she understood his dilemma to share the news since the new role rendered him incapable of acting as Bibhabati's lawyer in the future.

"I feel it's a conspiracy. The authorities kept delaying. Now, they moved Chakrabarti Babu away from the case with a posting in the High Court," she confided in her nephew.

By now, Bibhabati had gained enough experience in the legal system to get Pankaj Coomar Ghose, son of Sasanka Coomar Ghose, involved in the case. Since his father had represented the authorities, the case wasn't new for Pankaj Babu. He set off to London for the hearing.

The king's counsel for the defendants was W.W.K. Page, who understood the landscape of Calcutta well. The vibrant lawyer, D.N. Pritt, represented the plaintiff. Arabinda Guha flew to London to assist Pritt because he was a part of the plaintiff's team of lawyers since the beginning.

In 1945, the council heard the petition. Pritt argued against the leave to appeal since the trial court and the High Court had analysed the evidence and given judgments in favour of the plaintiff. There was no reason for another appeal where the issues and proofs stayed the same. However, Page argued the defendants deserved the last chance since the lower courts incorrectly admitted some pieces of evidence and improperly judged some aspects. Bibhabati was permitted to appeal.

A bench, constituting Lord Baron Thankerton, Lord Herbert du Parcq, and Sir Chettur Madhavan Nair, came into existence. Page proceeded to raise his argument against the judgment. He pointed out that Prof Maitra and the other professors at the sanitorium gave evidence based on hearsay about Kumar's death in Darjeeling. No one had identified the messenger who supposedly carried the news to the group. So, the judges shouldn't have included their statements as evidence. It would rule out the theory of Kumar's death between 7 to 8 p.m. on 8th May and thus negate the possibility of an attempted cremation at night.

W.W.K. Page also didn't buy the statement that the plaintiff's skin condition was that of an old syphilitic patient. His skin was mostly clear, with only three scars on the elbows. However, Ramendra Narayan suffered from tertiary-stage incurable syphilis. There was no possibility of the ulcer marks disappearing from his body.

The third point raised by Page was that Dr Caddy's report mentioned the eyes' colour as grey and not brown, which was the colour of the plaintiff's eyes. Thus, the evidence of similarity in physical traits didn't hold.

Since Justice Lodge felt the same way about the points Page mentioned, it was imperative to note all the High Court jury members hadn't agreed with the trial court's judgment.

Mr Page also clarified that Bibhabati gained control of the wealth after her husband's death. Irrespective of whether the man who returned was her husband, he couldn't claim back the property now.

Pritt argued Basu rightly included the evidence of the group of professors at the sanitorium under the laws of evidence. His argument steered towards the usual practice of the Privy Council not analysing the evidence in cases that received the same verdict in both the lower courts. He felt the same rule must be applied to this case since there was no ground for an exception. Over the next twenty-eight days, the arguments and counterarguments continued in front of the bench.

When Thankerton pronounced his judgment in concurrence with Nair and du Parcq on 30th July, 1946, he mentioned the complexities of the case and the magnitude of its impact. It was the usual practice of not reviewing evidence when both courts had concurrent findings. It was the court, not the lawyers, whose opinion needed to be concurrent. Dissent by a judge wasn't a valid reason to obviate the practice.

As per the bench, Basu had included the evidence within the limits of the Indian Evidence Act of 1872. The statement by the unidentified person didn't just include the news of Kumar's death heard by a specific set of people. But this man had also sought the help of the Maitra group to carry the body for cremation. Thus, it was evident someone at Step

Aside authorised the man to do the same. The evidence was admissible as per sec.114.

The council observed evidence of the usage of the words brownish and grey interchangeably by Kali Prasanna and the insurance agent, G.C. Sen. Kali Prasanna knew Kumar for years and noted his eyes as brown. Sen mentioned it as an identification mark in Dr Caddy's report, which the doctor had to submit to the insurance company. Sen clarified in court that he meant 'kata' eyes when he said grey. So, they were different colours in English used to describe the Kumar's 'kata' or cat's eyes. From Sen's testimony, it was clear Kumar was illiterate since he didn't understand what Dr Caddy spoke.

As regards his syphilis, the lower courts observed two marks on his right arm near the elbow and one on his left arm near the elbow. There was no definitive proof of scars on the plaintiff's legs since the evidence of the exact position of ulcers on Kumar's legs wasn't available. Besides, Dr Chatterjee, the expert on this disease, mentioned chances of recovery and no normality for syphilis, which the Privy Council took into consideration to conclude that the argument by Page didn't hold ground.

Since the arguments ruled out three out of five contentions, the board didn't find the appeal to take a deviation and review the evidence for the third time, convincing. Also, they stated that under the Limitance Act 9 of 1908, s.144, if the wife possessed the estate under the mistaken belief that her husband was dead, it wasn't adverse to the husband, whom she assumed was dead. So, the plaintiff had a right to reclaim his property. The privy council dismissed the appeal.

Bibhabati lost her last hope to regain her honour and property.

Epilogue

When Biswas analysed the trial court's judgment in detail, he noted a common point in the events that led the case to the High Court. The case centred around the plaintiff, whether he was an imposter or the prince of Bhawal. But the characters who pushed the case ahead were three women – Jyotirmayee Devi, Sarajubala Devi, and Bibhabati Devi.

If Jyotirmayee hadn't believed the sadhu to be her brother and gone ahead with her convictions, the case wouldn't have gained momentum. If Sarajubala hadn't financed the fight against the defendants in the High Court, he couldn't have afforded to fight the re-appeal. Bibhabati was the plaintiff's chief opposition. If she hadn't been so obstinate, it wouldn't have taken years for the man to prove his identity. The protagonist of his story was the sadhu turned plaintiff, proven to be Ramendra, and Satyen Banerjee played the antagonist with his associate, Dr Ashutosh Dasgupta. But these three women perfectly enacted their roles to keep the wheel of events rolling.

When the news of losing the case reached Bibhabati, she behaved with dignity, as always. Astrologers in Benares had told her about the impending loss. It prepared her for the worst. But they had also predicted an inevitable tragedy, which kept her hopes high.

By the time the judgment came, the plaintiff was living in Dharmatala separately from his wife, Dhara Devi, who resided in Maniktala. People thronged his house on 1st August 1946 after the final verdict reached him through a telegram on 31st July, 1946. The crowd wanted to celebrate his ultimate win – a decision agreed on by three courts which established him as Kumar Ramendra Narayan Roy, with no possibility of further doubts.

He visited the Thanthania Kali Bari in Calcutta the same evening to offer his prayers to Goddess Kali. As he was about to leave, he suffered a massive stroke and slumped on the floor, unconscious. Over the next two days, he was bedridden, while the doctors tried their best to save him. On 2nd August, the last of the surviving Kumars of Bhawal breathed his last in his home at sixty-five.

In her Lansdowne home, Bibhabati stood in her puja room, as warm tears ran down her cheeks. "The Goddess will never let an imposter win."

She had believed these words since the inception, but divine retribution had finally reinstated her faith. The courts could be wrong, but there could be no mistake in the Court of the Almighty. She believed the Goddess hadn't spared the culprit after his arrogance drove him to Kali Bari for puja.

Dhara Devi felt shattered at the turn of fate. Life gave her three years to be with her husband. She knew he was planning a trip to Jaidebpur soon. He wanted to regain control of his share since the estate manager held a power of attorney, and he only received a percentage of the income.

She arranged for his *shradh*, a second for the Second Kumar of Bhawal. Dhara Devi planned to hold it in Calcutta after ten days, as per the ritual. But she failed to organise the ceremony of feeding Brahmins and donating alms to the poor in Jaidebpur, as the estate manager informed her of his inability to withdraw money from the account. This power of attorney had lapsed after Kumar's death, leading to such a situation.

But the pious Hindu Brahmin widow Dhara Devi didn't give up. A month later, she sent money with a trusted source to Jaidebpur. On 2nd September, Hindu Brahmins were invited to and fed at Jaidebpur. Dhara Devi neither got a chance nor much time to know her husband well, but she remained devoted to his memory and the institution of marriage, even after his death.

Ram Narayan Roy, the adopted son of Ananda Kumari, gained a share of the estate after succeeding Mejo Kumar for a brief period. But the abolishment of the zamindari system in 1950 forced them to move to Calcutta. After 1960, he didn't even return to collect the rent.

The Court of Wards offered eight lakh rupees to Bibhabati as part of Ramendra's share since she was one of his widows.

Bibhabati was furious. "How dare they think I'll take this money? It belongs to an imposter, not my late husband. If I accept it, it'll mean I admit the cheater to be Mejo Kumar. That'll never happen in my lifetime."

Despite her lawyers trying to convince Bibhabati that it was rightfully her money since it came from her late husband's wealth, she returned the offer without a second thought.

Her nephew failed to appreciate her perspective, but he knew better than to argue with the matriarch. Some people still believed it was her trick to draw public sympathy towards herself since she had no requirement for money after her brother's death. But most people eventually lost interest in the lives of the prince turned sadhu labelled as an imposter declared as Ramendra Narayan, and his contriving wife portrayed as a helpless but dignified lady to the world.

A few months later, Basu heard that a forensic report of the dead plaintiff confirmed the match of nineteen (out of twenty-one) parameters of the physical identification data with that of Mejo Kumar. He was glad it validated his verdict on the case.

Twenty years passed before Bibhabati breathed her last and united with her brother Satyen in the sky. It remains a mystery if she met her husband there, and acknowledged him, or refused to believe his presence as a spirit, too.

Table of References

A. English books

(1) *An Imposter Prince* – Partha Chatterjee

(2) *A Prince, Poison, and Two Funerals* – Murad Fyzee

(3) *The Bhowal Case* – J.M. Mitra and R.C. Chakrabarty

(4) *The Bhowal Case (High Court Judgments)* – Edited by S.C. Dasgupta

B. Bengali books

(1) *Mejokumar – Ek Sanyasi Raja* – Ashim Himel

(2) *Bhawal Sanyasir Mamla* – Bishnucharan Ghosh and Sishir Paitandi

(3) *Rahasyabrita Bhawal Sanyasi* – Baridbaran Ghosh

C Articles

(1) 'The Bhawal case on Banglapedia' by Sirajul Islam

(2) 'The Legendary tale of the Bhawal Sanyasi' by Waqar A Khan in *Daily Star*

(3) 'A Prince rose who from the Dead' by Sreelata Menon in *Daily Star*, 2013

(4) Judgment of the Judicial Committee of Privy Council for Appeal No. 17 of 1945. Srimati Bibhabati Devi, Appellant v. Kumar Ramendra Narayan Roy and other respondents

(5) Judgment of Pannalal Basu Title Suit 38 of 1935 Ramendra Narayan Roy v. Bibhabati Devi and others

(6) Forensic Identification by Dr Anil Aggarwal Mystery Magazine Web, Fall 2003, Vol 1, Issue 2

(7) 'The Bhawal estate scandal' – *Dhaka Tribune,* November 7, 2014

(8) *The Statesman* archives

(9) *Amrit Bazar Patrika* physical archives at the National Library in Kolkata

Acknowledgments

The journey of my book would be incomplete without the support of the following people –

(1) My husband, Dr Tanmoy Banerjee, for being my Rock of Gibraltar.

(2) My son, Tuneer Banerjee, for his interest, enthusiasm, and love for my writing.

(3) My father, Prof Radhanath Chatterjee, for encouraging me to follow my heart.

(4) My father-in-law, Mr Somnath Banerjee, for believing in my creative endeavours.

(5) My mother-in-law, Mrs Aloka Banerjee, for supporting my career choices.

(6) My best friend, first reader, and soul sister, Ramya, for always having my back.

(7) My friends from the blogging and writing fraternity, for showering love on my writing journey over the years.

(8) My readers and friends, whose constant support and encouragement keeps me going.

(9) Best-selling author, wonderful friend, and the talented literary agent of The Book Bakers literary agency, Mr Suhail Mathur, for turning my dreams into reality.

(10) Mr Arup Bose from Srishti Publishers for his faith and support in getting this book out in the world. Ms Stuti Gupta, Ms Alisha

Verma Chopra, and the editorial team for their unrelenting efforts in bringing out the best version of my writing.

And,

(11) My mother, the late Mrs Debjani Chatterjee, for being my guardian angel. She's the reason I write. I lost her to a deadly disease thirteen years ago, but her memories and blessings keep me going.